School Bullying and Violence

School Bullying and Violence

Interventions for School Mental Health Specialists

GERALD A. JUHNKE
DARCY HAAG GRANELLO
PAUL F. GRANELLO

OXFORD
UNIVERSITY PRESS

OXFORD
UNIVERSITY PRESS

Oxford University Press is a department of the University of Oxford. It furthers
the University's objective of excellence in research, scholarship, and education
by publishing worldwide. Oxford is a registered trade mark of Oxford University
Press in the UK and certain other countries.

Published in the United States of America by Oxford University Press
198 Madison Avenue, New York, NY 10016, United States of America.

Library of Congress Cataloging-in-Publication Data
Names: Juhnke, Gerald A., author. | Granello, Darcy Haag, author. |
Granello, Paul F., author.
Title: School bullying and violence : interventions for school mental
health specialists / Gerald A. Juhnke, Darcy Haag Granello, Paul F. Granello.
Description: New York : Oxford University Press, 2020. |
Includes bibliographical references and index.
Identifiers: LCCN 2019052377 (print) | LCCN 2019052378 (ebook) |
ISBN 9780190059903 (paperback) | ISBN 9780190059927 (epub)
Subjects: LCSH: Bullying in schools—Prevention. | School
violence—Prevention. | School children—Mental health services.
Classification: LCC LB3013.3 .J82 2020 (print) | LCC LB3013.3 (ebook) |
DDC 371.5/8—dc23
LC record available at https://lccn.loc.gov/2019052377
LC ebook record available at https://lccn.loc.gov/2019052378

Disclaimer: The resources in this book are intended for use only as a tool to assist
clinicians/school-based professionals and should not be used to replace clinical judgment
or school-based policies and procedures. The information in this book is not provided as
legal advice and/or professional advice on specific situations. While we have attempted
to ensure the accuracy of information contained herein, we do not warrant that it is
complete or accurate, and we are not legally responsible for errors or omissions.

1 3 5 7 9 8 6 4 2

Printed by Marquis, Canada

Contents

Preface

If you are a school counselor, school social worker, school psychologist, clinical mental health counselor, social worker, psychologist, marriage and family therapist, pediatrician, psychiatrist, case manager, school administrator, or teaching professional who addresses the needs of school-age survivors and perpetrators of bullying and violence, this book is for you. *School Bullying and Violence: Interventions for School Mental Health Specialists* is based on our more than 80 years of combined clinical practice and supervision. The book has received praise from school counselors, school psychologists, school social workers, and other mental health providers who address the needs of this very special population.

This book is different from the rest. Unlike dull and tedious books that merely are academic in nature, *School Bullying and Violence* is theory driven and clinically oriented. Practical and useful clinical vignettes with detailed descriptions are packed into every chapter. These clinical vignettes demonstrate real-life interventions and techniques designed to augment your clinical skills and provide potentially helpful interventions for bullying and violence survivors and perpetrators.

The intent of the book is simple. Given the robust frequency of bullying and violence experienced by school students and the horrific emotional, interpersonal, and physical aftereffects, we want to help you devise the very best assessments and interventions for the students you serve. You are an expert on your students and their families, your schools, and your community. You understand what will work. Instead of eclipsing your expertise and clinical knowledge or telling you what to do, this book is designed to help us join you as you respond to your students' pressing bullying and violence experiences. Stated differently, we offer more than eight decades of combined experience to boost your clinical expertise and help your students. *School Bullying and Violence*'s interventions and strategies are designed to empower your students, schools, families, community, and you. This book skips mundane minutiae often found elsewhere. Instead, we provide critical information and potential strategies to consider when responding to student bullying and violence assessment and interventions. Each chapter is chockful of assessments or interventions specifically designed to help you provide a thoughtful and clinically relevant response to student bullying and violence issues.

The opening chapters address face-to-face clinical assessment and provide real-life methods for assessing immediate student needs. The book then moves into interventions for both individuals and parents. Over the years we have learned that the most potent interventions include both individual *and* parental or family interventions. However, there may be times when parental or family interventions are contraindicated or ill advised. These are discussed as well.

Another unique aspect of this book is our broad focus on all school mental health specialists and our use of the term "specialists" throughout the book. Although the book is relevant to school administrators, teaching professionals, and case managers, related to establishing protocols and responses, specialists have at least a master's degrees in one of the traditional mental health professions. Their graduate degrees require coursework specifically relevant to their students' developmental stages and assessment. In other words, specialists *are* experts. And we are not into political territorial battles. We believe no one profession serves the needs of all students who are bullied and victimized in our nation's schools. It has been our clinical experience that professionals who work with bullied students and who treat school violence perpetrators and victims come from many diverse and varied professional backgrounds. For example, professional counselors treating bullying and violence perpetrators and victims may have licenses such as Licensed Professional Counselor (LPC) or Licensed Professional Clinical Counselor (LPCC), or have certifications from the National Board of Certified Counselors such as Nationally Certified School Counselor (NCSC), National Certified Counselor (NCC), or Certified Clinical Mental Health Counselor (CCMHC). Additionally, it is not atypical for professional counselors working with bullied and victimized students to verbally identify themselves as school counselor, clinical mental health counselor, or marriage and family counselor.

Other professions, such as social work and psychology, have similar specializations and distinctions. For example, the National Association of Social Workers has a specialty credential, Certified School Social Worker Specialist (C-SSWS), for professionals providing services in schools. Thus, professional social workers responding to school violence concerns may have the C-SSWS or may simply use their state license as a Licensed Social Worker (LSW) or other such professional social work designation. Licenses and certifications for professional psychologists are similar. One can be a Licensed Psychologist (LP), a Nationally Certified School Psychologist (NCSP), or a Licensed Specialist in School Psychology (LSSP).

The intent of this book is to provide information to all licensed, master's, education specialist, and doctoral-level mental health professionals providing mental health services to student bullying and violence perpetrators and victims, no matter what their profession. We embrace the diversity of counselors, social workers, psychologists, and marriage and family therapists. Thus, instead of identifying only counselors, or social workers, or psychologists, or marriage and family therapists, we have used the generic term "specialist" for short, throughout the book. We have also interchanged the individual professions (counselor, social worker, psychologist, marriage and family therapist) within the clinical vignettes. We hope these changes increase the book's readability and ensure that all master's-level, licensed or certified specialists, no matter what their professional degree and background, are treated equally and fairly within the book.

Finally, as a former sous chef de cuisine and restaurateur who made dessert and ornate wedding cakes, and who established his first independent counseling practice in 1986, we understand that baking and clinical work have some overlapping similarities. Both involve precise, preplanned processes, and both take time. Cake baking requires at least two steps—baking the cake and decorating it after it fully cools. Attempting to decorate liquid cake batter or failing to allow adequate baking time for the cake to solidify and later cool is a recipe for disaster. We have found such beginning and advanced training steps helpful when training our master's and doctoral counselors. It is impossible to understand "how" to use cognitive-behavioral therapy or other interventions without first understanding "what" they are. Chapters 1, 5, and 7 "bake the cake," so to speak. They provide an overview of each topic and help the reader understand the "what" of that topic. These chapters give readers time to solidify and crystallize their understanding of the specific topic before moving on to the "how to" chapters (Chapters 2, 6, and 8).

These are just some of the things that make this book unique and dynamic. We trust that you will like these unique aspects, hope the book is helpful to you as you serve your students, and sincerely thank you for allowing us the privilege of serving you. We truly wish you the very best in your professional efforts to protect and help America's students and tomorrow's leaders.

Gerald A. Juhnke
Darcy Haag Granello
Paul F. Granello

Warning

Bullying and violence risk assessments and interventions are complex processes. It is impossible to identify all students who will ultimately bully or behave violently. Thus, the assessments and face-to-face clinical interviews described in this book should not be used as the sole methods to make a bullying or violence assessment or intervention. These assessments simply provide a "snapshot" in time and suggest potential immediate-risk levels that must be continually reevaluated by an experienced interdisciplinary mental health team. The described youth bullying and violence interventions should be viewed merely as partial components of a structured, multicomponent, and thorough youth bullying and violence prevention and intervention process facilitated by a safety and risk committee comprising, at a minimum, experienced and expert school mental health specialists (i.e., school counselors, clinical mental health counselors, school social workers, school psychologists, and marriage and family therapists), clinical supervisors, legal counsel, a student ombudsman or advocate, and a school administrative spokesperson. Remember: Always consult your clinical supervisor; school district legal counsel; professional liability insurance risk management carrier; licensed and certified, master's-level, school mental health specialist peers; and assigned school police or safety officers to ensure the greatest degree of safety and ultimate protection. Decisions related to this population should never be made by one individual; instead, a safety and risk committee approach should be used. Such high-risk committee decision making includes, at a minimum, the school mental health specialists and supervisors involved in the case, school administrators (e.g., school principals, vice principals), the student's teachers, systems of care services team members, parents, school safety officers, the school district's legal counsel, and potentially juvenile probation officers and a judge if warranted. The student in question should be considered for being allowed to return to the school milieu only if the safety and risk committee confidently concludes that (a) the student poses no imminent danger to others, (b) others within the school environment will be safe and not academically disrupted or threatened, and (c) sufficient structure and control can be arranged. Any return to school must be intensely structured. Previous freedoms experienced prior to the bullying or violent behaviors will likely never again be granted, and the student's school experiences will be significantly altered.

Acknowledgments

Life is filled with abundant blessings and sprinklings of challenges. Throughout this writing process we have been abundantly blessed by wonderful and supportive family members, friends, and professional colleagues. Specifically, we thank Deborah, Bryce, and Brenna Juhnke; Terri, Kevin, Kim, Christian, Brian, and Lauren Haag; and Alanna, Victor, Heather, Laura, Matthew, Jodi, and Andrew Granello. Their support and encouragement were monumental, and they endured many long absences as we toiled. Of course, we also recognize the influence of our loved ones and friends who have passed and the positive influence they continue to have on our lives and writings: Leon J. Granello, Leon V. Granello, Douglas M. Haag, Meryl Haag, Gerald Juhnke, Violet Juhnke, Nicholas Vacc, and Garry Walz. Their memories continually influence us and make us better people and professionals.

Additionally, Jerry wishes thank two of his incredible mentors: Dr. Alan J. Hovestadt and Dr. William Watson Purkey. Dr. Hovestadt is founder of Western Michigan University's Marriage and Family Program, a former president of the American Association for Marriage and Family Therapy Association, a renowned family-of-origin theorist, and a legendary marriage and family therapist and clinical supervisor. Alan supervised Jerry's doctoral dissertation and provided three-and-a-half years of live marriage and family clinical supervision to Jerry. Alan has been Jerry's academic and life mentor and friend for 31 years. He greatly enriched Jerry's clinical, supervision, and research skills. Dr. Purkey is the founder of invitational education theory and serves as Jerry's teaching mentor and life guide. William "supercharged" Jerry's teaching skills and taught Jerry how to "invite" learners to achieve their desired goals via "active" storytelling and metaphors. The duo co-presented and co-authored numerous presentations throughout the country and jointly authored and implemented grants, including a $250,000 grant with the District of Columbia's 15 most violent schools. From challenging Jerry to eliminate "boring overheads" to inspiring him to "live life to the fullest," William has been a significant life influence.

In addition to Alan and William, Jerry has been surrounded by many supportive and kind friends and professional colleagues during the writing of this book. These "superstars" are Dr. Darcy Haag Granello, Dr. Paul F. Granello, Dr. Richard S. Balkin, Dr. W. Bryce Hagedorn, Dr. Alan Shoho, and Brian Cadwallader, J.D. Each warrants special recognition.

Paul and Darcy Granello are close friends, and the opportunity to co-author this book with them has been a career highlight. Their support of Jerry's family and Jerry have gone far beyond recognizable boundaries. Their commitment to this book and their dedication to those who have been bullied and victimized are unequalled. Despite significant challenges, they helped champion this book to fruition.

Rick Balkin is another incredible friend and professional superstar who warrants special acknowledgment and thanks. Rick's support and encouragement have been exceptionally meaningful and are greatly appreciated. Rick is an expert researcher and counselor—and a Brazilian jiu-jitsu martial artist—who is highly committed to the needs of our nation's students. Rick provided valuable input and suggestions that greatly enhanced the end product. Thank you, Rick!

Bryce Hagedorn is the calm in any storm, and Jerry has been blessed to have him as a professional colleague and friend. Speaking with Bryce always helps reestablish the priority of helping students be substance free and safe.

Alan Shoho is the dean of the School of Education at the University of Wisconsin Milwaukee. His school leadership expertise and his commitment to current and future educators and students are noteworthy. He constantly reminds Jerry of the need to train counselors, educators, and administrators to respond to pressing school bullying and violence issues.

Brian Cadwallader is a law expert and a long-time friend and fellow skipper. Brian's comments and remarks continuously ensured that Jerry kept the book "practical," "real," and "relevant." His frank and realistic outlook on life was greatly appreciated and ensured the book stayed on target.

It is an honor and privilege to have such incredible, supportive, and caring professional friends who always come through and are dedicated to the students and faculty we serve.

Acknowledgment of two expert school psychologists is warranted as well. Both are professional colleagues at the University of Texas at San Antonio: Professor Jeremy R. Sullivan, Ph.D., LP, LSSP, NCSP, and Associate Professor Felicia Castro-Villarreal, Ph.D., LSSP. Their input and feedback were very appreciated. Thank you, Jeremy and Felicia. for your willingness to provide timely and sage advice to ensure the book was relevant for school psychologists.

Cheri Trahan Keene, M.Ed., LPC, and Gretchen McLain, MA, CSC, Jerry's research assistants, warrant recognition for their superior assistance. Thank you, Cheri and Gretchen, for your enthusiasm and investment of time and energy.

Paul, Darcy, and Jerry also thank Dana Bliss and the Oxford University Press team for their publication support and expertise. You made this writing and submission process superior.

We further recognize the following professional colleagues and friends who provided encouragement, support, wisdom, and suggestions: Dr. Rochelle Cade, Dr. Brian Canfield, Dr. Kenneth Coll, Dr. Ernest Cox, Jr., Dr. Russ Curtis, Dr. R. J. Davis, Dr. Thelma

Duffey, Dr. Sabina de Vries, Dr. Bradley Erford, Dr. David Fenell, Dr. John Geisler, Dr. Suzanne Hedstrom, Dr. Barbara Herlihy, Dr. Claudia Interiano-Shiverdecker, Dr. Brenda Jones, Dr. Mark Jones, Dr. Mehmet Akif Karaman, Mr. James Kennedy, Rev. John Kimmons, Dr. Simone Lambert, Dr. Stephen Lenz, Dr. Christopher Leeth, Dr. Ming Li, Dr. Jessica Lloyd-Hazlett, Ms. Gretchen McLain, Rev. Jerry Mitchell, Dr. Patrick Munley, Dr. Michael Moyer, Dr. Joe Olds, Rev. Greg Pentecost, Dr. Michelle Perepiczka, Dr. Paul Peluso, Rev. Phillip Rogers, Dr. Derek Robertson, Dr. Devon Romero, Dr. Catherine Somody, Dr. Joe Seelig, Dr. Carl Sheperis, Dr. Donna Sheperis, Dr. Robert Smith, Dr. Stacy Speedlin, Ms. Cheri Trahan Keene, Dr. Heather Trepal, Dr. Nancy Vacc, Dr. Richard Watts, Dr. Fangzhou Yu, and Dr. Elias Zambrano.

Finally, we thank those who allowed us to serve and counsel them during their times of crisis and overwhelming heartache. Bullying and violence represent times of great turmoil and emotional confusion. Our students allowed us to enter their world and learn from their bullying and violence experiences. They are the real heroes of this book. The many things we learned from them will allow our readers to add to their clinical knowledge, acumen, and wisdom. Our hope is the book will promote healing, speed recovery, and provide greater safety for all.

Introduction

Frequency and Definitions

Let's face it: Because you're reading this page, odds are good you believe school bullying and violence are problematic. Bullying has become epidemic among our nation's students. More than one out of five students report being bullied, and the incidence of bullying is highest among female students (Lessne & Yanez, 2016). The US Centers for Disease Control and Prevention (CDC, 2018) describes bullying as

> any unwanted aggressive behavior(s) toward a youth by another youth or group of youths, who are not siblings or current dating partners, involving an observed or perceived power imbalance. These behaviors are repeated, or have the potential to be repeated, over time. Bullying can happen in person and electronically (known as cyberbullying) and can occur at school or in other settings.

The three main bullying categories are verbal, social, and physical bullying (StopBullying.gov, 2019). Verbal bullying can be nearly any caustic or inappropriately hateful written comment or verbal remark made or shared. This includes making both clear threats (e.g., "I'm going to beat you to a pulp!") and veiled threats (e.g., "You should enjoy today, because you never can tell what may happen to you tomorrow"). Verbal threats can also include hurtful remarks (e.g., "You're the ugliest person I have ever seen!"). In comparison, social bullying revolves around interpersonal interactions and relationships. Included here are spreading rumors, embarrassing persons in public, and telling others not to befriend an identified person. Physical bullying can include anything from physically striking or kicking someone or pulling someone's hair to pushing, spitting on, or throwing things at someone.

Similar to physical bullying is school violence. According to the CDC (2016),

> School violence is youth violence that occurs on school property, on the way to or from school or school-sponsored events, or during a school-sponsored event. A young person can be a victim, a perpetrator, or a witness of school violence. School violence may also involve or impact adults.

School violence can include physically assaulting others via punching, hitting, choking, kicking, grabbing, scratching, or other behaviors where aggressive physical contact occurs (CDC, 2016). During the 2013–2014 academic year 65% of public schools reported one or more violent incidents, or an estimated 757,000 crimes, and 58% of public schools reported one or more physical fights without weapons (Musu-Gillette, Zhang, Wang, Zhang, & Odudekerk, 2017).

Such bullying and school violence numbers are alarming to most and grab national and local news headlines. However, we are assuming these numbers do not surprise you. If you are reading this book, you likely serve this population and understand the numbers of students within your school who experience bullying and school violence weekly. One middle school counselor reported to us that on his "typical" day, he has two or three students visit the counseling office due to either being bullied or fear of being bullied. He further said that one or two acts of student violence occur at his school weekly. When we asked about his district's much-publicized "zero tolerance" policy for bullying and fighting, he chuckled and reported that the policy, at best, was unequally implemented across the district's campuses and more likely was used as a political means to mitigate parental concerns.

Our desire in writing this book is to help you reduce the incidence of bullying and school violence in your school. However, until the time comes when there is no bullying or school violence, we hope that the assessments and interventions described herein provide useful resources to aid your clinical acumen, help you help survivors in your school, and help you promote healthy changes among those who present with mild to moderate bullying and violent behaviors.

Relevant Diagnoses

In our experience, many school counselors in training, as well as some practicing ones, do not like to diagnose students. Either they find diagnoses to be irrelevant or their schools do not allow them to diagnose. For the purposes of this book, however, readers may find it helpful to consider some diagnoses specific to school students who bully or are violent.

Jacobson and Gottman (1998) rocked the domestic violence and treatment communities when they classified domestic violence perpetrators into two broad but separately important groups: pit bulls and cobras. Both groups are pathological and potentially dangerous to their partners. Jacobson and Gottman classified the overwhelming majority of their batterer research group as pit bulls. These men were insecure and needy. They were dependent on their partners. Metaphorically, like a pit bull that intimidates by barking, growling, and showing its teeth, these men intimidated their partners. They overtly threatened their partners and ruled by clear and evident acts of intimidation with the unmistakable threat of violence.

In contrast, cobras represented a significantly smaller but far more dangerous group. Most cobras met criteria for antisocial personality disorder. Unlike noisy, snarling pit bulls, which are readily seen and therefore can be avoided, cobras are stealthy and covert. Their deadly bites come with little advance warning. According to Jacobson and Gottman, this antisocial group of batterers presented significantly greater lethality risk.

Although Jacobson and Gottman's pit bull and cobra metaphor is far too simplistic to address all the potential types of violent students school counselors encounter, it does establish an important point: There is a small subgroup of violent students who will not overtly present as a clear and present danger to others until they strike. This subgroup may not be clearly identified as an imminent danger until after they violently behave. In fact, members of this violent subgroup often understand how to skillfully deceive others and hide their true violent intentions. Many in this deceptive violent subgroup may meet criteria for conduct disorder. Clearly it is beyond the scope of this chapter to conduct an in-depth examination of this and all other disorders that may be related to violent students. However, because it may have clinical utility to consider conduct disorder, as well as other disorders we have encountered among this student perpetrator population, we will provide general descriptions of conduct disorder, oppositional defiant disorder, attention-deficit/hyperactivity disorder, and intermittent explosive disorder. We also provide a general description of posttraumatic stress disorder for student bullying and violence survivors.

Conduct Disorder

Jacobson and Gottman reported that the vast majority of cobras qualified for a diagnosis of antisocial personality disorder. However, students under the age of 18 cannot be diagnosed with formal personality disorders, according to the fifth edition of the American Psychiatric Association's *Diagnostic and Statistical Manual of Mental Disorders* (DSM-5; APA, 2013). Thus, antisocial elementary, middle, and most high school students are ineligible for this diagnosis due to their age. However, we have found conduct disorder strongly associated with later adult antisocial personality disorder diagnoses.

In the case of conduct disorder, the most predominant characteristic is a pattern of persistent behaviors in which students deny others' rights (e.g., the student initiates physical fights in an effort

to get what the student wants) or ignore major age-appropriate social norms (e.g., the student breaks into cars to steal electronics)
(APA, 2013). In particular, a conduct disorder diagnosis includes
four main categories: (a) aggressive behaviors that threaten or harm
other people or animals, (b) behaviors that cause damage to property,
(c) lying and stealing, and (d) full violation of societal rules or norms.

Students who meet conduct disorder criteria will likely have
checkered histories revolving around these four categories. Often,
they will be identified by both peers and teachers as threatening
or intimidating. Sometimes entry-level school counselors fail to
recognize students with conduct disorder because many graduate
assessment courses focus on overtly aggressive behaviors versus
"Machiavellian" behaviors. Hellions are far easier to identify; they
are the pit bulls described by Jacobson and Gottman.

Conversely, some Machiavellians initially present as budding
professionals or politicians, intelligent, able, and invested. These are
the cobras. They often dress well and present in respectful and polit-
ically correct ways. However, don't be fooled: Many Machiavellians
who meet criteria for conduct disorder are far more shrewd, cun-
ning, and scheming than their aggressive counterparts. Some
Machiavellians are initially so well liked by teachers and counselors
that inexperienced professionals are deceived into believing that
whatever claims are made about the student are unjustified and inaccurate. We know. We've been there.

More than 30 years ago, when I was an inexperienced counselor,
Kevin, a 10-year-old student, was referred to me. His grandmother,
Dorothy, initiated contact. Tearfully, Dorothy reported how Kevin's
parents had "temporarily" sent Kevin to live with her. She reported
Kevin's parents were going through a difficult divorce. According
to her, the divorce had "gotten way too ugly" for Kevin to stay.
Dorothy asked me to assess Kevin to determine how he was coping
with the move and his parents' divorce. I really liked Dorothy. She
reminded me of the way grandparents "should be"—invested in
their grandchildren, caring, nurturing, compassionate toward her

daughter who was caught in an awful divorce, and totally committed to the complete well-being of her young grandson. The only two things missing from our initial meeting were the American flag and Lee Greenwood's rendition of "God Bless the USA." I felt very positive about the referral and commended Dorothy for her interest in ensuring Kevin's healthy transition.

During our first joint session Dorothy and Kevin were exceedingly polite. When Dorothy introduced me to Kevin, he immediately stood. He shook my hand with a firm grip and said something like, "I am pleased to meet you, Dr. Juhnke. I like the paintings on the wall. Did you paint them yourself?" Kevin was well groomed, engaging, intelligent, and articulate and strikingly different from most of my 10-year-old students. He was like a candidate running for office without the tie. I queried Kevin and found him to be making a successful transition with no remarkable concerns or worries. He sat straight, began or ended most sentences with the word "sir," and made direct eye contact throughout session. At the session's conclusion, the grandmother and I met. She appeared relieved when I provided my clinical opinion that Kevin appeared to be adjusting well to the transition. However, when I reported no remarkable reason to meet again, she became visibly anxious. She immediately stated that I "needed" to meet monthly with Kevin "just to make sure" things were well.

When I stated my confusion and inquired why she wanted monthly sessions, she reported Kevin had "accidentally" shot his friend with a BB gun. The incident had reportedly occurred in the backyard of his parents' home in another state. Grandmother said the incident had been "completely blown out of proportion." After the victim's parents contacted the police, a juvenile probation officer was assigned to the case. The officer required monthly updates regarding Kevin to stem Kevin's detention. According to the grandmother, this was little more than a formality and the victim had not sustained any injuries.

I then invited Kevin to rejoin his grandmother and me back in the treatment room. Given Kevin's clinical presentation, I couldn't fathom this articulate and respectful student harming someone else. When I asked Kevin about the incident, he provided a detailed and benign story of erecting a target in the backyard with a neighborhood friend. According to Kevin, the boys took turns shooting the target until boredom set in, and then they began shooting soda cans. Unfortunately, one BB ricocheted off a soda can and struck his playmate in the face. The playmate was unscathed except for a small red mark to his cheek. Given the story details and my clinical impressions of Dorothy and Kevin, I simply *knew* they were telling the truth. It would be more accurate to say I *wanted* to believe Kevin was innocent. Little did I suspect that the saintly presenting grandmother most likely met antisocial personality disorder criteria and the grandson was the Machiavellian type of student with conduct disorder whom I would later describe to my counseling students during advanced master's and doctoral psychopathology courses.

The following morning I left a message for Kevin's juvenile probation officer. When the officer returned my call he recounted a significantly different story of a very violent Kevin with a checkered legal history. As a matter of fact, the story was so strikingly different that I requested the officer describe Kevin's physical appearance to ensure we were discussing the same person. There was no doubt. I had been duped.

My purpose in sharing this rather embarrassing story of my inaccurate initial assessment of Kevin is threefold:

1. We must be aware many Machiavellian-type students who present with conduct disorder can be eloquent at deception. Specific to this book's upcoming chapter on violence assessment, some students with conduct disorder will deny any intent to harm others. Instead, they will masterfully weave a relatively believable tale.

2. We must always verify the information and stories provided by potentially violent students who may meet conduct disorder criteria.

3. We must always consult with professional colleagues. Had I not spoken with Kevin's probation officer, I might have

written a glowing report and failed to ascertain the truth about Kevin for a long time.

Oppositional Defiant Disorder

Oppositional defiant disorder is another disorder we have found among some potentially violent students. It can be rather challenging to determine whether the student being assessed for oppositional defiant disorder is simply strong-willed or truly surpasses the minimal criteria threshold for the disorder. One of the chief distinguishing markers necessary to differentiate strong-willed students from those with oppositional defiant disorder is time. Students with oppositional defiant disorder must present with a general pattern of negativistic, hostile, and defiant behaviors that have been ongoing for at least six months (APA, 2013). Four or more of the following criteria must be present: The student often (a) loses his or her temper, (b) argues with adults, (c) actively defies or refuses to comply with adults' requests or rules, (d) deliberately annoys people, (e) blames others for his or her mistakes or misbehavior, (f) is touchy or easily annoyed by others, (g) is angry and resentful, and/or (h) is spiteful or vindictive. These criteria are met only if the behavior occurs more frequently than is typical with students of comparable age and development levels.

Attention-Deficit/Hyperactivity Disorder

In our experience, students diagnosed with attention-deficit/hyperactivity disorder (ADHD) are typically not intentionally violent. We have found that should they injure others, the injury was usually unintentional and frequently came about due to their hyperactivity. For example, an ADHD student may "jump" onto others standing in line and accidentally cause injury. However, it is rarely the student's intent to injure or harm others. When students diagnosed with ADHD do injure others, we have found there is frequently a comorbid diagnosis of either conduct disorder or oppositional defiant disorder.

The prominent feature with ADHD is an inability to maintain age-appropriate attention and an inability to concentrate on the specific task at hand. Symptoms such as inattention include behaviors like frequently (a) failing to pay close attention to details and making careless mistakes in schoolwork, work, or other activities, (b) having difficulty sustaining attention in tasks or play activities, (c) not seeming to listen when directly spoken to, (d) not following through on instructions and failing to finish schoolwork, chores, or duties in the workplace (not resulting from oppositional behaviors or an inability to understand instructions), (e) having difficulty organizing tasks and activities, (f) avoiding, disliking, or demonstrating reluctance to engage in tasks that require sustained mental effort, (g) losing books and items necessary for successful completion of tasks or activities, (h) being distracted by extraneous stimuli, and (i) forgetting daily activities (APA, 2013). Students qualifying for an ADHD diagnosis demonstrate hyperactivity by often (a) fidgeting with their hands or squirming in their seats, (b) leaving their classroom seats at times when being seated is expected, (c) running or climbing excessively in inappropriate situations, (d) having difficulty playing quietly during leisure activities, (e) being "on the go" or acting as if "driven by a motor," and (f) talking excessively. Symptoms of impulsivity must be noted as well. Such symptoms would include frequently (a) blurting out answers before questions have been completed, (b) having difficulty waiting one's turn, and (c) interrupting or intruding on others. Such symptoms must have persisted for at least six months (APA, 2013). Some symptoms need to have been present at or before age 7, and have been present in at least two separate settings (e.g., home and school) (APA, 2013). The symptomatology should also be creating significant impairment in social, academic, or occupational functioning or relationships (APA, 2013).

Intermittent Explosive Disorder

Another subgroup of violent and potentially violent students who warrant special consideration comprises those who meet criteria for intermittent explosive disorder. Frequently, these students will have histories of aggressive acts that are not premeditated. In other words, these students will act aggressively on the spur of the moment. Often students will report a sense or feeling of arousal or tension just prior to their aggressive outburst (APA, 2013). After the aggressive act they may truly feel compunction or remorse. At other times they may even report feelings of embarrassment related to their unexplained aggressive acts or may feel bewildered and unable to articulate exactly what brought the aggressive outburst to fruition. The fifth edition of the American Psychiatric Association's *Diagnostic and Statistical Manual of Mental Disorders* (DSM-5) lists specific criteria that are required for a diagnosis of intermittent explosive disorder (APA, 2013). These criteria include several episodes of impulsive behavior that result in serious damage to either persons or property, where the degree of aggressiveness is grossly disproportionate to the circumstances or provocation (APA, 2013).

Posttraumatic Stress Disorder

Although being bullied and experiencing school violence can be traumatic, depending on the exact circumstances, they do not automatically result in a diagnosis of posttraumatic stress disorder (PTSD). Readers are encouraged to review the DSM-5 for detailed PTSD diagnostic criteria and each of the diagnoses we have discussed. PTSD diagnostic criteria are broken into two classifications—one for children older than six years, the other for children six years and younger. For children older than six, general criteria include (a) exposure to actual or threatened death, serious injury, or sexual violence, (b) presence of intrusive symptoms that are associated with the trauma or that begin after the trauma, (c) persistent avoidance of stimuli associated with the trauma or beginning after the trauma, (d) negative alterations in cognitions and mood associated with the trauma or beginning or worsening after the trauma, (e) marked alterations in arousal and reactivity associated with the trauma, beginning or worsening after the trauma, (f) duration of disturbance more than one month, (g) the disturbance causes clinically significant distress or impairment in social, occupational, or other important areas of functioning, and (h) the disturbance is not attributable to the physiological effects of a substance or another medical condition.

For children six and younger the general criteria are similar and include (a) exposure to actual or threatened death, serious injury, or sexual violence, (b) presence of intrusive symptoms associated with the trauma, beginning after the trauma, (c) symptoms representing either persistent avoidance of stimuli associated with the trauma or negative alterations in cognitions and mood associated with the trauma, beginning or worsening after the events, (d) alterations in arousal and reactivity associated with the trauma, beginning or worsening after the trauma, (e) a duration of the disturbance over one month, (f) the disturbance causes clinically significant distress or impairment in relationship with parents, siblings, peers, or other caregivers or with school behavior, and (g) the disturbance is not attributable to the physiological effects of a substance or another medical condition.

Students Who Cannot Be Diagnosed

Students who bully or are violent and survivors of school bullying and trauma often do not neatly fit into created diagnostic categories. Factors such as fear, anxiety, frustration, social and cognitive intelligence, family, economic status, and social factors as well as social jockeying must be taken into full consideration when considering making a diagnosis. We believe students who do not warrant any of the above diagnoses should be protected from misdiagnosis. Many students we have counseled do not fulfill the above diagnoses. However, the intent of presenting these diagnoses is to ensure a full, detailed, and accurate understanding of all students who have experienced school bullying or violence and for perpetrators who bully or are violent.

Summary

This introduction provided general information regarding the frequency of bullying and school violence, defined bullying and school violence, and outlined potentially relevant diagnoses specific to bullying and school violence perpetrators.

References

American Psychiatric Association. (2013). *Diagnostic and statistical manual of mental disorders* (5th ed.). Arlington, VA: Author.

Centers for Disease Control and Prevention. (October 1, 2018). *Prevent bullying*. Retrieved from https.//www.cdc.gov/featers/prevent-bullying/index.html

Centers for Disease Control and Prevention. (2016). *Understanding school violence*. Retrieved from https://www.cdc.gov/violenceprevention/pdf/School_Violence_Fact_Sheet-a.pdf

Jacobson, N., & Gottman, J. (1998) *When men batter women: New insights into ending abusive relationships*. New York, NY: Simon and Schuster.

Lessne, D., & Yanez, C. (December 20, 2016). *Student reports of bullying: Results from the 2015 School Crime Supplement to the National Crime Victimization Survey*. Retrieved from https://nces.ed.gov/pubsearch/pubsinfo.asp?pubid=201715

Musu-Gillette, L., Zhang, A., Wang, K., Zhang, J., & Oudekerk, B. A. (2017). *Indicators of school crime and safety: 2016* (NCES 2017-064/NCJ 250650). Washington, DC: National Center for Education Statistics, U.S. Department of Education, and Bureau of Justice Statistics, Office of Justice Programs, U.S. Department of Justice.

StopBullying.com (May 30, 2019). *What is bullying?* Retrieved from https://www.stopbullying.gov/what-is-bullying/index.html

1

Clinical Interviewing
Is Not Conversation

We are "interviewed" nearly everywhere. When we walk into the newest, mega-super store, we are greeted by a 17-year-old "sales specialist" who "interviews" us to determine if we "should" purchase the store's deluxe discount card. According to this "expert" he can determine if our purchasing habits match an established buyer profile. Supposedly, if our profile is a match the deluxe discount card will save us hundreds of dollars. When we order printer cartridges from the company's customer service center somewhere in India, we are repeatedly "interviewed" by customer service representatives. Despite our continued protests the customer service operators claim they "must" interview us regarding our printing habits. This is supposedly done so they may "help" us determine if purchasing the company's "premium multi-printer cartridge pack" is best. Recently, a waitress "interviewed" us to determine if we were a "sophisticated enough wine connoisseur" to order the restaurant's overly priced specialty wine. Wanting merely to enjoy dinner without the need to be interviewed, we left.

We suspect our readers experience similar "interviews." Often such interviews are nothing more than casual, one-sided conversations conducted by persons who have an agenda to sell a product or service. Most of the time the persons doing the interviews are minimally invested in our well-being, and frequently they are far less expert than they claim. The detrimental result is a prevalent generalization among many people that interviews are little more than frivolous conversations conducted by noninvested nonexperts, attempting to benefit from our pressing needs.

However, when it comes to conducting face-to-face clinical interviews with bullied survivors and potentially bullying and violent students, this generalization is anything but true. Thus, specialists must understand the significant differences between general conversation and face-to-face clinical interviews.

Daily Conversation Compared to Face-to-Face Clinical Interviews

Some people see little difference between daily conversations and face-to-face clinical interviews. They view face-to-face clinical interviews as simple conversations. Little could be farther from the truth. Kadushin (1983) identified eight distinct differences between daily conversations and clinical interviews, and it is important for specialists to understand these critical differences:

1. The individual clinical interview has a specific intent and purpose.
2. The specialist directs the clinical interview and selects the content to be explored.
3. There is a nonreciprocal relationship between the specialist and the student in which the specialist questions the student and the student responds.
4. The specialist formally arranges the clinical interview meeting.
5. The clinical interaction mandates sustained attention to the clinical interview.
6. The specialist's behaviors are planned and organized.
7. In most situations, the specialist accepts the student's request for a clinical interview.

8. Discussion regarding emotionally charged and traumatic experiences is not avoided; in fact, they are discussed in detail.

Thus, there are striking and important differences between daily conversation and face-to-face clinical interviews. The most important difference is that clinical interviews are clinically and purposefully driven. The clinical purpose of face-to-face clinical interviews in this chapter is to assess a student's immediate bullying and violence risk. Only when such assessment is skillfully conducted can effective intervention follow.

Benefits of Face-to-Face Clinical Interview

In addition to these clear differences between daily conversation and face-to-face clinical interviews, clinical interviews enrich the assessment process and potentially provide robust student benefits. For example, clinical interviews are far more accommodating to students than computer-generated assessment instruments. Clinical interviews allow specialists to seek further student input and clarification related to unclear responses, conflicting statements, or expressed statements and presenting emotions (Balkin & Juhnke, 2017)—all vitally important when assessing bullied and potentially bullying and violent students. Thus, if a specialist is uncertain about a student's response during a face-to-face clinical interview, the specialist can restate the question or request clarification. In the case of potentially bullying or violent students, specialists can clarify bullying or violence ideation and potential harm toward specific students. Also, unlike computer-generated experiences, which promote little specialist–student interaction during the test-taking process, clinical interviews increase opportunities for student interaction and basic rapport building.

This is vitally important to students who have experienced bullying and may be reticent or anxious to engage in the counseling process. Potentially bullying and violent students may be embarrassed about their ideation, and the specialist can invite them to discuss what they are thinking and clarify their intent. Thus, specialists can help students describe thoughts and emotions that contribute to their bullying and violent behaviors ideation.

Moreover, highly anxious, emotional, or agitated students are typically better able to relate to specialists during face-to-face clinical interviews than when responding to computer-generated test questions. Therefore, specialists can verbally instruct panicked, fearful, or angry students how to slow their thinking and take control of their overwhelming emotions. Specialists can also verbally address the needs of fearful, angry or irritated students, recommending short student recesses to keep students engaged and focused on the clinical interview process. Thus, fearful and angry students receive necessary support that helps validate them and enhances the probability of successful data gathering.

Another clinical interview advantage is that specialists can directly observe students. They have front-row seats allowing them to view students' important nonverbal reactions to various subjects and topics during the interview. Undoubtedly, this is one of the most important benefits of face-to-face clinical interviews. For example, specialists can gain significant clinical impressions from students who avoid eye contact when asked about possible violent thoughts or who become agitated when asked about previously displayed bullying behaviors. Such nonverbal reactions clearly warrant further investigation and inquiry to ensure the best counseling treatment and support services are rendered.

Finally, during the clinical interview students have the freedom to openly express their fears, anxieties, and concerns. This is particularly relevant for students from diverse backgrounds. Here, clinical interviews present opportunities for persons from minority groups to provide a cultural context for their experiences and projected future behaviors. Hence, clinical interviews promote vital two-way communications between the specialist and the student. Most importantly, students are encouraged to educate the specialist about their presenting concerns within the students' culturally relevant context. In other words, students are not merely assessed by an external source—the school specialist. Instead, they actively contribute in the assessment process by teaching specialists about the cultural context in which concerns occur. Therefore, clinical interviews encourage students to mold counseling to their needs. Bullied survivors can learn they co-direct the counseling process by indicating their panic, anxiety, fear, anger, and needs. Likewise, potentially bullying and violent students learn they co-direct the counseling process by describing the thoughts and feelings that produce bullying and violent behaviors, and they learn they have the ability to change their bullying and violent thoughts, emotions, and behaviors.

Clearly, there are many potential benefits to using face-to-face clinical interviews, and we wholeheartedly believe in their use with both bullied survivors and bullying and violent student perpetrators. However, like all superior specialists, we understand that few things in life are purely good or bad. The same is true for clinical interviews. There are some potential limitations, and we would be foolish not to mention these. We believe the most likely limitation is potential error. As "live assessment instruments," specialists can be fallible. The specialist can unintentionally give certain cues such as facial expressions, voice inflection, and eye contact. Such behaviors could then lead the student to answer in an unintended manner or ignore responding to questions entirely. Also, the specialist may misperceive or misinterpret facial expressions, voice inflections, and other behaviors (e.g., looking away when questioned) and could misunderstand student behaviors as attempts to hide or disguise the truth. Also, some specialists may seem uninterested to students, and this could result in students disengaging altogether from the interview process.

However, we believe the benefits outweigh these limitations. Most importantly, we believe that using a semistructured question format within the face-to-face clinical interview process engages students and provides a balanced opportunity for feedback and discussion.

Helpful Face-to-Face Clinical Interview Question Types

Although there are many types of questions that can be effectively used in face-to-face clinical interviews with bullying survivors and bullying and violence perpetrators, three types of questions warrant discussion: (a) projective questioning, (b) circular questioning, and (c) direct questioning. Direct questioning is the most frequently used, but projective and circular questioning have great utility, especially when students are having difficulties expressing themselves, are guarded or defensive, or offer curt and truncated responses.

Projective Questioning

Specialists using projective questioning ask students to use from one to five words to describe someone (e.g., the bully), an experience (e.g., being bullied), a violent behavior (e.g., fighting), or a calming behavior (e.g., breathing exercises). For bullying and violent students, the primary intent is to gain an understanding of how to reduce and eliminate such behaviors. When counseling a bullied student, the primary intent is to gain increased understanding of the student's perceptions and potential for retaliation and suicide. With bullied students, projective questions can be used to promote effective treatment.

A common projective question for a bullied student would be, "What words would you use to describe the boy who bullied you?" Here, the intent is to learn the degree of anger the survivor holds against the perpetrator and the perception of harm the survivor believes was inflicted. Depending on the student's age, intelligence, and vocabulary sophistication, words like "wicked," "castrating," "repulsive," and "evil" would suggest substantial anger and robust feelings of victimization. Such a degree of anger and perceptions of victimization should be addressed via counseling. Also, depending on the exact bullying or violence experienced, survivors responding with such robust anger and victimization perceptions should be assessed for suicide and retaliation potential.

Another use of projective questioning is to promote student insight and learn how the student experienced either being bullied or perpetrating the acts of bullying and violence. Here, the specialist might ask a bullying survivor, "What three words would you use to describe how you felt when Tommy twisted your arm and called you names?" Should the student respond "scared," "afraid," and "frightened," the specialist might respond by comparing the degree of the feelings during the bullying event to the student's current feelings:

COUNSELOR: You used the words "scared," "afraid," and "frightened" to indicate what you were feeling when Tommy twisted your arm and called you names. On a scale of 0 to 10, with 0 meaning not scared, not afraid, and not frightened and 10 meaning very scared, very afraid, and very frightened, what score would you give?

STUDENT: It was a 10. I was very scared.

COUNSELOR: How about today when we talk about the bullying? Using the same scale, how "scared," "afraid," and "frightened" do you feel today resulting from the bullying?

STUDENT: I'm not scared any more. I would say a 3.

COUNSELOR: How did you reduce your scared, afraid, and frightened feelings from a 10 to a 3?

STUDENT: I guess I know Tommy's not going to hurt me anymore. He is not twisting my arm, and he is not calling me bad names. I am safe, and I know if anything like that happened again, I would go immediately to my teacher.

Here, the specialist is comparing the student's feelings during the bullying experience to his current feelings about the bullying experience. The specialist uses a 0-to-10 scale to help the student rate the event feelings. When it is determined that the student's feelings have significantly decreased, the specialist encourages insight by asking how the student reduced his scared, afraid, and frightened feelings. The student responds and also reports how he would react should he be similarly bullied again. This questioning has the potential to ensure students replicate helpful pathology-reducing strategies in the future.

Projective questioning can also be used with bullying and violence perpetrators. Here, the specialist asks the bully how it felt when perpetrating the bullying—for instance, "What three words would you use to describe how you felt when you twisted Kshawn's arm?" Should the student say "powerful," "in control," and "fulfilled," the specialist might respond by asking about other behaviors that engender similar feelings: "Based upon your responses, it sounds as though when you twisted Kshawn's arm, you felt powerful and in control. Tell me about other times in your life when you were not violent when you felt powerful and in control." The intent here is to help the student identify nonviolent times when he experienced similar positive feelings. If the student had responded by saying something like, "I never feel powerful or in control," it provides opportunities to explore nonviolent empowering behaviors that he could practice and use in the future.

Circular Questioning

Circular questioning is similar to projective questioning in that the specialist solicits students' perceptions and beliefs. However, this time, students are asked to describe themselves as they believe others experience them. The intent is not to learn students' perceptions of others, but rather to learn how students believe others experience them. Circular questioning is invaluable within the clinical interview process because it helps students identify and build on strengths they perceive others see in them. Furthermore, students can consider and address weaknesses they perceive others believe they demonstrate.

Frequently, students are quick to dismiss others' compliments, although they give considerable weight to unfavorable remarks and caustic statements. Circular questioning affords specialists the opportunity to learn what students think others believe about them. Noted strengths can be built upon. Unfavorable perceptions can be considered and dismissed or needed improvements can be defined.

When initiating circular questioning, it is important to learn whom students consider most important. This can be accomplished by asking a simple question such as, "Rosa, which three people mean the very most to you?" Once these persons are identified, circular questioning can be used to understand how students believe each of the three persons perceives them. Here, circular questioning begins with the most important person and continues to the third most important person. Thus, the specialist might say, "Rosa, you said your father is the most important person in your life. If your father were sitting here right now, what would he say are your most positive attributes and skills?" This question is important because it encourages students to identify attributes and skills that they believe persons important to them would identify. The specialist can then begin building upon such noted attributes and skills within the counseling process. For example, should Rosa state, "My daddy would say that I am intelligent, smart, and kind," the specialist might ask how she could use these positive attributes and skills in other ways that would bring about her life goals without the use of violence. Thus, the intent is to use such perceived attributes and skills to replace students' violent behaviors with nonviolent behaviors that engender feelings of success and accomplishment.

On the other hand, should students be unable to state any positive attributes or skills that they believe others perceive in them, the specialist might say, "It sounds as though you may not know what attributes or skills this very important person sees in you, Rosa. Let's think about it in another way. What attributes or skills would you like your father to see in you?" Here, the intent is to learn how students wish to be perceived by significant others. Once these attributes and skills are listed, the specialist might ask, "Rosa, I'm wondering. What things would you need to begin doing so others who you really care about could begin noticing your many already existing favorable attributes and skills?" At this point, the specialist can help students identify ways in which such attributes and skills can be demonstrated.

Finally, specialists can use circular questioning to encourage new student behaviors by having students describe their perceptions of how their bullying or violent behaviors perceive them. For example, the specialist might say,

> "Reggie, this is the second time this year that you have been suspended from school because of your violent behaviors. You say you want to go to college, become a lawyer, and make lots of money. But, because you got into another fight on school property and threatened Vice Principal Harris, you are suspended from school and your grades are dropping. You told me your mother cried because of your fighting and your little brother cries because he doesn't want you to fight at school anymore. Given all of this, if fighting could talk, how would it describe you?"

Should Reggie indicate that fighting would describe him as "weak" and "stupid," the specialist might then ask, "How would you need to begin acting so fighting would know you are strong and smart?" The intent is to have students identify new behaviors that would indicate they are initiating their nonviolent behaviors and are committed to them.

Directive Questioning

In directive questioning, the specialist queries students about themselves, their violent behaviors, and their presenting concerns. In other words, instead of asking students how they believe others perceive them or how the specialist could be helpful to persons presenting with their violent behaviors, students directly respond to the specialist's questions. A likely query might be:

> "John, I've heard you say others perceive you as being violent and you don't like that. However, according to you, some people you had been friends with no longer want to be your friends because of your violent behaviors. Therefore, my question to you is, 'Are you ready to exchange your previous violent behaviors for new nonviolent behaviors?'"

These questions have particular merit because they provide specialists direct student self-report and allow students to provide important information regarding their beliefs and concerns. Self-report is vital to any clinical interview because it also allows specialists to gain an understanding of the student's commitment to counseling and willingness to participate in treatment.

Using the above example, if John stated, "No, I'm not willing to stop hitting people and getting in their face," the specialist might respond by stating something like:

"I guess I am a little confused, John. You told me that you lost some close friends because you were fighting. You specifically told me Charlie no longer wants to be your friend because you broke his arm. You also told me your mother called the police and had you removed from her home because you hit her in her face with your fist and threatened to kill her. Help me understand how it is helpful to continue your violent behaviors."

Here the specialist is using information from previous directive questioning to confront John about his indication he does not wish to change his violent behaviors. The intent is to attempt to get John to understand that he was the one who previously reported he wished to change his behaviors and to create potential cognitive dissonance related to his past and current statements.

Conversely, should John respond by saying, "You know what? I am ready to exchange my previous violent behaviors for new, non-violent behaviors," the specialist could again respond with directive questioning by asking something like "I'm glad to learn you want to give up your old way of acting for new and more effective ways of behaving. What is the first old, violent way of acting you are going to give up, and how are you going to interact in new ways that aren't violent?" Again, the specialist is using directive questioning to have John identify the exact behaviors he will change. Directive questioning also gives John the opportunity to identify a list of new behaviors from which he could select should he become violent again.

Our Face-to-Face Clinical
Interview Experiences

We have found face-to-face clinical interviews to be indispensable part of the assessment process. They allow us to quickly secure vital information related to bullied and violence survivors (e.g., where they are being bullied or victimized, who is bullying or harming them). In the case of bullying or violent students, we can further ascertain the manner of intended harm against potential victims (e.g., bullying, fighting), where the behaviors have occurred or will occur (e.g., at the bus stop, in the gym), and the identities of current or intended victims. Clinical interviews also ensure students receive a thorough face-to-face clinical assessment. At the conclusion of that clinical assessment, a context is created in which to view student symptomatology identified by more traditional, broad-spectrum assessments such as the Minnesota Multiphasic Personality Inventory–Adolescent–Restructured Form, the Minnesota Multiphasic Personality Inventory–Adolescent, or the Million Adolescent Clinical Inventory.

Here, for example, a more traditional assessment instrument might suggest the student responded in a manner consistent with others of the same age who are feeling hopeless, angry, hostile or depressed, or who are experiencing familial stressors (Juhnke & Balkin, 2017). Endorsing question responses in such a manner on a testing instrument is not the same as being hopeless, angry, hostile, and depressed and experiencing familial stressors. Simply stated, these question responses only suggest the student responded like persons who are feeling this way. Thus, the clinical interview is used as a means to support or remove the broader generalizations generated via testing instrument (Balkin & Juhnke, 2017; Juhnke & Balkin, 2017). More importantly, however, information generated by traditional testing instruments need to be placed within the context of the information gathered during the face-to-face clinical interview. In other words, the face-to-face clinical interview serves as the foundational lens of all assessments. Every other assessment piece is filtered through this foundational lens. Information that does not fit the foundational lens is considered and then discarded if perceived inaccurate. Information that matches the information gathered via the face-to-face interview is retained and used to supplement the specialist's clinical judgment and treatment plans.

Face-to-face clinical interviews provide multisystemic contexts that aid specialists in understanding bullying survivors' fears and concerns. For bullying and violent perpetrators, these multisystemic contexts are also important. Therefore, it is important to understand bullying and violent behaviors within the contexts of the many systems in which students are immersed (e.g., family, school, neighborhood, gang). Only by understanding such multisystemic contexts from the student's point of view can specialists fully comprehend the stressors experienced by students and their experiences of being bullied or perpetrating bullying and violence. Equally important, clinical interviews allow specialists to quickly engage bullied and potentially bullying and violent students. Such engagement promotes opportunities for students to interact within a therapeutically safe and inviting professional relationship that fosters important healing and change.

In general, both bullied and bullying and violent students we have interviewed readily participate in clinical interviews, even when they have flatly refused to participate in more traditional psychological testing. Thus, when we believe students have been bullied or demonstrate a potential for bullying or violence, we begin by engaging them in general conversation. Once students perceive we are invested in helping them resolve their pressing concerns, they generally become more comfortable talking to us. Only then do we ask students about their experiences. With bullied students, we ask about their current condition and how they are doing. With bullying and potentially violent students, we ask if they would be willing to help us understand how the bullying and violent behaviors are helpful. After all, what child or adolescent doesn't want to tell others about what he or she is going through or perceived injustices or feelings of ill treatment?

Once we respond to any potential student questions related to the proposed clinical interview process, we describe the purpose of the clinical interview. It is critical to indicate that the interview's purpose is to learn how the specialist can be helpful to the student.

For bullied students, we focus on their immediate physical, emotional, and interpersonal needs. For bullied students who were sexually abused or who report shame or embarrassment, we also assess for potential suicide risk or retaliation toward the perpetrator. For bullying and violent students, we determine if they pose an immediate threat or danger to others.

The student also needs to be informed regarding how the obtained information will be used. The specialist indicates that the information gathered via the clinical interview will be used to (a) ensure the student's safety as well as the safety of others, (b) learn whether further assessment is warranted, (c) determine whether a secure or more structured environment such as a hospital, foster care, or juvenile detention setting is necessary, and (d) determine what school policies or laws may have been broken and if the acts warrant police investigation. Both students and parents must be informed about confidentiality limitations; they must be told that the specialist who perceives a threat of danger is required to respond accordingly. Such responses may require (a) breaking confidentiality by informing student-identified victims (e.g., students, parents of students, teachers, administrators), (b) making required reports to agencies such as Child Protective Services, school officials, or the police, and (c) advocating that the student be removed from school grounds or evaluated for placement in a restrictive environment to ensure the student's or others' safety. If information derived from the clinical interview is to be used in any other manner, that intended use must be clearly described to both students and parents. If the student is a minor, which is nearly always the case, we require written permission from the student's parents to conduct the assessment. Such parental permission is always obtained prior to the interview process with a witness's signature.

Should bullied students or their parents indicate an unwillingness to participate (a rarity, given that most students and parents we encounter report either "relief" that someone "finally cares" or "appreciation" for our sincere and respectful interest in the student), we typically seek clarification of their concerns and encourage them to return in the future when they are feeling more comfortable with the assessment process. For bullying and violent students and their parents who do not consent to the assessment process, we simply remind them that nonparticipating students likely will be expelled or suspended from school for a very lengthy time and will be required to complete a battery of psychological tests and interviews before they are considered potentially eligible to return. Nonparticipating students who are perceived to be at risk for bullying and violent behaviors may even be placed in more restrictive settings where they will be monitored and assessed until sufficient information can be gathered to make an informed determination about their violent risk potential.

The intent of these statements is not to threaten or intimidate; rather, the statements merely reflect reality. When school administrators are faced with bullying and potentially violent students who refuse to participate in the assessment process and whose parents refuse to require the students to participate, the school must act to ensure its students' safety and to insulate the school district from liability risks. Thus, until it is determined that students who are identified as warranting an assessment are not imminent bullying or violence risks, it is likely they will be prohibited from returning to school. When presented with such information and the gravity of the situation, most students and their parents comply with the assessment process.

Empowering Students During the Interview

Often bullied and bullying and violent students feel disempowered and defensive. We have found it important to explain to students that they control the clinical interview and may stop the interview at any time. Only on infrequent occasions have we ever had students actually stop a clinical interview. However, giving students both the permission and authority to stop the interview seems to dispel most student concerns and reminds them that they control the assessment interview process.

Should students request the interview be stopped, we typically respond to the request and later query them regarding the reasons for the requested stoppage. For example, are the students becoming exhausted from the questions, are they overwrought with emotions, are they embarrassed, or do specific questions engender unpleasant memories? Often, we ask those stopping the interviews if they wish to take a short break or if they would like to discuss another topic area specific to the clinical interview. We find it important to stay with students and engage them in nonclinical conversation if such conversations are not threatening or bothersome to the student. Here our intent is to continue to build rapport and continually engage students in general conversation. During this time, we ask questions related to persons perceived as being supportive to them (e.g., friends, teachers, family members) and activities they enjoy (e.g., sports, games, extracurricular activities). Once the students again seem comfortable and able to proceed, we reinitiate the clinical interview.

Should students refuse or be too emotionally distraught to continue the interview, the specialist should note what questions prompted the request to discontinue the interview. For example, were the questions related to a girlfriend or boyfriend? If so, gathering further information specific to this person and potential issues surrounding this area would be important. Should students refuse to continue the interview or respond to queries related to the disconcerting subject area, clarifying data might be obtained via clinical interviews with family members or friends.

Summary

This chapter addressed issues specific to face-to-face clinical interviews, including differences between face-to-face clinical interviews and general conversation, and potential benefits and limitations of face-to-face clinical interviews. Three common face-to-face questioning types were described: projective questioning, circular questioning, and direct questioning. Clinical vignettes demonstrated how each could be effectively used. We highlighted the indispensable clinical utility of face-to-face interviews as a means to quickly engage students and to gain multisystemic contexts for both the perpetrator and survivor. Such engagement gives students the opportunity to interact within a therapeutically safe and inviting professional relationship that fosters important healing and change. Clinical interviews are also used as a means to support or remove the broader generalizations potentially generated via testing instruments.

References

Balkin, R. S., & Juhnke, G. A. (2017). *Assessment in mental health*. New York, NY: Oxford University Press.

Juhnke, G. A., & Balkin, R. S. (2017). *The Minnesota Multiphasic Personality Inventory-2 and Minnesota Multiphasic Personality Inventory-2-Restructured Form: An essential primer for non-psychologist mental health professionals*. San Diego, CA: CreateSpace.

Kadushin, A. (1983). *The social work interview* (2nd ed.). New York, NY: Columbia University Press.

2

Clinical Interviewing with Violence and Bullying Behavior

This chapter builds upon the foundational "what" information provided in Chapter 1. It will describe vital core questions that are easily integrated into face-to-face clinical interviews with bullying survivors and bullying and violence perpetrators. The chapter provides an overview of two mnemonics—the 2WHO-SCAN and the VIOLENT STUdent Scale—and how they can be used to assess key intervention strategies. Both are intended to augment the specialist's clinical judgment and promote a positive clinical intervention.

Student Survivor Core Questions

Face-to-face clinical interviews have long been reported as demonstrating significant assessment utility and have been used within successful clinical practice (Vacc & Juhnke, 1997). Most frequently, they focus on the specific behaviors, symptoms, or events being assessed within the interview. For bullied and violence survivors, clinical interview topics revolve around (a) their immediate safety and physical needs, (b) what happened, (c) how the bullying or violent behaviors have affected the student, (d) stopping the victimization of this and other student survivors, and (e) identifying other students who may currently be or were bullied or victimized by the same perpetrator.

The 2WHO-SCAN Mnemonic

To address these core questions and address the pressing needs of bullying survivors, the 2WHO-SCAN bullying mnemonic was created (Juhnke, Juhnke, & Henderson, 2013). Mnemonics are words or combinations of letters, numbers, or symbols used to aid recall and memory. Typically, each mnemonic letter, number, or symbol relates to a specific assessment or intervention factor. Patterson, Dohn, Bird, and Patterson's (1983) and Juhnke's (1994) seminal research demonstrated the effectiveness of mental health trainees using mnemonics as part of the suicide assessment process. Their findings indicated that counseling students who used mnemonic memory aids (e.g., SAD PERSONS, Adapted-SAD PERSONS) were clinically and statistically better able to recall important risk factors than those who simply learned multiple assessment factors without a mnemonic. These researchers further found that students who used mnemonics conducted more thorough assessments and more accurately scored corresponding clinical vignettes.

Today, mnemonics are broadly used as a means to recall important factors and sequences and to remember relevant instructions. For example, the American Association for Suicidology (2013) encourages counseling professionals to use the mnemonic "IS PATH WARM" when assessing suicide risk. Medical professionals frequently use mnemonics such as "Every Little Boy Must Pray" to help providers remember the specific order of drugs to be given when attempting to resuscitate patients whose hearts have stopped (epinephrine, lidocaine, bretylium, magnesium sulfate, procainamide) (C. Weiner, personal communication, February 6, 2012). Law enforcement professionals use mnemonics such as GO WISELY to help them thoroughly investigate a crime scene (grounds, object, warrant, identification, station, entitlement, lawfully, year) (D. Macintosh, personal communication, February 7, 2012). Given research demonstrating the benefits of mnemonics and the widespread use of mnemonics in many professions to aid factor recall and memory, the authors believed creating and using the 2WHO-SCAN mnemonic would help supervisees better remember important bullying assessment factors and intervene with survivors of bullying.

2WHO-SCAN (pronounced "too scan" or "tü skan") was designed to help specialists remember seven critical assessment factors and intervention steps (Balkin & Juhnke, 2013; Juhnke, Granello, & Granello, 2010). Each letter corresponds to a specific step for assessing a bullying survivor and intervening in a bullying situation:

> <u>W</u>hat is necessary to physically stabilize the bullied student? and
>   <u>W</u>hat happened?
> <u>H</u>ow has the bullying affected the student?
> <u>O</u>ptions for intervention
> <u>S</u>top the bullying behaviors
> <u>C</u>harges and interventions for the bully
> <u>A</u>nother bullying survivor
> <u>N</u>otify parents and guardians

Specialists are strongly encouraged to use additional assessment and intervention measures depending on the student's specific needs and the exact bullying situation. The 2WHO-SCAN mnemonic and each of the seven stages are presented next.

Step 1: What Is Necessary to Physically Stabilize the Bullied Student? and What Happened?

The first question ("What is necessary to physically stabilize the bullied student?") is used to ensure immediate student safety. Thus, immediate medical care is sought if bullied students have experienced physical injuries that warrant medical attention.

Only after medical needs have been addressed and the student's physical condition has stabilized do specialists move to the second "what" question ("What happened?"). This second question reminds specialists to gather facts about the bullying incident and understand the details of what happened. Minimally, this question includes: (a) who bullied the survivor, (b) where the bullying occurred, (c) when the bullying occurred, and (d) any other bullying the student has experienced.

Step 1 of the assessment and intervention might go something like this:

SOCIAL WORKER: Sonja, are you hurt? Do you need me to call an ambulance?

SONJA: No, I am fine. I just hurt my arm when I got pushed down.

SOCIAL WORKER: Tell me what happened.

SONJA: Summer and Ginger have been bullying me. Today, they called me names and pushed me down.

SOCIAL WORKER: When did that happen?

SONJA: It started on the bus. Ginger grabbed my purse, and Summer made fun of the way I talk. Then, when I walked inside the school at first bell, Summer pushed me to the ground, and Ginger spit on me and laughed at me.

SOCIAL WORKER: Where did this happen?

SONJA: At the entrance to the dance studio.

SOCIAL WORKER: How long has this been going on?

SONJA: It all started about two weeks ago when I started dating Summer's old boyfriend, Oscar.

SOCIAL WORKER: Is this the first time you've been bullied?

SONJA: Yeah! I don't like it.

The first "what" question was specific to stabilizing the student. The second "what" question was specific to gathering simple facts rather than focusing on the student's emotions or symptoms. The specialist needs to understand the survivor's bullying experiences within the context of what occurred.

Step 2: How Has the Bullying Affected the Student?

After ensuring the student's safety and understanding the facts of the bullying, the specialist finds out how the student has been affected by the bullying. Here, the specialist seeks to determine potential emotional, cognitive, or interpersonal struggles specific to the bullying and any coping behaviors the student has found helpful. Thus, the specialist might say something like:

SOCIAL WORKER: Sonja, tell me a little about how the bullying has affected you.

SONJA: I hadn't really thought about it.

SOCIAL WORKER: It sounds as though you haven't really had the time to think how the bullying has affected you. So, as you think about the bullying, how do you think it may have affected you?

SONJA: Well, I have been crying a lot, and skipped dance class, because I am scared to attend.

SOCIAL WORKER: Tell me about the crying.

SONJA: I have dance first period. I get so scared about Summer beating up on me that I start to cry. I can't concentrate or do my homework, because I know Summer and Ginger are just going to push me around, steal my dance bag, or ridicule me.

SOCIAL WORKER: That sounds pretty rough.

SONJA: It has been really bad. I get so scared my body literally shakes.

SOCIAL WORKER: Tell me what things you have done to stop the shaking and move through the fear.

SONJA: I tell myself that I am going to get through this and say, "What doesn't kill me makes me stronger."

SOCIAL WORKER: It sounds like your self-talk makes you stronger.

SONJA: It has been very helpful.

SOCIAL WORKER: What are you saying to yourself right now?

SONJA: That I am safe and I am not going to let Summer or Ginger bully me any longer.

SOCIAL WORKER: Good. I want you to be safe. Besides the crying and skipping dance class, have you noticed any other ways the bullying has affected you?

SONJA: I have noticed my friends have left me. Summer and Ginger bullied them when they were around me, so they have kind of left me to protect themselves.

SOCIAL WORKER: Which friends? [Bullied friends will be addressed in Step 6.]

SONJA: Clare and Anna. They stopped hanging around me because Summer and Ginger bullied them too.

SOCIAL WORKER: Have others left you because of the bullying?

SONJA: No, just Clare and Anna, but I bet they will start hanging around me again once Summer and Ginger stop bullying me.

SOCIAL WORKER: You said that since the bullying began you've cried a lot and Clare and Anna have stopped hanging around you. Has the bullying affected you in other ways or have you noticed anything else?

SONJA: No. That's about it.

In this vignette, the specialist simply asks the survivor how the bullying has affected her. He also responded to Sonja's statements in a factual manner. The intent is to focus on the facts versus emotions about the bullying. The specialist validates the student throughout the vignette and helps her identify her coping behaviors and strengths. Also, the specialist continues to ask how the student has been affected by the bullying until the student reports all the effects she has noticed. The specialist finally summarizes the overall effects noted by the student.

Step 3: Options for Intervention

In this step the specialist identifies available counseling options for the bullied survivor. The specialist may wish to consider different combinations of counseling modalities such as individual, group, or family counseling. Given the differences in children's and adolescent's developmental needs along the lifespan continuum, family counseling may be particularly important for younger students and their parents. Some schools may not provide necessary moderate- to long-term counseling options, or group or family counseling options. Thus, depending on the survivor's immediate needs and available counseling services in the school district, the specialist may need to identify treatment options in the community and facilitate a seamless and supportive referral.

Step 4: Stop the Bullying Behaviors

This step is focused on stopping the identified perpetrators from bullying again. The information gathered in Step 1 provides information about who the perpetrators are, the location of their bullying behaviors, the times the bullying occurred, and what the perpetrators did. Here, specialists need to share information with the school principal, campus resource officer, teachers, and other administrators and staff (e.g., bus drivers, custodians) regarding what happened and ensure a jointly developed intervention designed to stop the identified perpetrators from repeating their bullying behaviors. In addition, safety procedures are implemented in the locations where the bullying occurred and at the times the survivor was bullied (e.g., at first bell). For instance, Sonja reported that she experienced bullying on the bus and at the entrance to the dance studio at first bell. In this case, Sonja's school bus driver and her dance instructor would be informed of the bullying. Campus resource officers, faculty, or other appropriate staff should also be placed on the bus, at the bus arrival point, and at the entrance to the dance studio at first bell to ensure the safety and protection of all students. Such placements will likely diminish once administrators determine the bullying behaviors are no longer occurring at the identified locations and times. However, continued monitoring of these locations should continue (e.g., security cameras).

Step 5: Charges and Interventions for the Bully

Most schools have zero tolerance policies for bullying behaviors. Depending on the severity of the incidents and the injuries to survivors, bullying behaviors may also result in criminal or civil charges. As in Step 4, school administrators, legal counsel, and school resource officers must notified of the bullying behaviors and incidents. However, unlike Step 4, this step is focused on ensuring that the school district's policies as well as corresponding local laws are followed. The intent is not to seek punishment but rather to ensure the survivor's safety and rights and to make certain all students in the school are adequately protected. Depending on the outcome of those policies and laws, but before the bullying perpetrator is allowed to return to school, he or she should be required to participate in psychological assessment and counseling. Before the perpetrator is allowed to return to school, the outcomes of those assessments and the counseling experience should find the perpetrator at minimal risk of continued bullying behaviors.

Step 6: Another Bullying Survivor

Bullying perpetrators typically do not limit their bullying behaviors to one person. Often friends of the bullying survivor or others with whom the bullying perpetrator has frequent contact have been or will be bullied. In Step 2, Sonja reported that her friends Clare and Anna were intimidated by the bullying perpetrator. In this case the specialist should speak with Clare and Anna to provide them an opportunity to discuss being bullied should they wish:

PSYCHOLOGIST: Hi, Clare, I am Mr. Acousta. I am the psychologist for seventh- and eighth-graders at James Madison Middle School. I think I saw you Thursday afternoon at the basketball game. How are you?

CLARE: Oh! Hi, Mr. Acosta. Yes, that was a good game.

PSYCHOLOGIST: I like it when we win.

CLARE: Me too.

PSYCHOLOGIST: How are things going?

CLARE: Pretty good. I am having some struggles in science, but who isn't?

PSYCHOLOGIST: Seventh-grade science can be challenging! Is there anything I can do to help?

CLARE: Nah, I just need to pay attention and read Mr. Bryce's required handouts.

PSYCHOLOGIST: I bet that will help. Hey, Clare, I have heard stories about some kiddos intimidating or bullying others here at Madison. Have you heard about any bullying or experienced anything like that?

CLARE: I don't know if I should say anything, but I think Sonja Jones had a couple things happen. Don't tell her I said anything, though.

PSYCHOLOGIST: What kinds of things?

CLARE: Ever since Sonja started dating Summer Smith's old boyfriend, Oscar, Summer and her friend Ginger have been really picking on Sonja.

PSYCHOLOGIST: How about you, Clare? Has anyone been picking on you?

CLARE: Not really.

PSYCHOLOGIST: And "not really" means . . .

CLARE: Anna Arnold and I used to hang around with Sonja a lot, but Summer and Ginger have been causing so much trouble, Anna and I don't ride the bus any more. We try to stay away from Sonja, Summer, and Ginger. It is really their thing, not ours.

PSYCHOLOGIST: Did Summer or Ginger ever threaten or hurt you?

CLARE: No.

PSYCHOLOGIST: Is that a "no, they never threatened or harmed you" or a "no, I don't want to talk about it"?

CLARE: (Giggles) It is a "no, they never did anything to me."

PSYCHOLOGIST: How would you let me know if they ever threatened or harmed you?

CLARE: I would come to your office. But really, they have never done anything to me.

PSYCHOLOGIST: OK, Clare. Thanks for being so helpful to me. You know if you ever want to talk or if you ever need any help, come down to my office or speak with Ms. Kimmons at the front desk.

CLARE: I know. Everything is fine. I just don't need anything, but if I do need something, I will talk with you. I know where your office is.

This vignette demonstrates how the specialist invites Sonja's friend, Clare, to discuss any potential bullying she may have experienced. Here, the specialist connects with the student by first introducing himself and then commenting on Thursday's middle school basketball game. The student recognizes the specialist and responds to his comment. Once the student engages in conversation, the specialist asks a very generic, nonleading question, "How are things going?" He did not discuss the bullying first or those involved (i.e., Sonja, Summer, Ginger, Oscar, or Anna). Instead, the question he poses is very general and nondescript, with no hint of the bullying topic or the potentially involved students. This is done to maintain confidentiality and ensure Clare's response is not driven by a leading question.

Had Clare reported being bullied, the specialist would have immediately used the 2WHO-SCAN. However, given that Clare does not respond to the generic question, the specialist asks a more specific question related to bullying. This time Clare indicates Sonja may be involved but asks the specialist not to say anything to Sonja. Instead of promising confidentiality or anonymity, the specialist simply eclipses the request and asks, "What kinds of things?" Clare describes the situation with Sonja but fails to indicate whether she has experienced bullying herself. The specialist then personalizes the question and asks, "How about you, Clare? Has anyone been picking on you?" Clare's response is, "Not really." The specialist gently challenges Clare's response and seeks clarification. As a result of this challenge, Clare divulges what she witnessed and how she responded to Summer and Ginger's bullying of Sonja. This time the specialist asks Claire if she was threatened or hurt by Summer or Ginger. Clare's response is "No." Again, the specialist seeks clarification and Clare denies being threatened or harmed by Summer or Ginger. Instead of dropping the discussion, the specialist asks, "How would you let me know if they ever threatened or harmed you?" This is an excellent response and demonstrates a meta-communication intervention. Thus, Clare reports that if she needed help she understands how to contact the specialist and clarifies that she did not experience bullying. The specialist ensures Clare understands how to get help by indicating a potential alternative female specialist, Ms. Kimmons, should Clare feel uncomfortable speaking to him.

In addition to speaking with Clare and Anna, the specialist may consider talking to other potential bullying survivors who rode the same bus as Sonja and the bullying perpetrator, or other potential bullying survivors who entered the school dance studio around first bell. Specialists should continue to maintain confidentiality and not divulge the identities of the bullying survivor or the accused perpetrator to students. However, specialists should interact with students at these identified locations and make themselves available to others who may have experienced the bullying behaviors.

Step 7: Notify Parents and Guardians

This step is designed to ensure that the parents of both the bullying survivor and the perpetrator are notified of the situation. Parents of bullying survivors can help provide vital information regarding their children and can aid in monitoring of the survivor's recovery. Often the parents of the survivor want immediate resolution and a guarantee the survivor will never again be bullied. Specialists must be cautious in their responses and should not promise complete safety. Instead, the specialist can report steps taken to protect the survivor from further bullying. Also, parents of bullying survivors can seek criminal charges or civil court actions.

Parents of bullying perpetrators should be informed of the bullying behavior and the school district's policies regarding bullying behaviors. Although some parents of bullying perpetrators are empathic toward their child's victims, in our experience most parents support their children who demonstrate bullying behaviors. Often these parents strongly advocate for their children and blame teachers, administrators, and staff for allowing the bullying behaviors to occur. On more than one occasion we have experienced parents who exhibited intimidating behaviors or refused to follow or support school district bullying policies. In such situations when parents are failing to take parental authority and control of their children, specialists should speak with school legal counsel about involving child protective services.

Bullying and Violence Question Core

In this chapter, the "question core" or central focus of clinical interviews related to bullying and violence perpetrators comprises three core areas—(a) the frequency of violent thoughts, (b) the strength of violent thoughts, and (c) the duration of violent thoughts—and an ancillary substance abuse/addictions area.

Frequency of Violent Thoughts

How often does the student have thoughts of violence toward others? Are they infrequent (i.e., once a year), occasional (i.e., three or four times a year), or markedly frequent (i.e., two or more times per hour)? We ask such questions in a straightforward manner.

FAMILY THERAPIST: John, you say you have had thoughts of stabbing Brian. It is 9 o'clock a.m. now. How many times have you thought about stabbing Brian today?

STUDENT: I don't know . . . probably 30 times.

FAMILY THERAPIST: So, you've had thoughts of stabbing Brian 30 times today?

STUDENT: Yes.

FAMILY THERAPIST: What time did you get up today?

STUDENT: About 7:30.

FAMILY THERAPIST: So, between 7:30 and 9 a.m. today, you have thought about stabbing Brian about 30 times?

STUDENT: Yep. Maybe more.

FAMILY THERAPIST: How many more?

STUDENT: Maybe 35 or 40 times. I just keep thinking about stabbing that punk.

FAMILY THERAPIST: Did you have thoughts about stabbing Brian yesterday?

STUDENT: Yes. When I saw Brian stealing my backpack yesterday afternoon, I kept thinking to myself, "I am going to stab that punk."

FAMILY THERAPIST: Before that time, had you thought about stabbing Brian?

STUDENT: Nope. It all started yesterday after I saw him take my backpack off the bus.

FAMILY THERAPIST: How many times did you think about stabbing or hurting Brian yesterday after you got off the bus?

STUDENT: Lots of times. I just kept thinking about it and thinking about it. Maybe 100 times or more. I guess I kept thinking about it until I fell asleep. Then, I thought about stabbing him first thing when I got up this morning. He might steal from others, but that is the last time he will steal from me.

In this vignette we learn that the violent behavior ruminations began as a result of the student's belief that Brian had stolen his backpack. The student reports that "100 times or more" last night he "thought about stabbing" Brian, and today he has already thought about stabbing Brian on 30 or more occasions. This violent thought frequency is clearly noteworthy and warrants immediate intervention to ensure Brian's safety.

Strength of Violent Thoughts

The specialist is looking to ascertain the strength or intensity of the violent thoughts. Is the violent thought only nonchalantly considered (e.g., "I could punch Sarah!")? Or is it so powerful that the student concentrates and ruminates on it (e.g., "I hate Sarah and must kill her")? At more extreme strength levels students feel they "must" or "should" act on their violent thoughts. Depending on the student's age and development, we often find it helpful to ask questions using a scale from 0 to 10, with 0 representing a total lack of strength or intensity and 10 representing overwhelming strength that causes violent rumination:

COUNSELOR: Alex, on a scale of 0 to 10, where 0 indicates you just simply thought about stabbing Brian but had no intention of really stabbing him and forgot about stabbing him immediately after thinking of it, and 10 meaning that you not only thought about stabbing Brian but that you actually intended to stab

Brian, what kind of score would you say matches your thoughts last night of stabbing Brian?

STUDENT: Beats me . . . I guess I'd give myself a 9. If he had been standing by me, I would have stabbed him. Each time I thought about stabbing him, I would think to myself, "Yes, I'm going to stab that punk!" and I would think about how he would feel the pain.

COUNSELOR: So, I'm hearing you say that it wasn't like, "I'm thinking about stabbing Brian," then thinking about other things for a while or thinking to yourself, "OK, I'm over thinking about stabbing Brian now. I'm not really going to stab him. I'm going to think about something else now."

STUDENT: Right. As soon as I would think about stabbing that punk, I would start thinking about when I would stab him and who would be there. When my mom called she asked me to make dinner for my kid sister. I had to stop thinking about stabbing Brian. But, as soon as I fed my sister, I began drawing pictures of what I was going to do to him. You know, it was something like a cartoon. Frame one, I would stalk him in the hall. Frame two, I would push him against his locker, Frame three, I would stab him in the neck. I couldn't stop thinking about it.

Here we note Alex's robust violent thought strength and intensity. Alex self-reports a significant intensity level (i.e., 9). He describes ruminating on his violent thinking and even drawing pictures of the intended stabbing. Each picture frame reflects part of Alex's premeditated violence plan. Such intensity again reveals a need for immediate intervention.

Duration of Violent Thoughts

Although the duration and the strength of violent thinking may initially present as somewhat similar, with some potential overlap, duration means the amount of time the student considers the violent act. In other words, when the student thinks about behaving in a violent manner, how much time does he or she commit to truly thinking about the violence? Is the violent thought merely fleeting and brief, or does the student dwell on it? Thus, we are seeking to determine if the violent thoughts are fleeting or sustained in duration. Sustained violent thoughts or ruminations typically result in elaborate schemes on how to carry out the violent behaviors. Well-delineated violence plans require sustained attention specific to the intended violent act. Such sustained attention requires time or duration.

COUNSELOR: When you initially thought about stabbing Brian, how long did you think about it?

STUDENT: I couldn't stop thinking about it.

COUNSELOR: What do you mean?

STUDENT: It was like, "Man, I want to pulverize that punk and make him pay for stealing my backpack." You know, I would just sit there and think about it.

COUNSELOR: So, each time you thought about stabbing Brian you would think about it for—what, maybe 30 seconds or a minute at the most?

STUDENT: No. I would just sit there and think about it over and over again. I bet I sat there for at least 30 minutes just thinking about how mad I was at him and how I wanted to smash his punk head in for stealing my things.

COUNSELOR: When you went to bed last night, did you think about stabbing Brian then?

STUDENT: I couldn't even sleep! I kept thinking about what he had done to me and how I was going to make him pay for what he did to me. All night I kept thinking to myself, "You've got to quit thinking about breaking this guy apart because you've got to get some sleep."

It is strikingly evident that the duration of Alex's violent thoughts was significant. Thus, based on Alex's responses to the three violence core queries specific to frequency, strength, and duration, there is little doubt that he poses a clear and imminent danger to Brian.

Substance Use/Addiction

An ancillary substance abuse–violence area has become increasingly important in recent years. Specifically, we have found a robust correlation among violence ideation and violent behaviors when students are under the influence.

Alcohol

When we first began to assess potentially violent students, we primarily assessed for alcohol abuse. Certainly, any student under the influence of any substance can become violent, but we noted that students abusing alcohol often had increased impulsivity, diminished self-control and appropriate boundary-setting abilities, an inability to effectively use verbal skills, increased combativeness, and tendencies toward argumentative and aggressive behaviors when under the influence. Certainly not all students under the influence of alcohol become violent, but a sizeable portion of those under the influence of alcohol act in violent ways. Therefore, students who abuse alcohol are at increased risk of violent behaviors.

We have expanded our substance abuse assessment with violent and potentially violent students to assess not only alcohol but also two other substance groups that seem particularly correlated with student violence: (a) central nervous system stimulants and (b) steroids.

CNS Stimulants

Stimulants, such as cocaine and methamphetamines, increase hyperactivity and restlessness. Some students report that while under the influence their minds "race." This racing seems to increase the risk that they will ruminate over perceived injustices and will have thoughts of violent behaviors toward others. Over time stimulant abuse can result in paranoia, paranoid delusions, or hallucinations, all which can further contribute to violent behaviors.

Steroids

Anabolic–androgenic steroids are more commonly known simply as "steroids." Testosterone is one of the most widely known steroids, which enhance muscle growth via individual cell protein synthesis. Aggression, violence, and "roid rage" are correlated with steroid use. Due to the potential for violence among students who abuse steroids, such steroid abuse should be investigated.

Extreme bravado is one overarching clinical presentation we have occasionally seen in potentially violent students abusing any of these three substances (especially stimulants and steroids). These students often "get in your face." They brim with a menacing presence and present with an air of defiance designed to intimidate and threaten. Frankly, when students present in such a manner there is only a paper-thin insulator between unsustainable safety and certain detonation. Students displaying such extreme bravado along with substance abuse warrant a restricted environment with detoxification and addictions treatment.

The VIOLENT STUdent Scale

The VIOLENT STUdent Scale (Table 2.1) was created by Juhnke and published in 2000. Juhnke's intent was to create an atheoretical,

Table 2.1 VIOLENT STUdent Scale

Violent or aggressive history

Isolation or feelings of being isolated

Overt aggression toward or torturing of animals

Low school interest

Expressions of violence in drawing or writing

Noted by peers as being "different"

Threats of violence towards others

Social withdrawal

Teased or perceptions of being teased, harassed or "picked on"

Use that is inappropriate or inappropriate access to firearms.

---

semistructured violence assessment scale that specialists could easily and quickly implement during a face-to-face clinical assessment. Proper use of the VIOLENT STUdent Scale ensures that critical violence risk questions are investigated. The scale generates both the potentially violent student's suggested risk for immediate violent behaviors and general clinical intervention guidelines (Juhnke, 2000).

Risk Factor Clusters

The VIOLENT STUdent Scale is based on 10 student violent risk factor clusters identified within the literature by the US Departments of Education and Justice (Dwyer, Osher, & Warger, 1998) and by the Federal Bureau of Investigation's National Center for the Analysis for Violent Crime/Critical Incident Response Group (Supervisory Special Agent Eugene A. Rugala, personal communication, August 31, 1998). These 10 high-risk factor clusters are as follows:

1. **Violent or aggressive history.** Students with violent or aggressive histories are at greater risk of perpetrating violence or aggression toward others. Thus, they are identified within this scale as being at increased risk for potential violent or aggressive behaviors.
2. **Isolation or feelings of being isolated.** The vast majority of students who isolate themselves from peers or who appear friendless typically are not violent. However, within the high-risk factor cluster suggesting increased potential for violence, isolation or feelings of being isolated can be associated with students who behave violently toward their peers. For this reason, students isolating themselves or reporting feelings of being isolated from others should be considered at greater risk.
3. **Overt aggression toward or torturing of animals.** There is a high correlation between violence and students who demonstrate aggression toward animals or torture animals. Hence, students who present with either of these factors should be considered at increased risk of violence.
4. **Low school interest.** The risk factor could come from any of a multitude of reasons that by themselves may not evoke violent behaviors. However, in combination with other risk factors noted in this scale, students presenting with low school interest may be unable to perform as well as they desire and may feel frustrated by such inability. These students may also perceive themselves as belittled by those performing more favorably. Thus, when challenged to increase their performance or when feeling harassed by those performing at higher levels, these students may become violent. For these reasons, this factor has been included.

5. **Expressions of violence in drawing or writing**. Violent students often indicate their intentions before acting violently via drawings or writing. Such expressions of violence should be assessed immediately and should not be easily dismissed.

6. **Noted by peers as being "different."** On many occasions after student violence, peers and others will note that the perpetrating student was labeled as being "different" from peers or being associated with some group that was noted as being "different." Hence, students frequently labeled by peers as being "weird," "strange," "geeky," and so forth may be at increased risk.

7. **Threats of violence toward others.** Any threat of violence toward others should be immediately assessed and appropriate interventions should be taken to ensure safety. Direct threats such as "I'm going to kill him" as well as veiled threats such as "You better enjoy yourself this morning, because your life may come to a quick end after third period today" clearly are inappropriate and warrant immediate assessment.

8. **Social withdrawal.** Withdrawal from peers and familial supports can indicate the student is experiencing any of a number of concerns (e.g., depression, helplessness) that warrant further assessment and intervention. When combined with other risk factors, social withdrawal may signal potential violence toward others.

9. **Teased or perceptions of being teased, harassed, or "picked on."** Violent students often have hypersensitivity toward criticism. They report perceptions of being teased, harassed, or picked on by those they were violent toward. Thus, when hypersensitive students present with other identified risk factors, the potential for violence increases.

10. **Use that is inappropriate or inappropriate access to firearms.** Students inappropriately using firearms (e.g., shooting at buses, airplanes, people) or having inappropriate access to firearms clearly have the potential to act violently and to do so

with a high degree of lethality. Again, this factor by itself may suggest little, but when combined with other risk factors, it suggests an increased potential for violence.

Scoring and Intervention Guidelines

Each of these 10 risk factors can receive a score between 0 (complete absence) and 10 (significant manifestation or presence), for a total of 0 to 100. Proposed intervention guidelines are based on the total number of points received (Table 2.2). The intended purpose of this scale is to augment the school specialist's clinical judgment. In other words, the specialist's clinical judgment supersedes the VIOLENT STUdent Scale scoring and intervention guidelines, and general mass application of this scale among the general student population at large who are not perceived as violent would engender an unacceptable percentage of false-positive responses. Therefore, the scale should only be used when a student is perceived as being at risk for violent behaviors and the corresponding general clinical guidelines represent a minimal standard of care logically determined in conjunction with the school safety and risk committee. Should the school safety and risk committee perceive that the scale's general intervention guidelines are too lax and fail to adequately ensure the restrictive standard of care deemed most appropriate for the presenting student, the intervention guideline should be adjusted accordingly and the student should be placed in a restrictive environment that best matches the immediate violence threat.

Thus, students who are perceived to be at risk of behaving violently but have a lower score (0 to 9) may very well have suspicious responses, which may indicate the student is attempting to present in a favorable and nonviolent fashion. Such scores suggest the student is indicating an absence of violent risk factors. The

Table 2.2 VIOLENT STUdent Scale Scores and General Clinical Guidelines

Score	Clinical Guidelines
70+ points	Immediate removal from general school environment; structured living environment required
40 to 69 points	Counseling with close follow-up required; collaborative meeting with parent(s) or guardians; formalized psychological testing warranted; evaluate and strongly consider structured living environment placement, depending on student's (a) willingness to participate in counseling, (b) cooperation in follow-up arrangements and sincere commitment to enter into a "no harm" contract, and (c) family support
10 to 39 points	Assess immediate danger to self and others; counseling and follow-up counseling offered and strongly encouraged; parental contacts established; additional psychological testing if perceived necessary; "no harm" contract
0 to 9 points	Consult with clinical supervisor and professional peers to determine whether (a) the student was attempting to present self in an overly positive, nonviolent manner and needs more formalized psychological assessment and follow-up intervention, or (b) to provide the student with information on how to contact the specialist in case a future need arises.

primary issue with such low scores is the incongruence between the specialist's initial concerns related to the student's violence risk, which originally incited the violence assessment, and the student's current score, which suggests little risk. Consulting with a clinical supervisor and professional peers can help clarify whether the specialist's original concerns were likely unfounded or whether such concerns suggest that the student's responses to the VIOLENT STUdent Scale questions are suspicious.

Should the specialist's original concerns seem unfounded, the student should be provided information about how to contact specialists in the future should he or she perceive feelings of anger or intent to harm others. Two follow-up meetings with the student to reassess the student's risk for harm to self and others as well as the student's current situation are warranted. The first follow-up should occur within 24 hours of the first assessment, the second 48 to 72 hours after the first follow-up meeting. The specialist should document these meetings and the outcomes of those assessments.

Should the student's responses appear suspicious, additional assessment is clearly warranted. Depending on the outcome of such additional assessment, appropriate interventions should be conducted to ensure the student's and others' safety.

Certain risk factors, even by themselves, warrant immediate investigation and intervention. For example, any student making violent threats toward others should at a minimum participate in further formalized psychological testing, counseling with case management, and parental conferencing until the school safety and risk committee and the specialist all determine the student is not an imminent risk to self or others. Although these steps will not prevent all forms of violence, they are a way to provide a reasonable safety standard.

Students perceived to be at risk for violence with scores between 10 and 39 should be assessed related to immediate danger to harm an identified person or persons. Participation in follow-up counseling should be strongly encouraged as a means to address any presenting concerns, parental contacts should be established, and additional psychological testing should be encouraged if perceived as necessary. Follow-up visits by the school specialist can be used to monitor the student's immediate condition and ensure that appropriate services are made available should a change in the student's condition warrant more intense interventions. Giving students a business-size card with the local 24-hour crisis telephone number printed on the front can provide students with the means to obtain help should they need it. A "no harm contract" may also be useful. Here, students make a promise to the school specialist and trusted family members that they will call the 24-hour crisis hotline should they feel overwhelmed, "angry enough" to hurt someone, or "intent" on harming someone.

Those perceived at risk and receiving scores between 40 and 69 points are required to participate in counseling with close follow-up services. Specialists are obligated to contact parents or guardians whenever a child is considered to be a danger to self or others. A thorough risk assessment should occur anytime a student indicates intent to harm others. Intent may become manifest in a number of ways. A student may make a verbal statement (e.g., "I'm going to kill Shannon tonight with my dad's gun") or may indicate homicidal intent in written work (e.g., journals, assignments). Artwork depicting the student demonstrating violent behaviors (e.g., dousing a fellow student with gasoline and igniting him) deserves further investigation and warrants contacting parents or guardians. Thus, even students with these moderate scores should be evaluated and strongly considered for placement in more structured environments (e.g., foster care, group homes, or psychiatric hospitals specializing in the treatment of violent children) where opportunities to harm others are reduced and effective treatment for those with potentially violent behaviors can occur.

Certainly, students with these scores warrant more formalized psychological testing and likely a more structured school and home environment. The requirement for increased structure within the current living environment or a more restricted environment such as a psychiatric hospital depends on a number of factors, including the school specialist's confidence in the follow-up arrangements and the student's and parents' willingness to comply with comprehensive treatment recommendations (e.g., individual counseling, family counseling, substance abuse counseling). Should the student and the student's family fully support the comprehensive treatment recommendations and a more structured living environment is deemed unnecessary at the time, a school interdisciplinary team should be mobilized to develop an academic and socialization support network. Child protective services should also be notified if neglect or abuse is suspected.

Scores of 70 or greater suggest significant environmental turmoil and emotional stressors. These students are at significant risk of violence toward others and are likely unable to function adequately without direct intervention and intense structure. Those whose scores are at the extreme end of this risk continuum warrant immediate removal from the general school environment and placement in a structured living environment (e.g., specialized foster care, inpatient psychiatric hospital) to ensure safety to peers and self. Of course, such a placement would require parental support. Should the student be deemed an immediate danger to self or others and the parents are unwilling to appropriately support evaluation for a more structured living and learning environment, child protective services should likely be notified. In many cases child protective services can intervene to ensure the child is placed in a safe environment until the immediate danger to self or others disappears.

Clearly, the presence of a single 10-point factor does not mean a student will behave violently. However, a clustering of high-risk factors suggests increased risk. Also, high scores on single factors such as low school interest or isolation may not by themselves suggest violence risk but may suggest a student's need for more general counseling services. Finally, students identified as imminent future victims or targets of violence and their parents or guardians should be notified about such specific and intended threats. The need for student and parental contact as well as the best method in which this contact should be made (e.g., telephone call, registered letter) should be discussed with a clinical supervisor, legal counsel, and the school safety and risk committee.

The VIOLENT STUdent Scale will not identify every violent student; no assessment scale will. The intent of the scale, however, is to augment the specialist's clinical judgment and to provide a general template for the face-to-face clinical assessment that also includes the violence question core and traditional psychological testing. The next part of the face-to-face clinical interview should include direct input from family members and persons who know the student well.

Face-to-Face Clinical Family Interviews

Benefits of a Family Interview

Face-to-face structured clinical interviews can also help the specialist better understand students' familial supports. Specifically, family clinical interviews provide a nonthreatening opportunity to interact with students' families. Such interaction can reduce family members' possible defensiveness, encourage students to see their family systems as more helpful and less caustic, and serve as part of the counseling intervention itself. Thus, direct, nonthreatening questions can be used to gain additional information about the student's violent ideation and behaviors. Family members may be able to provide their thoughts or observations related to precipitating events or behaviors that seem to frequently occur prior to the student's violent behaviors or verbal threats.

SOCIAL WORKER: You say you have heard Ricky threaten to kill his younger brothers and sisters. What kinds of things do you see happening or hear being said just before he makes such threats?

MOTHER: Well, he usually says those things because his younger brothers are goofing around and not helping him get dinner ready.

SOCIAL WORKER: So, Ricky, what are you thinking or saying to yourself when your brothers are goofing around and not helping you get dinner ready?

RICKY: I'm thinking, "Mom, why am I always the one who has to get dinner ready for them? It is unfair. I've got a lot more homework to do, and my homework is harder than theirs. Why can't they make dinner on nights before my tests? How am I going to get to college if I can't study? They should be making dinner, not me. It's not fair."

SOCIAL WORKER: So when you were at school and threatened to kill Marco, were you saying or thinking to yourself that something wasn't fair?

RICKY: Exactly! I was saying to myself, "It is not fair that Marco is rich. He never has to work at home or babysit his brothers and sisters. He always has time to do his schoolwork, and when he doesn't understand his homework his parents get him a tutor. It is not fair.'"

In this sequence the mother provides direct observations of behaviors occurring immediately prior to Ricky's threats to his younger siblings. The specialist asks Ricky about potential precipitating self-talk that engendered his threats at home. Then, the specialist asks him about having the same "It's not fair" self-talk prior to threatening Marco. Once such precipitating violence self-talk can be identified, the specialist and student can establish ways to disrupt or dilute the self-talk and change the previously occurring violent behaviors associated with the self-talk.

Clinical interviews can also be used to engender change. For example, during a family interview with a potentially violent student and his parents, the specialist might ask something like this:

"Ricky indicates that he is the oldest son in this family and suggests that at times he enjoys participating in a parenting-like role with his younger brothers and sisters. Yet, there seem to be times when Ricky finds some family responsibilities overwhelming, and he becomes angry. Certainly, there are times when all of us have responsibilities which we don't find enjoyable. However, I am

wondering, should Ricky feel overwhelmed or angry, would you
be willing to hear his concerns and talk with him?"

This question has specific relevance. First, the specialist points
out that "at times, he enjoys participating in a parenting-like role"
and follows up with the indication that at one time or another, "all
of us have responsibilities which we don't find enjoyable." These
statements are noncondemning to the parents and remind Ricky
that not all responsibilities are enjoyable. These statements also
imply that the parenting role is the parents' responsibility, not
Ricky's. Thus, Ricky can be a parenting helper, but he cannot be a
parent and should not be expected to behave like one.

Second, the specialist uses the phrase "should Ricky feel
overwhelmed or angry." Here, the word "should" indicates that
these feelings may not occur in the future. Thus, it suggests to Ricky
and his parents that he might not have these feelings in the future.
In contrast, using the word "when" would suggest that Ricky will
have these feelings. This would mistakenly suggest that Ricky will
definitely feel overwhelmed or angry in the future.

Finally, the specialist asks Ricky's parents if they would be
willing to listen to his concerns and talk with him, should he
feel overwhelmed or angry. Again, this question is phrased in a
noncondemning manner. Few parents we have counseled have
said they would be unwilling to listen to their child's concerns or
feelings. As a matter of fact, most parents with whom we interact
truly love their children and desire opportunities to engage them
in conversation. Therefore, if Ricky's parents said they would be
willing to listen to Ricky's concerns and feelings, we would ask
them how he should present these concerns to them. For example,
we might say,

"Roberto and Marie, I hear you say you would be very willing
to listen to Ricky should he have any concerns or should he feel
overwhelmed or angry. Should Ricky ever have those feelings in

the future, how would you want him to indicate such concerns or feelings?"

Here, the intent is to have Ricky better understand that his parents want to hear his concerns and learn how he can appropriately present his concerns or feelings to his parents in a nonthreatening, nonviolent manner. The intent is also to have his parents become more aware of how Ricky may present his concerns or feelings, and to encourage their listening commitment.

On rare occasions, we have had parents say they are unwilling to listen to their son's or daughter's concerns or feelings. Typically, these parents present as rather immature and angry, and they frequently state that their children have relatively few required responsibilities compared to the many significant demands their children place on them. A dialog might go like this:

MOTHER: No, I am not willing to hear Ricky's concerns or talk with him when he feels overwhelmed or angry. He has no "real" concerns, and he shouldn't feel angry. Ricky lives a life of Xbox games, Coca-Cola, HBO, and loud music. I work two jobs, and he doesn't lift a finger around the house. Ricky throws a fit whenever I ask for just a little help. I go to work at 7 a.m., get out at 3:30 p.m., and race to my second job, where I wait tables and endure rude people from 4:30 until 8:00 o'clock at night. Ricky sleeps until 9 a.m., usually is tardy for his first hour class, refuses to take care of his three younger siblings, and refuses to grow up.

SOCIAL WORKER [VALIDATING THE MOTHER]: It sounds as though you're working very hard and feeling unappreciated. What do you really want from Ricky?" [The intent of this question is to open previously closed communication between Ricky and his mother and continue to assess the family's needs.]

MOTHER: What do I really want from Ricky? I want him to be a man, to quit whining, and to help with household and parenting duties.

SPECIALIST: Ricky, what do you hear your mom asking you to do?

RICKY: She just wants me to be her slave and work like a dog around the house.

SPECIALIST: Maybe I am wrong, but I don't hear her asking you to be a slave or to work like a dog. Mom, are you asking Ricky to be a slave or work like a dog?

MOTHER: No, I just want some help around the house.

SPECIALIST: Help me understand exactly what you want Ricky to do.

Thus, the specialist would attempt to have the mother indicate in realistic, concrete, behavioral terms the specific charges she wishes Ricky to complete. The specialist could help the mother and Ricky establish a token economy: If Ricky completes identified tasks within a specified timeframe (e.g., each night by 5 p.m.), he would receive meaningful privileges like watching HBO movies approved by his parents.

The intent of these vignettes is again to demonstrate how clinical interviews serve a number of important purposes. Clinical interviews assess Ricky's and his mother's specific needs and provide vital information related to family dynamics. Furthermore, the assessment process can be used to reduce family members' defensiveness while encouraging students to see their families in a more helpful manner. Finally, the assessment process can actually serve as part of the clinical intervention itself or can provide a segue into an intervention such as a token economy.

Family Interview Contraindications

Not all families are sufficiently functional or invested to participate in family interviews with violent or potentially violent students. We use two factors when deciding whether to initiate family interviews.

First, we talk with the student being assessed. Specifically, we discuss the potential utility of inviting parents into the face-to-face clinical interview and describe how parents have been helpful in the past. We might say something like:

> "Ricky, some of the students we have previously interviewed have found it helpful to invite their parents to participate in the interviews. Often parents can provide their thoughts about their sons or daughters and describe what types of things are going on at home. This frequently is helpful. At other times some students are frustrated over things at home. They want change. Having mom or parents here allows students the opportunity to voice the ideas and suggestions they have for change. I think it would be helpful to have your parents here. What are your thoughts about asking your parents to participate?"

We *ask* for Ricky's thoughts about inviting his mother or father's participation rather than *telling* him he will allow his parents to participate. Asking whether Ricky wishes parental involvement empowers Ricky. As professional specialists who are not part of the criminal justice system, we are unable to require parental involvement in the assessment. We cannot force parents to participate in the family interview, nor can we force students to request that their parents be included in the interview. Instead, we present the potential benefits of involving the parents.

Some students quickly accept this parental involvement invitation; others do not. We believe that for this initial violence assessment, it is the student's decision whether to invite his or her parents to participate. Of course, the potential consequences of inviting or not inviting the parents are the student's as well. The reality is that the parents will certainly be contacted by school administration if their child has acted violently or is perceived to be at imminent risk. Administrators have no choice. Violent or imminently violent students will not be allowed to return to the school milieu without significant parental involvement. Students who readily accept parental involvement often perceive parental support or anticipate the interview session will allow them to influence their familial dynamics in a helpful way. When students agree to the family interview, we obtain a release of confidential information and invite the parents to actively engage in the face-to-face family clinical assessment.

When students deny a desire for parental involvement and refuse to provide releases, we frequently find significant family dysfunction. Sometimes this dysfunction is engendered by the student's psychopathology (e.g., substance use disorder, conduct disorder, oppositional defiant disorder). At other times, the dysfunction results from chaos within the family system itself, often due to a parent's addiction or personality disorder such as antisocial or borderline personality disorder. Therefore, the second factor we use when deciding whether to initiate family interviews is if the student will be in danger if the parents are involved or if extreme parental psychopathology is evident. Should we suspect the parents would likely present with addictions issues or florid personality disorders based on student or teacher report, our primary assessment revolves around the student with limited or no parental input. No matter the perceived psychopathology, parents are encouraged to engage in treatment either for themselves or their children.

The third factor decision to invite parents may ultimately be determined by state laws or school district rules and policies. Thus, the safety and risk committee should make the ultimate decision based on what is best for the student, the other students in the school, and legal counsel directions and advice.

An Important Reminder

You have diligently worked to attain your graduate degree and your professional license. Don't risk losing your license! Unless you are an expert in school violence and law, *always* consult your school district's legal department and attain authorization before implementing any assessment or intervention specific to a student who presents with a suicide or violence risk. In this day and age when lawyers themselves hire other expert legal counsel to ensure they are protected from liability risks, it is clear that specialists should always consult on any matter that has potential liability risks and should carry quality professional liability risk insurance.

Summary

This chapter described vital core questions that can easily be integrated into face-to-face clinical interviews with student survivors and bullying and violence perpetrators. The 2WHO-SCAN and the VIOLENT STUdent Scale mnemonics were introduced and explained.

References

American Association of Suicidology. (2013). *Know the warning signs*. Retrieved from https://www.suicidology.org/resources/warning-signs

Balkin, R. S., & Juhnke, G. A. (2013). *The theory and practice of assessment in counseling*. Columbus, OH: Pearson.

Dwyer, K., Osher, D., & Warger, C. (1998). *Early warning, timely response: A guide to safe schools*. Bethesda, MD: National Association of School Psychologists.

Juhnke, G. A. (1994). Teaching suicide assessment to counselor education students. *Counselor Education and Supervision, 34*(1), 52–57. doi:1.1002/j.1556-6978.1994.tb00310.x

Juhnke, G. A. (2000). *Addressing school violence: Practical strategies and interventions*. Austin, TX: Pro-Ed.

Juhnke, G. A., Granello, D. H., & Granello, P. F. (2010). *Suicide, self-injury, and violence in the schools: Assessment, prevention, and intervention strategies*. Hoboken, NJ: John Wiley & Sons.

Juhnke, G. A., Juhnke, B. A., & Henderson, K. (2013). Using the 2WHO-SCAN mnemonic to respond to bullying survivor's needs. *VISTAS 2013*. Retrieved from http://www.counseling.org/docs/vistas/using-the-2who-scan-mnemonic-to-respond.pdf?sfvrsn=2

Patterson, W. M., Dohn, H. H., Bird, J., & Patterson, G. A. (1983). Evaluation of suicidal patients: The SAD PERSONS Scale. *Psychosomatics, 24*(4), 343–349. doi:10.1016/S0033-3182(83)73213-5

Vacc, N. A., & Juhnke, G. A. (1997). The use of structured clinical interviews for assessment in counseling. *Journal of Counseling & Development, 75,* 470–486. doi:10.1002/j.1556-6676.1997.tb02363.x

3

Motivational Interviewing

When bullying and high-risk students are assessed as a clear and imminent danger to others within the school milieu, the response is undeniably evident: They must be removed from the school milieu until they present no imminent danger to themselves or others. More challenging, however, are students who wish to return to school yet present with a history of mild to moderate bullying or violence or with mild to moderate bullying or violence ideation. It is even more challenging when the parents, not the student, demand that the student return without sufficient investment or desire by the student to do so. How do specialists work with these students once it has been determined they may return to the school milieu?

It is the responsibility of the school safety and risk committee to determine if students are allowed the privilege of returning to the school milieu. Each bullying and post-violent student and every student presenting with bullying or violent ideation must be individually assessed and reviewed by the school's safety and risk committee. The duty of each school safety and risk committee is to ensure students do not pose a danger or threaten the safety of themselves or others. Concomitantly, threatening behaviors or actions that potentially create chaos or jeopardize the learning milieu cannot be tolerated. Thus, the safety and risk committee should *consider* allowing the student to return only if the committee members, after thorough and comprehensive assessment and evaluation, agree the student (a) is sufficiently committed and able to be consistently bullying and violence free, (b) has the necessary cognitive-intellectual, social, interpersonal, emotional, and psychological skills, functioning, and abilities, and familial and/or other supports to be and to remain consistently bullying and violence free, and (c) poses no threat, danger, or risk to self or others.

A number of factors should automatically eliminate bullying and post-violent students, as well as students with past or present bullying or violent ideation, from school return. For example, depending on the exact situation and presenting issues, students with current or past delusions, paranoia, hallucinations, or mania likely should be eliminated as school return candidates. Depending on the specific circumstances, students meeting criteria for diagnostic disorders such as conduct disorder, schizophrenia, bipolar disorder, and similar "not otherwise specified" disorders likely should be ruled out. Students with access to guns or lethal means to harm others are also not candidates for return. This is especially true if they used guns, knives, weapons, or other means to intimidate, bully, or be violent to others in the past or present, or have ideation reflecting those means to harm others (e.g., ideation of using the student's or parent's gun to shoot others, ideation of using the student's parent's car to ram peers). Students with gang involvement or involvement with others who have police histories, and students with previous arrests or checkered histories, also are ruled out from treatments described for the purposes of this book. Substance-using students, especially those who have used or currently use anabolic steroids, alcohol, central nervous system stimulants (e.g., cocaine, methamphetamines), or hallucinogens (e.g., lysergic acid diethylamide [LSD], heroin), likely should not be allowed to return. Past bullying or violent behaviors that were severe, as well as severe ideations, rule out students from return to school. Examples of such behaviors or ideations include behaviors and thoughts such as homicide, rape, torture, or kidnapping. Certainly, this is not a comprehensive list, but it does provide examples for potentially ruling out school return.

Every safety and risk committee decision must consider local and state laws, school district policies, and student rights and must ultimately ensure safety for all. Based on our more than

80 years of combined clinical experiences, we believe motivational interviewing (MI), cognitive-behavioral therapy, and systems of care interventions hold significant promise as treatment interventions for students not ruled out by the above criteria. This chapter provides a general overview of MI, with clinical vignettes demonstrating how to use MI interventions with students and their families and significant others. The interventions can be adapted, as necessary, to the student's needs and uniqueness. We believe face-to-face, interpersonal counseling with such students provides a means to help reintegrate them back into school while continually monitoring their behaviors and addressing their presenting violent or bullying ideation. Specifically, we believe MI interventions are evidence-based counseling practices that potentially can be used to help these students remain free from bullying, violence, and violent ideation.

Evidence-based practices have gained national attention (American Psychological Association Presidential Task Force on Evidence-Based Practices [APAPRFEBP], 2006; American School Counseling Association [ASCA] National Model, 2005; Barlow, 2000; Carey & Dimmitt, 2008; Carey, Dimmitt, Hatch, Lapan, & Whiston, 2008; Cooper, Benton, Benton, & Phillips, 2008; Gysbers & Henderson, 2006; Hazler, Hoover, & Oliver, 1991; Hoover & Hazler, 1990; Messer, 2004; Sink, 2009; Wampold & Bhati, 2004; Weisz, Jensen-Doss, & Hawley, 2006). In response, national counseling associations such as the ASCA and the American Psychological Association and national agencies such as the Substance Abuse and Mental Health Services Administration (SAMHSA) strongly encourage specialists to select and use evidence-based counseling theories, models, and practices (ASCA, 2005; SAMHSA, 2012). One evidence-based practice encouraged by SAMHSA is MI (2012). SAMHSA identified MI as one of only a limited number of clinically proven practices in its National Registry of Evidence-Based Programs and Practices (NREPP) (SAMHSA, 2012). Evidence-based practices in the NREPP have demonstrated effective treatment outcomes. They have been successfully used in multiple replicated randomized clinical trials or their effectiveness has been demonstrated via meta-analysis where repeated clinical significance and statistical significance were attained in different randomized clinical studies (APAPRFEBP, 2006; Chambless & Ollendick, 2001).

Although MI's effectiveness and utility had been well documented via numerous individual studies (Baer, Kivlahan, Blume, McKnight, & Marlatt, 2001; Bernstein et al., 2005; Borrelli et al., 2005; Carroll et al., 2006; Dunn, Droesch, Johnston, & Rivara, 2004; Foley et al., 2005; Levensky, Forcehimes, O'Donohue, & Beitz, 2007; Marlatt et al., 1998; Monti, Colby, Barnette, Spirito, & Rohsennow, 1999; Rubak, Sandbaek, Lauritzen, & Christensen, 2005; Senft, Polen, Freeborn, & Hollis, 1997; Vasilaki, Hosier, & Cox, 2006) and by its inclusion in SAMHSA's NREPP, Lundahl, Kunz, Brownell, Tollefson, and Burke (2010) summarized MI's clinical value and efficacy via a large meta-analysis. Their meta-analysis included findings from 119 MI randomized research studies done over a 25-year period. The results clearly demonstrated MI's broadly noted evidence-based utility. Specifically, Lundahl et al.'s (2010) findings indicated MI had a positive impact on targeted substance use outcomes (e.g., alcohol abuse, cannabis use, cocaine dependence, tobacco use) and health-related behaviors (e.g., diet, exercise, obesity, safe sex). These researchers confirmed what many counseling professionals already knew: MI can be an effective and useful treatment practice and has utility even with challenging populations that perceive no or limited benefit for change (Juhnke & Hagedorn, 2006).

Despite wide recognition that MI is an effective, evidence-based practice, there exists a paucity of literature describing how to use it with school-aged bullying or violence perpetrators. Bullying and violence are major threats that negatively impact students, classrooms, and schools (Dao et al., 2006; Davis et al., 2018; Due & Holstein, 2008; Espelage & Holt, 2007; Fry et al., 2018; Haynie et al., 2001; Marshall, Varjas, Meyers, Graybill, & Skoczylas, 2009;

Nansel, Craig, Overpeck, Saluja, & Ruan, 2004; Nansel, Overpeck, Pilla, Ruan, Simons-Morton, & Scheidet, 2001; Olweus, 1997; Olweus, 2003; Reuter-Rice, 2008; Rubens, Miller, Zeringue, & Laird, 2019; Sourander et al., 2009; Srabstein & Piazza, 2008). Two surveys in particular reflect bullying's widespread occurrence. From September 2016 through December 2017, Kann et al. (2018) surveyed a nationally representative sample of US 9th- through 12th-graders and found that 19% of them had experienced bullying on school property in the preceding 12 months. In 2012, Schneider, O'Donnell, Stueve, and Coulter found that over 25% of 20,406 9th- through 12th-graders in Massachusetts reported experiencing school bullying behaviors in the preceding 12 months. These percentages suggest that bullying behaviors are increasing. This seems especially true when comparing Schneider et al.'s 2012 finding to Nansel et al.'s 2001 finding that 11% of the adolescents reported being a bullying victim. The implications for specialists are clear: We need effective interventions that will truncate bullying and violent behaviors and restore school safety.

As counselor educators who are licensed by our states and who have additional national certifications, we counsel and clinically supervise specialists who counsel in schools. Via these experiences we have found MI to be an indispensable intervention. This is especially true with school bullying and school violence perpetrators who do not identify their bullying or violence as problematic. Thus, the intent of this chapter is to provide specialists a practical, step-by-step guide describing how to use MI with students. Clinical vignettes are incorporated to demonstrate how MI can be implemented within sessions.

Basic Tenets

Rollnick and Miller (1995) developed MI from Prochaska and DiClemente's transtheoretical change model (1982). Four basic tenets govern the use of MI and are employed throughout the bullying counseling process: (a) expressing empathy, (b) rolling with resistance, (c) developing discrepancy, and (d) supporting self-efficacy.

Expressing Empathy

Specialists establish a welcoming and positive environment, build rapport with bullying and violent students, and seek to understand the perpetrator's mindset. Given that most specialists are familiar with person-centered theory, expressing empathy for bullying and violent students and accepting students without contempt should not be a surprise. We have found that as bullying and violent students experience empathy, their defenses lessen and they become more willing to engage in the MI process. When this happens, students begin to discuss their bullying and violent behaviors without fear of condemnation, and specialists can better understand the underlying reasons for the behaviors.

Rolling with Resistance

The central theme of this second tenet is continual communication with the bullying and violent student without arguing or debating. Ineffective treatment providers often label students "resistant" when behaviors are perceived as defiant or rebellious. Rollnick and Miller (1995) take a different approach: They suggest that clients become resistant when they believe specialists do not understand their situation. Thus, Rollnick and Miller encourage specialists to roll with client resistance by accepting what the client says and encouraging the client to talk via simple reflections of client statements in a neutral manner:

STUDENT: I refuse to stop punching others.
SPECIALIST: You don't intend to stop punching others right now.

According to Rollnick and Miller (1995), arguing with clients will only entrench the targeted behaviors.

Developing Discrepancy

According to Miller, Zweben, DiClemente, and Rychtarik (1992, p. 8), "Motivation for change occurs when people perceive a discrepancy between where they are and where they want to be." Thus, instead of telling bullying and violent perpetrators why they should stop their behaviors, the authors of MI encourage specialists to ask questions and make statements to help perpetrators identify their own reasons for change. Specifically, specialists are encouraged to actively listen to students; pay special attention to stated discrepancies between how they think, act, or feel, and behave; and ask questions that highlight or emphasize the discrepancies related to their bullying and violent behaviors. For instance:

SPECIALIST: So help me understand. You say you want to be a nurse. However, you say you will never stop pushing others around. Help me understand that.
SPECIALIST: I keep hearing you say that you want to stop threatening your friends. However, you keep threatening them. How is that working for you?

In both situations, the specialist is pointing out the incongruence between the student's bullying and violent behaviors and the student's stated goals or desires. Thus, the student's own statements serve as fertile ground for self-examination between the stated discrepancies.

Supporting Self-Efficacy

Rollnick and Miller (1995) believed clients are more likely to invest, follow through, and accomplish freely selected behaviors they believe are attainable. Stated differently, if clients believe new or unattainable behaviors are forced on them, they are less likely to engage in the behaviors and likely will not bring the behaviors to fruition. Thus, specialists will need to optimistically encourage students, remind them of their past successes, and affirm all attempts to stop bullying and violent behaviors.

The Model

MI has six change stages: (a) precontemplation, (b) contemplation, (c) determination, (d) action, (e) maintenance, and (f) relapse.

Precontemplation

Unlike more traditional theories where clients commonly seek counseling to eliminate or reduce perceived noxious symptoms (e.g., depression, anxiety, panic), MI was designed to address drinking and drug-using behaviors. Because clients often experienced such behaviors as enjoyable rather than problematic or bothersome (Rollnick & Miller, 1995), they did not wish to stop.

These perceptions are strikingly similar to our experience with bullying and violent students: They enjoy bullying and violence and do not perceive these behaviors as problematic or bothersome. These students are in the precontemplation stage. They do not perceive a need to change their behaviors. In this stage, specialists begin MI by encouraging perpetrators to self-explore and explain the potential risks, costs, or sanctions associated with continued bullying and violence. This is done without demanding that the bullying and violence stop. For example:

SCHOOL COUNSELOR: Robby, have you noticed when you punch and shove other students in the hall you are sent to the principal's office and lose your freedom and privileges?

ROBBY: So?

SCHOOL COUNSELOR: So, I'm wondering if Principal Lanford explained the school's no-bullying policy to you.

ROBBY: No. He just said I shouldn't punch or shove other kids in the hall.

SCHOOL COUNSELOR: Did he explain what will happen if you punch or shove other students?

ROBBY: No, he just told me not to do it.

SCHOOL COUNSELOR: Punching, shoving, harming, threatening, or intimidating qualifies for bullying behaviors within the district's no-bullying policy. The school district has established a zero-tolerance policy for bullying. That means any student who bullies other students by doing things like threatening, intimidating, yelling, pushing, shoving, or punching another student will be suspended from school for the second offense and possibly expelled from school for a third or later offense. Do you understand your behaviors of punching and shoving other students in the hallway are defined as bullying by the district's no-bullying policy and you may be suspended or expelled from school because of your bullying behaviors?

This vignette demonstrates how specialists describe bullying in simple, clear words and clearly explain bullying sanctions. Thus, they provide a clear definition of bullying behaviors and inform students about the school's or district's bullying policies and sanctions. Students learn their behaviors fulfill the bullying definition. Once they realize their behaviors match the described bullying definition and they understand they were bullying, students move from the precontemplation to the contemplation stage. In other words, they move from ignorance of their behaviors as fulfilling bullying and violent criteria to awareness of their bullying and violent behaviors with corresponding district sanctions.

Contemplation

Contemplation, the second MI stage, is an ambivalent stage. Here, students begin to understand more fully that their behaviors are defined as bullying or violent behaviors. They have not yet decided to change their bullying or violent behaviors or they are undecided if they will continue such behaviors. Therefore, the intent of the specialist's questioning in the contemplation stage is to help students more thoroughly understand the good and bad parts of their bullying and violent behaviors and to amplify and enlarge students' discussions of the "bad parts" of such behaviors. This is done until it is fully evident to students that the costs of bullying and violence clearly outweigh possible benefits and they understand that it is illogical to continue their bullying and violent behaviors.

The contemplation stage intervention is typically initiated by querying students about perceived positives resulting from the targeted bullying and violent behaviors:

SOCIAL WORKER: You tell me that you've been beating kids up your whole life. There must be some positive things experienced from beating up others. Tell me about some of those positive things.

ROBBY: I don't know. I just do it. Beating other kids up just comes naturally to me, I guess.

SOCIAL WORKER: One thing I have learned as a specialist is that people do what they like to do or they do things they perceive are rewarding. What are some of the rewards you experience from beating up kids?

ROBBY: Well, one thing is everybody knows who I am and nobody messes with me or pushes me around.

SOCIAL WORKER: OK. Beating up on other kids makes it so people know who you are and it ensures no one messes with you or pushes you around.

ROBBY: Yeah. And it makes me feel good about myself, like I'm big enough to take care of myself.

SOCIAL WORKER: How's that helpful?

ROBBY: It makes me feel good about myself, because I know I can take care of myself and that makes me feel grown up.

Here the specialist indicates the student would not bully and be violent without some perceived benefits. The student's first response is he does not know why he bullies and is violent to other students. The specialist gently confronts him. First, she makes a benign but intentional remark, indicating that people behave the way they do when they perceive rewards for those behaviors. Then, she asks about the potential rewards the student experiences from his bullying and violent behaviors. The student's response is clear: When he bullies others, they know who he is and stay out of his way. His intimidation of others provides a reputation that ensures fame among his peers and freedom from their control. For this bullying student, such behaviors enable him to feel positive about himself. He equates the positively experienced feelings to being adult-like. These are important perceived benefits and, if left unaddressed, could sabotage effective treatment and render counseling ineffective.

Failure to ask about potential positives from the targeted behaviors typically results in unrealistic change expectations and continued bullying and violent behaviors. Thus, it is important to encourage students to honestly list perceived benefits of their behavior. In a later MI stage, the specialist will return to these perceived benefits and help the student identify new behaviors designed to attain the same or similar benefits via more socially acceptable and healthy behaviors.

Once the perceived benefits have been thoroughly discussed, the specialist asks the student about the "not so good" things about bullying. Here, the specialist might discuss the identified school sanctions that have occurred (e.g., school suspensions) as well as potential future sanctions (e.g., school expulsion). However, the specialist also investigates the student's other negative perceptions or feelings about bullying:

PSYCHOLOGIST: You've said you sometimes like to bully other students because it often scares them. When others are scared of you, they in turn give you space. I am wondering: Are there some not-so-good things you experience when you bully and scare other students?

ROBBY: Like what?

PSYCHOLOGIST: Well, do you ever find yourself feeling lonesome or by yourself because other students are scared of you?

ROBBY: Yeah. Sometimes after I beat up a kid and scare everybody, nobody wants to hang around me. I don't like being by myself all the time. It's not like I'm going to beat everybody up.

PSYCHOLOGIST: So, sometimes after you beat up others, you find nobody will hang around you. What is that like for you?

ROBBY: I don't like it. I get lonesome and sometimes can't find anyone who will talk with me. A few days ago at lunch, no one would sit by me in the cafeteria. I wasn't really lonesome, but it's boring without having anyone sit by you at lunch.

PSYCHOLOGIST: I bet that was boring and not fun. What other not-so-good things do you find happen when you beat up on other kids?

ROBBY: When Principal Rodriguez calls my mom and suspends me for fighting, she makes my life miserable.

PSYCHOLOGIST: How does she do that?

ROBBY: She makes me stay in my room, wash the car, clean the bathrooms, and make dinner and stuff like that. She also takes away my iPhone and won't let me use the computer to get on Facebook. I hate it.

PSYCHOLOGIST: Sounds miserable. What other not-so-good things happen?

The goal is to help students understand the significance of the negative aspects of their behaviors and to begin to question whether the costs of bullying and violence outweigh potential positives. Other examples of questions used in the contemplation stage may include:

"What are the worst things you experience by bullying or being violent to other students?"

"What will happen if you continue to bully others and get permanently expelled from school?"

"When you get older and punch people, what do you believe the police will do?"

"What kind of job will you get if you get expelled from school for bullying and have an arrest record for fighting?"

"How would your life improve if you didn't have to bully or be violent toward other students?"

Determination

After students discuss the negative outcomes of their bullying behaviors and the potential benefits of changing their behaviors, they move into a transitional stage between the contemplation and the action stages: the determination stage. The intent of this stage is to help students prepare to act and obtain support from family and friends to move from bullying and violent behaviors to more socially acceptable ways to behave. For example, students might begin reducing the frequency of their bullying or violent behaviors, they might ask friends or family for advice about socially acceptable behaviors their friends and family use instead of bullying or violence, or they might explore with the specialist perceived barriers to changing their behaviors. One common process in this stage is having students explore and identify new antibullying and antiviolence behaviors that they might use. For instance, if a student said he bullied because he needed space, the specialist might say,

FAMILY THERAPIST: Last time we talked, you indicated when you needed more space you bullied others by threatening or scaring them. I wonder what you might be able to do instead of bullying other students.

ROBBY: I don't know.

FAMILY THERAPIST: Some students who need space ask the librarian for one of the private reading rooms. Other students have told me that when they need space they go to the café, purchase a milk or water, and sit alone and read a book or surf the net on their mobile phone. And I know other students who come to my office and sit in the waiting room when they need space. I wonder if any of those things or something else might work for you, Robby. What would work best when you need your space?

ROBBY: I think I would go to the librarian and ask to read in the private reading room.

FAMILY THERAPIST: Do you think that would work?

ROBBY: I think it would.

FAMILY THERAPIST: What would happen if the private reading room were being used?

ROBBY: I guess I could come to your office and talk with you.

FAMILY THERAPIST: Are those things you would really do, or are you just saying those things?

ROBBY: I would really do them, and I think they would work.

In this vignette, the specialist asks about nonbullying and non-violent behaviors the student could implement. The student is stumped. The specialist then describes options used by other students. The student says he could use option one. The specialist challenges him by asking what he would do if option one were unavailable. The student says he would then use the third option. This exchange is most helpful because it provides options and has the student identify exactly what he can do to address his bullying behaviors in the future. In other words, the student is learning how to prepare to make important changes in the next MI stage.

Action

In previous stages students considered whether they wished to change their behaviors, identified the costs and benefits of their behaviors, made a commitment to stop their behaviors, and may have even begun to prepare to change based on some small modifications in their previous behaviors. However, they have not sufficiently changed their previous behaviors or attained nonbullying or nonviolent stability. In the action stage, students actively change their behaviors and begin actively implementing new antibullying and antiviolence behaviors. Here, the specialist might encourage small change steps and focus on praising the student for his accomplishments:

COUNSELOR: Instead of making gigantic changes, sometimes it is easier and more effective to identify smaller changes that lead to bigger ones. What small steps are you using to help you eliminate your bullying?

ROBBY: For one thing, when I start to get angry and think about punching people, I think, "What will happen if I do?"

COUNSELOR: What do you mean?

ROBBY: Well, I don't want to get kicked out of school and lose any opportunity to go to college. So, when I start getting angry, I just walk away and say to myself, "I'm not going to punch him out and lose my chance at getting into college."

COUNSELOR: Does that help?

ROBBY: Yes! If I punched another kid, I would be expelled from school and lose my 3.2 grade point average. If I get kicked out of school and lose my 3.2 grade point average, I might as well flush my dreams of being a doctor goodbye, because no college will accept me.

COUNSELOR: So in addition to walking away, what else do you do?

ROBBY: I also call my mom and tell her that I almost punched a kid out, but didn't.

COUNSELOR: How does that help?

ROBBY: My mom is pretty cool. She tells me that I did the right thing and verbally praises me. That makes me feel like I did a good thing, and she is proud of me. So, I don't have the urge to punch anyone out. I feel good about myself.

Maintenance

The primary goal of the maintenance stage is to help the new antibullying and antiviolent behaviors become ingrained, repetitive habits. The idea is to sustain these new behaviors while addressing the student's potential discouragement about how slowly progress comes or recurring bullying or violent thoughts:

ROBBY: There are times when I get frustrated and think it would be easier to beat up some of these other kids rather than trying to change.

COUNSELOR: However, you have made very good progress. Don't give up now after you've done all this work, Robby. How many weeks has it been since you have beat someone up?

ROBBY: Three weeks.

COUNSELOR: That is really good. I see lots of progress, Robby. Tell me how, even when you felt frustrated in the past, you stayed focused on your new antibullying behaviors and did not give up.

This is an important interchange. First, Robby reports his frustration and his belief that sometimes it would be easier not to change. The specialist acknowledges Robby's statement but immediately lauds him for his progress. Then, the specialist asks a therapeutic question designed to remind Robby of the length of his success. Again, the specialist praises Robby and reports progress. Next, the specialist asks how Robby has stayed focused and not returned to his previous bullying behaviors. This question is designed to help Robby understand how he has eliminated his bullying behaviors and the things he did to continually focus on his goal. Once Robby is reminded of these helpful behaviors, he can remember how to use them in his current situation. Students often favorably receive such affirmation, praise, and encouragement, which help remind them how successful they have become and encourage students to repeat and reuse previously helpful methods.

Relapse

The final MI stage is relapse. Interestingly, Rollnick and Miller depathologized this stage and made it part of the solution rather than the problem. In other words, they encouraged specialists and clients to understand that relapse is not to be feared. Instead, it is an intricate part of the long-term antibullying and antiviolence process. Thus, when students relapse to previous bullying or violent behaviors, specialists do not chastise, threaten, or embarrass them. Instead, specialists report relapse as a normal part of the change process and address the potential feelings of demoralization experienced by students and use the triggers leading to relapse as learning opportunities for longer-term bullying elimination.

SOCIAL WORKER: Lots of my students feel they failed when they relapse and chose to bully.

ROBBY: You can say that again. My mom and little brother
cried when I was suspended again for punching out Stevey
Wisneski.

SOCIAL WORKER: I am sure you felt that way. But relapsing is just a
part of learning how to really eliminate those bullying behaviors.

ROBBY: What do you mean?

SOCIAL WORKER: Well, many students think they have eliminated
their previous bullying behaviors and feel like they don't have
to continue to strive to eliminate bullying from their repertoire
of actions. Once they let their guard down, they revert back to
their previous bullying behaviors. So, what did you learn from
this brief slip back into bullying?

ROBBY: I learned that I've got to walk away from people when they
start to get on my nerves, before I punch them out.

SOCIAL WORKER: So how will you do that?

Again, this is another important therapeutic interchange
designed to promote the student's understanding that relapse is not
failure. More importantly, helping the student learn from his re-
version to bullying behaviors is critically important. Here, the specialist raises the subject of potential student feelings of failure by
saying other students who relapsed into bullying behaviors often
feel they have failed. This normalizes Robby's feelings. The specialist also therapeutically reframes the bullying relapse as a "slip"
and indicates slips are part of the long-term bullying elimination
process. Specifically, the specialist asks what Robby will do next
time he considers reverting to his bullying behaviors. This question is designed to engender insight. First, it indicates Robby had a
choice whether to bully or not. Second, it is designed to help Robby
identify more helpful behaviors that will promote his long-term
bullying recovery. In this case, Robby learned he can "walk away"
when people are getting on his "nerves."

Summary

This chapter described how to use MI to address perpetrators of school bullying and violence. MI is a proven, evidence-based treatment that holds promise with these perpetrators. The chapter provided a general overview of the basic MI tenets and practical, step-by-step directions describing how to use it with school-age perpetrators of violence. We have found MI to be a viable treatment option for school-age perpetrators that fits well with most school settings.

References

American Psychological Association Presidential Task Force on Evidence-Based Practices. (2006). Evidence-based practice in psychology. *American Psychologist, 61*(4), 271–285. doi:10.1037/0003-066X.61.4.271

American Counseling Association. (2005). *The ASCA national model: A framework for school counseling programs* (2nd ed.). Alexandria, VA: Author.

Baer, J. S., Kivlahan, D. R., Blume, A. W., McKnight, P., & Marlatt, G. A. (2001). Brief intervention for heavy-drinking college students: Four-year follow-up and natural history. *American Journal of Public Health, 91*(8), 1310–1316. doi:10.2105/AJPH.91.8.1310

Barlow, D. H. (2000). Evidence-based practice: A world view. *Clinical Psychology: Science and Practice, 7*, 241–242. doi:10.1093/clipsy.7.3.241

Bernstein, J., Bernstein, E., Tassiopoulos, K., Heeren, T., Levenson, S., & Hingson, R. (2005). Brief motivational intervention at a clinic visit reduces cocaine and heroin use. *Drug and Alcohol Dependence, 77*, 49–59. doi:10.1016/j.drugalcdep.2004.07.006

Borrelli, B., Novak, S., Hecht, J., Emmons, K., Papandonatos, G., & Abrams, D. (2005). Home health care nurses as a new channel for smoking cessation treatment: Outcomes from Project CARES (Community-Nurse Assisted Research and Education in Smoking). *Preventive Medicine, 41*(5/6), 815–821. doi:10.1016/j.ypmed.2005.08.004

Carey, J., & Dimmitt, C. (2008). A model for evidence-based elementary school counseling: Using school data, research, and evaluation to enhance practice. *Elementary School Journal, 108*, 422–430. doi:10.1086/589471

Carey, J. C., Dimmitt, C., Hatch, T. A., Lapan, R. T., & Whiston, S. C. (2008). Report of the National Panel for Evidence-Based School

Counseling: Outcome research coding protocol and evaluation of student success skills and second step. *Professional School Counseling, 11*, 197–206. doi:10.5330/PSC.n.2010-11.197

Carroll, K. M., Ball, S. A., Nich, C., Martino, S., Frankforter, T. L., & Farentinos, C. (2006). Motivational interviewing to improve treatment engagement and outcome in individuals seeking treatment for substance abuse: A multisite effectiveness study. *Drug and Alcohol Dependence, 81*, 301–312. doi:10.1016/j.drugalcdep.2005.08.002

Chambless, D. L., & Ollendick, T. H. (2001). Empirically supported psychological interventions: Controversies and evidence. *Annual Review of Psychology, 52*, 685–716. doi:10.1146/annurev.psych.52.1.685

Cooper, S. E., Benton, S. A., Benton, S. L., & Phillips, J. C. (2008) Evidence-based practice in psychology among college counseling center clinicians. *Journal of College Student Psychotherapy, 22*(4), 28–50. doi:10.1080/87568220801952214

Dao, T. K., Kerbs, J. J., Rollin, S. A., Potts, I., Gutierrez, R., Choi, K., . . . Prevatt, F. (2006). The association between bullying dynamics and psychological distress. *Journal of Adolescence Health, 39*, 277–282. doi:10.1016/j.jadohealth.2005.11.001

Davis, J. P., Dumas, T. M., Merrin, G. J., Espelage, D. L., Tan, K., Madden, D., & Hong, J. S. (2018). Examining the pathways between bully victimization, depression, academic achievement, and problematic drinking in adolescence. *Psychology of Addictive Behaviors, 32*(6), 605–616. doi:10.1037/adb000394

Due, P., & Holstein, B. E. (2008). Bullying victimization among 13- to 15-year-old school children: Results from two comparative studies in 66 countries and regions. *International Journal of Adolescent Medicine and Health, 20*, 209–221. doi:10.1515/IJAMH.2008.20.2.209

Dunn, C., Droesch, R. M., Johnston, B. D., & Rivara, R. P. (2004). Motivational interviewing with injured adolescents in the emergency department: In-session predictors of change. *Behavioral and Cognitive Psychotherapy, 32*, 113–116. doi:10.1017/S1352465804001110

Espelage, D. L., & Holt, M. K. (2007). Dating violence and sexual harassment across the bully-victim continuum among middle and high school students. *Journal of Youth and Adolescence, 36*, 799–811. doi:10.1007/s10964-006-9109-7

Foley, K., Duran, B., Borris, P, Lucero, J., Jiang, Y., Baxter, B., . . . Sonleiter, N. (2005). Using motivational interviewing to promote HIV testing at an American Indian substance abuse treatment facility. *Journal of Psychoactive Drugs, 37*, 321–329. doi:10.1080/02791072.2005.10400526

Fry, D., Fang, X., Elliott, S., Casey, T., Zheng, X., Li, J., . . . McCluskey, G. (2018). The relationships between violence in childhood and education outcomes: A global systematic review and meta-analysis. *Child Abuse & Neglect, 75*, 6–28. doi:10.1016/j.chiabu.2017.06.021

Gysbers, N. C., & Henderson, P. (2006). *Developing and managing your school guidance and counseling program* (4th ed.) Alexandria, VA: American Counseling Association.

Haynie, D. L., Nansel, T., Eitel, P., Crump, A. D., Saylor, K., Yu, K., & Simons-Morton, B. (2001). Bullies, victims, and bully/victims: Distinct groups of at-risk youth. *Journal of Early Adolescence, 21,* 21–29. doi:10.1177/0272431601021001002

Hazler, R. J., Hoover, J. H., & Oliver, R. L. (1991). Student perceptions of victimization by bullies in schools. *Journal of Humanistic Education and Development, 29,* 143–150. doi:10.1002/j.2164-4683.1991.tb00018.x

Hoover, J., & Hazler, R. J. (1991). Bullies and victims. *Elementary School Guidance and Counseling Journal, 25,* 212–219. Retrieved from http://www.jstor.org.libweb.lib.utsa.edu/stable/42874015

Juhnke, G. A., & Hagedorn, W. B. (2006). *Counseling addicted families: An integrated assessment and treatment model.* New York, NY: Brunner-Routledge.

Kann, L., McManus, T., Harris, W. A., Shanklin, S. L., Flint, K. H., Queen, B., . . . Ethier, K. A. (2018). Youth risk behavior surveillance—United States, 2017. *Morbidity and Mortality Weekly Report, 67*(8), 1–114. doi:10.15585/mmwr.ss6708a1

Levensky, E. R., Forcehimes, A., O'Donohue, W. T., & Beitz, K. (2007). Motivational interviewing: An evidence-based approach to counseling helps patients follow treatment recommendation. *American Journal of Nursing, 107*(10), 50–58. doi:10.1097/01.NAJ.0000292202.06571.24

Lundahl, B. W., Kunz, C., Brownell, C., Tollefson, D., & Burke, B. L. (2010). A meta-analysis of motivational interviewing: Twenty-five years of empirical studies. *Research on Social Work Practice, 20*(2), 137–160. doi:10.1177/1049731509347850

Marlatt, G. A., Baer, J. S., Kivahan, D. R., Dimeff, L. A., Larimer, M. E., Quigley, L. A., . . . Williams, E. (1998). Screening and brief intervention for high-risk college student drinkers: Results from a 2-year follow-up assessment. *Journal of Consulting Clinical Psychology, 66*(4), 604–615. doi:10.1037/0022-006X.66.4.604

Marshall, M. L., Varjas, K., Meyers, J., Graybill, E. C., & Skoczylas, R. B. (2009). Teacher responses to bullying: Self-reports from the front line. *Journal of School Violence, 8,* 136–158. doi:10.1080/15388220802074124

Messer, S. B. (2004). Evidence-based practice: Beyond empirically supported treatments. *Professional Psychology: Research and Practice, 35,* 580–588. doi:10.1037/0735-7028.35.6.580

Miller, W. R., Zweben, A., DiClemente, C. C., & Rychtarik, R. G. (1992). *Motivational enhancement therapy manual: A clinical research guide for therapists treating individuals with alcohol abuse and dependence.* Rockville, MD: National Institute on Alcohol Abuse and Alcoholism.

Monti, P. M., Colby, S. M., Barnette, N. P., Spirito, A., & Rohsenow, D. J. (1999). Brief intervention for harm reduction with alcohol-positive older adolescents in a hospital emergency department. *Journal of Consulting and Clinical Psychology, 67*, 989–994. doi:10.1037/0022-006X.67.6.989

Nansel, T. R., Craig, W., Overpeck, M. D., Saluja, G., & Ruan, W. J. (2004). Cross-national consistency in the relationship between bullying behaviors and psychosocial adjustment. *Archives of Pediatric and Adolescent Medicine, 158*, 730–736. doi:10.1001/archpedi.158.8.730

Nansel, T. R., Overpeck, M., Pilla, R. S., Ruan, W. J., Simons-Morton, B., & Scheidt, P. (2001). Bullying behaviors among US youth: Prevalence and association with psychosocial adjustment. *Journal of American Medical Association, 285*, 2094–2100. doi:10.1001/jama.285.16.2094

Olweus, D. (1997). Bully/victim problems in school: Facts and interventions. *European Journal of Psychology of Education, 12*, 495–510. doi:10.1007/BF03172807

Olweus, D. (2003). A profile of bullying at school. *Educational Leadership, 60*(6), 12–17. Retrieved from http://www.ascd.org/publications/educational-leadership/mar03/vol60/num06/A-Profile-of-Bullying-at-School.aspx

Prochaska, J. O., & DiClemente, C. C. (1982). Transtheoretical therapy: Toward a more integrative mode of change. *Psychotherapy: Theory, Research, and Practice, 19*, 276–288. doi:10.1037/h0088437

Reuter-Rice, K. (2008). Male adolescent bullying and the school shooter. *Journal of School Nursing, 24*(6), 350–359. doi:10.1177/1059840508324577

Rollnick, S., & Miller, W. R. (1995). What is motivational interviewing? *Behavioural and Cognitive Psychotherapy, 23*, 325–334. doi:10.1017/S135246580001643X

Rubak, S., Sandbaek, A., Lauritzen, T., & Christensen, B. (2005). Motivational interviewing: A systematic review and meta-analysis. *British Journal of General Practice, 55*(513), 305–312. Retrieved from https://bjgp.org/content/55/513/305

Rubens, S. L., Miller, M. A., Zeringue, M. M., & Laird, R. D. (2019). Association of bullying, victimization, and daytime sleepiness with academic problems in adolescents attending an alternative high school. *American Journal of Orthopsychiatry, 89*(4), 508–517. doi:10.1037/ort0000305

Schneider, S. K., O'Donnell, L., Stueve, A., & Coulter, R. (2012). Cyberbullying, school bullying, and psychological distress: A regional census of high school students. *American Journal of Public Health, 102*, 171–177. doi:10.2105/AJPH.2011.300308

Senft, R. A., Polen, M. R., Freeborn, D. K., & Hollis, J. F. (1997). Brief intervention in primary care setting for hazardous drinkers. *American Journal of Preventive Medicine, 13*(6), 464–470. doi:10.1016/S0749-3797(18)30143-0

Sink, C. A. (2009). Specialists as accountability leaders: Another call for action. *Professional School Counseling, 13*(2), 68–74. Retrieved from https://www.schoolspecialist.org/asca/media/asca/LeadershipSpecialist/SchoolSpecialis tsAsAccountabilityLeaders.pdf

Sourander, A., Klomek, A. B., Niemela, S., Haavisto, A., Gyllenber, D., Helenius, H., . . . Gould, M. S. (2009). Childhood predictors of completed and severe suicide attempts: Findings from the Finnish 1981 Birth Cohort Study. *Archives of General Psychiatry, 66,* 398–406. doi:10.1001/archgenpsychiatry.2009.21

Srabstein, J., & Piazza, T. (2008). Public health, safety, and educational risks associated with bullying behaviors in American adolescents. *International Journal of Medicine and Health, 20,* 223–233. doi:10.1515/IJAMH.2008.20.2.223

Substance Abuse and Mental Health Services Administration (SAMHSA). (April 5, 2012). *SAMHSA's national registry of evidence-based programs and practices.* Retrieved from http://www.nrepp.samhsa.gov/ViewIntervention.aspx?id=130

Vasilaki, E. I., Hosier, S. G., & Cox, W. M. (2006). The efficacy of motivational interviewing as a brief intervention for excessive drinking: A meta-analytic review. *Alcohol & Alcoholism, 41,* 328–335. doi:10.1093/alcalc/agl016

Wampold, B. E., & Bhati, K. S. (2004). Attending to the omissions: A historical examination of evidence-based practice movements. *Professional Psychology: Research and Practice, 35,* 563–570. doi:10.1037/0735-7028.35.6.563

Weisz, J. R., Jensen-Doss, A., & Hawley, K. M. (2006). Evidence-based youth psychotherapies versus usual clinical care: A meta-analysis of direct comparisons. *American Psychologist, 61,* 671–689. doi:10.1037/0003-066X.61.7.671

4

Cognitive-Behavioral Therapy

Like motivational interviewing (described in Chapter 3), cognitive-behavioral therapy (CBT) is an evidence-based treatment (American Psychological Association Presidential Task Force on Evidence-Based Practices, 2006; Carey & Dimmitt, 2008; Carey, Dimmitt, Hatch, Lapan, & Whiston, 2008; Development Services Group, Inc. [DSGI], 2010; Wampold & Bhati, 2004; Weisz, Jensen-Doss, & Hawley, 2006) that has significant utility when addressing the needs of school bullying and violence perpetrators. In this chapter we will provide an overview of CBT with clinical vignettes demonstrating how to use CBT interventions with students, their families, and their significant others. Similar to motivational interviewing, the CBT interventions we describe should be adapted to match each student's needs and uniqueness.

Definition

CBT is the most evidence-based form of psychotherapy (DSGI, 2010), and "strategies of CBT have been used successfully to forestall the onset, ameliorate the severity, and divert the long-term consequences of problem behaviors among young people" (p. 2). Little (2005) reported that CBT variations are the most widely used treatment interventions in the criminal justice field. This is especially true related to "violence and criminality" (DSGI, 2010, p. 2) where CBT is typically the first-choice mental health intervention. Sukhodolsky, Solomon, and Perine (2000) found that aggressive elementary school students participating in CBT experienced a reduction in teacher-reported aggressive acts and self-reported enhanced anger control.

We have found CBT to be effective with clients we have counseled as well as our clinical supervisees' clients who present with bullying and violent behaviors. Adding to our firm belief that CBT is useful for treating student perpetrators of bullying and violent behaviors are two large meta-analyses suggesting the same. The first meta-analysis was conducted by Hofmann, Asnaani, Vonk, and Fang (2012). Their meta-analysis of 106 different studies examined the efficacy of CBT among both adults and children. These researchers found that CBT was effective and results were generally "very strong" (p. 427), especially related to "anger control problems" (p. 427). We have found that anger control problems are especially relevant to students who bully and are violent toward their peers.

The second significant meta-analysis was conducted by Henwood, Chou, and Browne (2015) and was specific to the effectiveness of CBT for anger management. These researchers reviewed 14 independent studies. Their results suggested that CBT was effective at decreasing violent reoffending, even though the findings were "not always statistically significant" (p. 287). In other words, although statistical significance may not have been met in some of these studies, clinical significance was sufficiently demonstrated. Further, the researchers found a significant reduction in risk for violent recidivism. Thus, those who had been violent and participated in CBT were assessed after treatment as less likely to repeat their previous violent behaviors.

As was the case with motivational interviewing, CBT is widely recognized within the mental health professions. Also like motivational interviewing, there appears to exist a paucity of research literature specific to the use of CBT with students presenting with bullying or violent behaviors. However, as experienced specialists and researchers, we believe that CBT, like motivational interviewing, can be helpful to reduce bullying and violent behaviors toward other students.

Basic Tenets

CBT combines cognitive therapy (Beck, 1995; Beck, 1999) and behavioral therapy (Bandura, 1977; Skinner, 1974). The basic tenet suggests that cognitive thoughts can generate intense, pathological emotions; these powerful emotions then engender behaviors designed to ameliorate or quell the extreme emotional discomfort (Sudak et al., 2016). Cognitive-behavioral interventions encourage clients to first identify these underlying pathological cognitions and later the pathological and harmful behavioral patterns associated with these painful cognitions. Using CBT, specialists help clients replace the underlying faulty and pathological cognitions with healthy cognitions. Once these are exchanged, specialists help clients replace the previous resulting harmful behaviors with new, healthy behaviors. The key for specialists, then, is helping bullying or violent students to change their underlying pathological cognitions and to identify precipitants for the resulting unhealthy behaviors. These precipitants can then be used as "warning signals" to students that promote new and healthier ways of thinking and responding.

In Chapter 3's vignette, Robby's pathological thoughts and cognitions engender intense emotions. Here, his bullying and violent behaviors may be highly influenced by these pathological cognitions and intense emotions. He reported that his bullying and violent behaviors "make" him feel good about himself. Hence, effective change will require changing his thoughts and cognitions from indicating he is vulnerable, exposed, defenseless, endangered, unsafe, and unprotected to indicating he is protected, safe, shielded, confident, and valued and respected by others.

Goals

Specialists using CBT have three primary goals (Juhnke & Hagedorn, 2006).

First, specialists working with bullying and violent students help students understand (1) how their pathological cognitions and thoughts create intense and powerful "response emotions" and (2) how their behavioral responses are designed to protect and insulate them from the emotional pain of these caustic cognitions and thoughts. Often, we help students identify what they say to themselves just prior to their bullying or violent behaviors toward peers. In our experience, students who bully and are violent often say to themselves things like, "He's making fun of me" or "I can't let her get away with humiliating me in front of my peers." It has further been our experience that even when these students do not recall internalized talk, they typically can identify the "feelings" experienced prior to their bullying or violent behaviors. Here, they report feeling ridiculed, mocked, or angered just prior to their bullying and violent behaviors.

Second, specialists provide a safe and welcoming environment where students can feel comfortable enough to consider and learn how their bullying and violent behaviors are connected to negative consequences (e.g., feeling lonesome and unloved, being expelled from school) and positive consequences (e.g., feeling empowered and confident).

Finally, specialists help students explore and implement new, healthier ways of thinking and acting that reduce the probability of bullying and violence.

Interventions

One of the primary interventions is helping students recognize triggers (e.g., negative self-talk, thoughts, feelings, behaviors, situations, interactions) occurring immediately prior to bullying and violent behaviors. Frequently, the students we have counseled can identify internalized conversations they have with themselves and emotional (e.g., feeling angry, feeling hurt) or physical (e.g., feeling their face flush, feeling their heart pound) signals that fore-tell their upcoming bullying or violent episodes. Hence, a student like Robby described in the earlier vignette may say he feels angry, irritable, or "mad" before he lashes out and recognizes his internal dialog. Thus, the specialist might say something like this:

PSYCHOLOGIST: Often students report talking to themselves in-ternally before they bully or act violently. I'm wondering what things you say to yourself just before bullying or being violent.

ROBBY: Like what?

PSYCHOLOGIST: Well, maybe you have said to yourself something like, "If this kid doesn't back off, I'm going to beat up on him" or something like that.

ROBBY: I can't recall ever saying that to myself before. However, I sometimes get mad at a punk and say to myself, "He is making fun of me or ridiculing me." That's just before I get angry and punch him.

PSYCHOLOGIST: So before you punch someone you find yourself thinking, "Hey! He is making fun of me." And, you are feeling angry about it?"

STUDENT: Yeah!

PSYCHOLOGIST: That is interesting. So you do some self-talk about what's going on and you experience some pretty intense feelings before you bully and become violent.

ROBBY: That's for sure! I talk to myself about what I'm feeling and know when I'm going to punch someone before I actually do it.

PSYCHOLOGIST: Tell me about the fire alarm at school. What does it do?

ROBBY: Weird question, but OK, I'll play. The fire alarm makes a loud, obnoxious screeching sound. It tells you to get out of the school because the school is on fire.

PSYCHOLOGIST: I'm wondering, Robby. When you start to have internal conversation about someone making fun of you and when you start noticing yourself getting angry, isn't that like the school fire alarm indicating your emotions are on fire and telling you to walk away from the other kid or you will bully the other kid or become violent?

ROBBY: I never thought of it that way.

PSYCHOLOGIST: You're smart, Robby. So what could you do when you start to feel angry and start to have an internalized conversation about bullying or being violent to another kid?

ROBBY: I guess I could walk away.

PSYCHOLOGIST: What will you have to do to simply walk away from the other kid?

ROBBY: I guess I just have to say to myself something like, "He's a loser. I need to just blow him off and walk away." Then, just walk away from him.

PSYCHOLOGIST: So, when will you begin walking away?

The specialist is helping Robby think about using his internal cognitive dialog and his feelings of being "mad" like a school fire alarm. When he finds himself talking to himself about being angry with another student or feeling "mad" about another student, he can use these baseline triggers as alarm indicators to get him to move away from the other student rather than bullying or being violent.

Three important points regarding this vignette:

1. The specialist starts by stating, "Often students report talking to themselves internally before they bully or act violently. I'm wondering what things you say to yourself just before bullying or being violent?" Thus, the specialist does not ask "if" Robby has such internal dialog; asking "if" will typically lead to denial. Instead, the specialist states that others "report" such dialog, which allows Robby to consider if he, like others, uses internal dialog.

2. The specialist states, "You're smart, Robby. So what could you do when you start to feel angry and start to have an internalized conversation about bullying or being violent to

another kid?" By telling Robby he is "smart," the specialist acknowledges something positive about Robby. Somewhat similar to cognitive dissonance (when a client holds two contradictory beliefs), we have found it is more difficult for clients to dismiss our questions when we say something positive about them first. In other words, it would be easier to ignore or dismiss the specialist's statements if the statements were all negative. However, when presented this way, the question to Robby has greater meaning. By phrasing the question this way, the specialist suggests that a "smart" person like Robby is capable of making better choices, and asks what he will do next time he experiences the bullying and violence triggers. This is powerful and encourages a thoughtful response.

3. Finally, the specialist does not simply allow Robby to provide a response. Instead, the specialist pushes for change and asks, "So, when will you begin walking away?" Again, this is a powerful intervention. It indicates Robby is capable of making such changes in his behaviors "when" he is ready.

Specialists also encourage students to recognize people (e.g., Janet in science class, Boyd in metals class, younger or smaller students), places (e.g., the hallway outside science class, on the school bus, at the bus stop, in the cafeteria line, at the football stadium), and times (e.g., immediately before math class, Monday mornings, Friday afternoons after school) when they bully and violence occurs. The discussion might go like this:

FAMILY THERAPIST: So, Robby, help me understand. Do you ever find yourself bullying other students when you are around certain people?

ROBBY: What do you mean?

FAMILY THERAPIST: I guess I'm wondering if you ever find yourself around the same people when you bully or get violent.

ROBBY: Janet in science class is usually around when I beat up other kids.

FAMILY THERAPIST: Is Janet beating up other kids with you or is she simply around when you bully and are violent?

ROBBY: She never beats up the others, but she usually tells me what the other kids are saying about me. Then I go after them.

FAMILY THERAPIST: Help me understand.

ROBBY: On Friday afternoons after we score each other's science tests, Janet tells me who laughs about my low test scores. I go find the kids she said laughed at me and punch them out.

In this vignette, Robby identifies Janet not as a fellow bully, but as an informant. The information provided about Janet's behaviors helps the specialist better understand how to intervene and potentially change the Friday science test scoring between students. At other times, students will report others who often co-bully or who help instigate or co-perpetrate violent behaviors. When such co-perpetrators are identified, specialists can advocate for environmental and structural changes that distance the co-perpetrators and reduce the probability of continued bullying and violence synergy.

Just as important is identifying people who are present when Robby is *not* bullying. Learning what these folks are doing to quell or lessen his bullying and violent behaviors is vital and helps the specialist create new, effective interventions as well.

SCHOOL COUNSELOR: Robby, tell me about the people you hang around with when you don't find yourself bullying or being violent.

ROBBY: I never bully when I'm around my big sister.

SCHOOL COUNSELOR: Really. I wonder why you never bully when you are around your big sister.

ROBBY: We are always having fun, and she makes me feel really important. And, she wouldn't put up with my bullying anyone. She is always about being fair and respectful of other people.

SCHOOL COUNSELOR: How does she make you feel really important, Robby?

ROBBY: She listens to me. She never laughs at me. She always asks me how I am doing. Usually, we are having so much fun together, I just am enjoying myself and not feeling like others are making fun of me or ridiculing me.

Robby's responses suggest he cognitively interprets his positive interactions with older sister in a positive way without resulting negative response emotions. Hence, promoting increased interactions between Robby and his older sister is a logical intervention. Helping Robby identify others like his sister who behave and generate similar positive interactions can be useful. In both cases, increasing interactions that Robby cognitively interprets as positive will decrease opportunities and time for bullying and violent behaviors.

Further, it is important to learn the places (e.g., the hallway outside the principal's office) and times (e.g., immediately after class) where bullying and violent behaviors are *not* occurring. The specialist might say something like:

SOCIAL WORKER: Robby, tell me about the places and times of day you when you do not bully.

ROBBY: I don't bully at home, and I never get in fights in the morning.

SOCIAL WORKER: That is interesting. Help me understand why you don't bully at home.

ROBBY: First, you have to understand my momma. She won't put up with any fighting. And she has threatened to kick me out of the house if I fight with my brothers, sisters, or her.

SOCIAL WORKER: How does she let you know she really means business when she says she won't put up with any fighting?

ROBBY: My big brother used to get in fights with us. She told him one time, "You mess with them boys one more time, and I will kick your sorry butt out of this trailer." He didn't pay any attention to her—and she kicked him out that night.

SOCIAL WORKER: When she tells you something, you know she means it.

ROBBY: Yes, sir. That is the truth!

SOCIAL WORKER: So how do you know the difference between when she means business and when she say something but doesn't mean business?

ROBBY: When she doesn't mean business, she smiles. When she means business, there is no doubt. She doesn't smile, she doesn't look happy, and her voice is stone cold.

SOCIAL WORKER: How is that different than when your teachers or principal tell you to stop bullying or hitting?

ROBBY: You see, they are always nice. They always smile. With my momma, there is no smile, and there is no "nice" when she means business. And her punishment is going to be severe, final, and over the top. I know that I can keep getting away with things here at the school, and they really won't do anything that harsh. But with my momma, it is a whole different story.

This vignette is packed with vital information. Robby knows precisely when and where he does not bully. He clarifies the difference between his mother establishing rules and teachers establishing rules. His mother does not smile when she means business, and her sanctions for noncompliance are immediate and forceful. It would be important to discuss these findings with the principal and teachers regarding how they present rules and directives to Robby. They must understand that although they may be well meaning when smiling and implementing policies or instructions specific to what Robby is to do, acting like his mother (i.e., no smiles, not attempting to be friendly, giving clear directives) will help him understand they mean business.

Throughout our clinical experiences, we have found that persons who bully and behave violently often remember how their previous actions and behaviors produced feelings of empowerment and reduced angry and anxious feelings. These memories make it more likely that they will repeat these pathological behaviors to provide relief from intense emotions and to engender feelings of control. Helping students replace their faulty cognitions and find other means to feel empowered, reduce feelings of anger and anxiety, and increase perceptions of control can be very important. Therefore, the specialist might ask something like:

PSYCHOLOGIST: Robby, when you discuss the triggers that occur prior to your bullying and violent behaviors and when you report the feelings you have immediately following those behaviors, it sometimes seems like you find bullying and violence provide you with a sense of power and control and reduce your feelings of anxiety. What things other than bullying and violence do you find that bring about those thoughts and feelings of power, control, and order in your life?

ROBBY: I don't know.

PSYCHOLOGIST: Tell me about a time recently when you felt powerful and in control when you weren't bullying or being violent.

ROBBY: I can't really think of any, except when I'm with my big sister. It's not like I feel powerful with her, but I don't feel like she is making fun of me or trying to take advantage of me.

PSYCHOLOGIST: So when you're with your big sister you feel comfortable and safe. So what are you saying to yourself when you are with her?

ROBBY: I'm really not having that internal dialog you talked about earlier. I'm just thinking to myself, "This feels good. She really cares about me. She wants what's best for me." That's what I'm thinking.

PSYCHOLOGIST: OK, that makes sense. What would have to happen for you to think others really care about you and want what's best for you?

ROBBY: I guess I'd have to start to think that others weren't making fun of me or trying to put me down because I'm stupid and stuff.

PSYCHOLOGIST: So, what would you have to start saying to yourself to begin thinking that others weren't making fun of you or trying to put you down?

The specialist initiates this discussion by asking Robby about behaviors other than bullying and violence that engender cognitions and feelings of power and control. If Robby had identified cognitions and behaviors that produced such feelings, the specialist would have encouraged him to increase the frequency of those cognitions and behaviors and role-played these cognitions and behaviors with him. Unfortunately, Robby could not identify any such cognitions and behaviors. However, the specialist learns that Robby feels comfortable and safe when he is with his sister. Therefore, the specialist asks Robby about his internal cognitive dialog when he is with his sister. The specialist next attempts to help Robby identify cognitions and behaviors he could initiate to engender experiences like those he has with his sister. Robby's response is that he would have to think others were not making fun of him or putting him down. The specialist immediately asks Robby what he would have to say to himself to initiate these cognitions. The purpose is to have Robby identify and replace his faulty cognitions and behaviors with new, healthy cognitions and behaviors.

Trigger List

The student makes a comprehensive list of all triggers for bullying and violence and describes them cognitively and behaviorally. The most powerful triggers and the most frequent ones are identified. With the help of the specialist, the student ranks the severity of each trigger on a scale of 0 ("When I experience this trigger I rarely bully or become violent") to 10 ("When I experience this trigger, I bully or become violent"). Next, the student ranks the frequency of each trigger, again on a scale of 0 ("I rarely experience this trigger") to 10 ("I experience this trigger constantly all day"). The highest priority is assigned to triggers identified as being the most powerful and the most frequent. In other words, triggers noted as both foretelling inevitable bullying or violent behaviors and the most frequent ones are assigned the greatest importance and addressed first.

Establishing Trigger Baselines

The severity and frequency of identified triggers serve as baselines that can be used to measure progress. In other words, these baselines allow students and specialists to track the efficacy of CBT. Should students report a decrease in trigger severity and frequency, progress is being made and the CBT interventions being used should continue. Conversely, should the severity and frequency of triggers increase, treatment and interventions warrant reconsideration, revisiting, and revision.

Nonbullying and Nonviolent Lists

In addition to the trigger list, the specialist should help the student construct "nonbullying" and "nonviolent" lists. As discussed earlier in the chapter, the emphasis is on identifying thoughts, feelings, behaviors, people, places, and situations when students do not bully and are not violent. The purpose of these lists is to help students identify different ways of positively experiencing life without the need to bully or become violent. Bullying and violent students often can identify when they do not bully or become violent. Often these occur when the students are (1) interacting with respected and admired adults, family, friends, and peers, (2) jointly participating with others in activities they are highly invested and activities they find interesting and rewarding, and (3) not experiencing over-whelming emotions such as hatred, anger, anxiety, embarrassment, or danger. These lists provide ideas on how students might better cope with experiences that commonly lead to their bullying or violent behaviors by instead describing how they think, feel, and behave when they are not responding to their pathological and intense emotions.

Positive Consequences

Unfortunately, rewards and positive consequences of bullying and violence are often ignored or inappropriately minimized by specialists. This is a significant treatment error that sabotages counseling efficacy and disinvests active participation. Bullying and violent students frequently experience multiple rewards and positive consequences for their inappropriate and harmful behaviors. These positive consequences can vary greatly depending on the specific student and his or her relationships and circumstances. Perceived attention and support by family, professionals, and peers and escape from responsibilities, duties, and classes can be key reasons students bully and become violent. Honest discussion regarding the potential loss of these perceived positive consequences is important. Therefore, the specialist can ask questions such as, "What positive things do you experience when you bully?" or "What is it like to assault the smaller students in your class?" The intent of such questions is not to have students romanticize their harmful behaviors; instead, the specialist is learning "how" these behaviors are pleasurable, "why" such behaviors are repeated, and "how" such behaviors are helpful to the student. Once the "hows" and "whys" are answered, the specialist can begin working to address the inappropriate thoughts and harmful emotions that generate the antisocial behaviors.

For example, should a 13-year-old boy indicate that bullying peers provides him friendships, the specialist and student may work to identify other ways the student can make friends without bullying. Given the importance adolescents place on peer acceptance and their desire to "fit in," this can be a daunting challenge. However, failing to address this bullying student's needs for friends destines the counseling process to limited success at best.

Negative Consequences

When reviewing negative consequences resulting from bullying and violent behaviors, it is helpful to first ask about the presenting circumstance that brought the student into counseling and then link the presenting circumstances to the bullying and violent behavior.

FAMILY THERAPIST: Robby, I know Principal Smith referred you to my office. As I understand the situation, you got in a fight at Friday night's basketball game against Reagan High School. Help me understand what that was like for you.

ROBBY: It was awful. I was in the stands when a kid from Churchill flipped me the bird. I got so mad I grabbed him and started kicking him. The next thing I knew, the rent-a-cops knocked me to the ground and handcuffed me. I was so embarrassed. Now, I'm kicked out of school for a week, I can't go with my friends to any more athletic events, and I'm grounded. Everyone is calling me stupid for fighting. My older sister is so mad at me for fighting that she doesn't want anything to do with me, and my grandfather keeps telling me how much I've disappointed him and hurt my entire family. I hate it!

FAMILY THERAPIST: That sounds rough.

ROBBY: Yeah . . . pretty rough.

FAMILY THERAPIST: What have you learned from this, Robby?

ROBBY: I've learned not to start fights, and I've learned not to get caught fighting at the basketball games.

FAMILY THERAPIST: Tell me about other times you had bad things happen when you've gotten in fights.

ROBBY: Really, I can't think of anything bad.

FAMILY THERAPIST: Sometimes students tell me they have lost friendships or no one wants to be around them because of their temper or fighting. Has anything like that happened to you, Robby?

ROBBY: No. I really don't have any friends and no one likes to be around me.

FAMILY THERAPIST: You seem to be articulate and smart. How is it that you don't have friends or that no one likes to be around you?

ROBBY: I don't know. I make friends and then when I get angry and threaten them, they don't want to be around me anymore.

FAMILY THERAPIST: So, how is it helpful to get angry and threaten others?

ROBBY: I guess it's not.

FAMILY THERAPIST: What would you have to do to change that?

ROBBY: I could not swear at them and not intimidate them to remain my friend.

FAMILY THERAPIST: That's interesting, Robby. I am a believer that our thoughts and actions either move people closer to a relationship with us or farther away from us. So, when I'm thinking, "I'm going to be nice to this person and say a couple nice things," I anticipate they will like it and want to hang around me. Once they start hanging around me, then I say to myself, "This person likes to be respected by me," and so I act in a manner that demonstrates that respect.

ROBBY: Yeah. I could do something like that.

The specialist first attempts to help Robby understand the link between fighting and negative consequences. The specialist reports the school principal referred Robby to counseling because of Robby's fighting. Robby proceeds to describe a litany of negative consequences resulting from his fighting at the basketball game.

Next, the specialist asks Robby what he learned from the experience. Interestingly, Robby reports he learned not to "start fights" or "get caught fighting." In other words, Robby does not take responsibility for his fighting behaviors and instead minimizes his responsibility. The specialist does not confront Robby and instead proceeds to ask about other negative things that have occurred when Robby has gotten into fights. Robby is unable to identify any associated negative events, so the specialist asks about "lost friendships" or people not wanting to be around Robby due to his anger. Robby's response is that he does not have friends and other students do not want to associate with him. The specialist acts puzzled and seeks Robby's clarification.

Robby reports that his threatening behaviors end friendships. When asked how his angry and threatening behaviors help, Robby admits these behaviors do not help establish or maintain the relationships. When asked what he would need to do differently, Robby identifies behaviors he would eliminate. We have found such "elimination behaviors" less than beneficial: Working to "not" do something is inefficient and often keeps bullying students focused on the problem versus the solution. It is akin to saying, "Whatever you do, do not think about an ice cream sundae. Do not think about the vanilla ice cream with fudge cascading down the creamy ice cream scoop. And, whatever you do, don't think about the whipped cream atop the ice cream or the red cherry on top of the whipped cream."

Were you thinking about an ice cream sundae before you read the previous sentences? Probably not. However, you are now. This same thing happens to many of our bullying and violent students. When we ask them to not think about bullying or not be violent, the bullying and violent behaviors are at the foreground of their thoughts and behaviors. Instead, the specialist in this vignette provides examples of new cognitions and active behaviors. In other words, the specialist provides a potential "menu" of options that Robby can consider. We have found this particularly useful when students do not know how to make friends or have a limited thought and behavior reference related to friendships.

Contingency Contracting

We believe contingency contracting can be an efficient and effective intervention with students who have a history of bullying and violence. Nonbullying and nonviolence contingency contracts are clearly worded contracts that precisely describe acceptable and unacceptable behaviors specific to bullying and violent behaviors. With the help of school legal counsel, the principal, teachers, and other invested personnel (e.g., coaches, school resource officers), the specialist meets with the student and the student's parents to describe the contract and to review the list of acceptable behaviors as well as sanctions for failing to meet the contracted behaviors. Sanctions such as school expulsion are stated as well as potential rewards for full compliance (e.g., being allowed to return to classes at school, being allowed to participate in extracurricular activities such as sports or music, being admitted to school events such as dances and sporting events).

At the beginning of each school day and immediately following lunch period, students and their parents meet at a specified school location (e.g., specialist's office). At that meeting students verbally commit to their parents and the specialist or other designee (e.g., principal) that they will remain bullying and violence free at school and on school grounds. Students reiterate their commitment to immediately go to a previously identified and designated school location (e.g., specialist's office, principal's office) should they begin to have violent thoughts or feel as though they might become violent. The contingency contracting process might go like this:

COUNSELOR: Robby and Ms. Max, thank you for meeting this morning before class. Robby, please begin by promising your mom and me that you will not bully or act violent toward others today.

ROBBY: You know I won't.

COUNSELOR: Robby, I need you to look right at your mom and tell her you promise her that you will not bully or act violently toward anyone today.

ROBBY: OK. Mom, I won't beat anyone up today or bully anyone.

COUNSELOR: Thank you, Robby. Do you believe him, Ms. Max?

MS. MAX: My son doesn't lie, and he will not break his promises to me.

COUNSELOR: Thank you, Ms. Max. Robby, will you look at me and make the same promise?

ROBBY: Sure. Mr. Jones, I will not bully anyone or be violent toward anyone today.

COUNSELOR: Thank you, Robby. Can you also promise your mom and me that if you start to feel or think about bullying someone or acting violently you will immediately come to the specialist's office and inform us?

ROBBY: Yeah. Mom and Mr. Jones, if I feel like bullying someone or beating someone up, I will come to your office and let you know what's going on.

COUNSELOR: Thank you, Robby, for your promises and commitment to staying violence free. Because of your willingness to make these promises, the school's risk committee is granting you permission to attend school this morning and participate in band. The risk committee wants me to remind both your mom and you that this is a time for learning and helping you achieve your dream of going to State and earning your music degree. Remember, however, that any bullying or violent behaviors will result in your final school expulsion and you cannot return to Northern Hills. Do you understand, Robby?

ROBBY: Yes, I get it.

COUNSELOR: Ms. Max?

MS. MAX: I understand. Robby won't cause any problems.

This vignette demonstrates how the specialist might facilitate contingency contracting. The specialist begins by thanking Robby and his mother for meeting. Then, he asks Robby to make the nonbullying, nonviolence promise. Robby responds, "You know I won't [bully]." The specialist does not accept this response, but instead of arguing with him, the specialist simply asks Robby to look at his mother and make the promise. Having Robby look at his mother when he makes the promise is significant. Can it guarantee Robby will comply? No, but it reminds Robby he is making a promise to someone he values and who is important to him. When Robby complies, the specialist then asks Robby's mother if she believes him. This question is not asked at each meeting, but in this case it provides the mother an opportunity to clarify any concerns she might have. For example, the mother might say something like, "I'm not sure if I believe him. Before we came to school this morning, Robby was swearing and acting very aggressive toward me." In this case, the specialist might ask follow-up questions to ensure Robby will not be aggressive at school. Thus, the specialist might say something like, "Robby, it sounds like your mom has some concerns. Can you help us understand what happened?" This will allow Robby to clarify and respond to the specialist's questions. Only when (a) Robby clarifies he does not intend to harm others and will not become violent and (b) the specialist and Ms. Max believe Robby is not in danger of harming others can Robby return to the classroom.

Returning to the above vignette, Robby's mother says she believes her son. The specialist asks Robby to repeat his nonbullying and nonviolent promise to the specialist. The specialist continues by having Robby promise that should Robby think about or feel like bullying or being violent, he will immediately come to the counseling office and inform the specialist. Again, Robby complies, and the specialist thanks Robby for making his promises. The specialist reminds him and his mother that because of his promises, Robby is granted the privilege of attending school and participating in band. This quid pro quo provides the privilege of attending school and participating in a valued and enjoyed extracurricular activity, and reminds Robby of his goal of graduating from high school and earning his music degree at the state university. This process is time and labor intensive, but it reminds the student and his mother that in exchange for being nonviolent, Robby can participate in school and pursue his dream of earning his music degree.

Some parents may object to the frequency of participation and argue that their participation is unnecessary and unwarranted. However, we believe the return of previously violent or bullying students to school is a privilege, not a right. If the parents petitioned to have their previously violent and bullying child return to school, daily parental participation is warranted and helps ensure daily communication and collaboration among the student, the parents, and the school. For example, if Robby's mother objects to participating, the specialist might respond:

MS. MAX: There is no way I'm going to participate in this "contingency contracting" thing twice a day! I have a job and need to work. Robby can do this by himself.

SOCIAL WORKER: Ms. Max, two things I have come to appreciate about you are your frankness and your devotion to Robby. I know you are very committed to your son, and your commitment is one of the reasons we even considered allowing Robby back into Northern Hills High. Robby's previous violent behaviors at Northern Hills caused bodily injuries to three younger students, as well as Robby's expulsion from Northern Hills High and his 60-day incarceration at Thomas Hill Juvenile Facility. We know you want the very best for Robby, and we do too. One of the issues you indicated earlier and prior to Robby's violent behaviors was a lack of communication among Robby, you, and Northern Hills High faculty and staff. These daily meetings ensure open communication between all parties and are designed to help Robby remain violence free and participate in a school he is familiar with. Based on our previous conversations, this is what you reportedly want as well. As the devoted and caring mother you are, your daily participation is crucial.

This response might not result in the mother's continued participation, but it reminds her of the violent behaviors that resulted in the contingency contracting and the purpose of keeping communications open among her, Robby, and the school.

Summary

This chapter provides a succinct overview of CBT and describes how to use this modality to address perpetrators of school bullying and violence. CBT is the most researched and evidence-based treatment and holds significant promise for addressing bullying and violence perpetrators. CBT tenets are outlined and practical, step-by-step directions are given describing how to use CBT with this population.

References

American Psychological Association Presidential Task Force on Evidence-Based Practices. (2006). Evidence-based practice in psychology. *American Psychologist, 61*(4), 271–285. doi:10.1037/0003-066X.61.4.271

Bandura, A. (1977). *Social learning theory.* Englewood Cliffs, NJ: Prentice-Hall, Inc.

Beck, A. (1999). *Prisoners of hate: The cognitive basis of anger, hostility, and violence.* New York, NY: HarperCollins Publishers, Inc.

Beck, J. S. (1995). *Cognitive therapy: Basics and beyond.* New York, NY: Guilford.

Carey, J., & Dimmitt, C. (2008). A model for evidence-based elementary school counseling: Using school data, research, and evaluation to enhance practice. *Elementary School Journal, 108*, 422–430. doi:10.1086/589471

Carey, J. C., Dimmitt, C., Hatch, T. A., Lapan, R. T., & Whiston, S. C. (2008). Report of the National Panel for Evidence-Based School Counseling: Outcome research coding protocol and evaluation of student success skills and second step. *Professional School Counseling, 11*, 197–206. doi:10.5330/PSC.n.2010-11.197

Development Services Group, Inc. (2010, September). *Cognitive-behavioral treatment, literature review.* Washington, DC: Office of Juvenile Justice and Delinquency Prevention. Retrieved from https://www.ojjdp.gov/mpg/litreviews/Cognitive_Behavioral_Treatment.pdf

Henwood, K. S., Chou, S., & Browne, K. D. (2015). A systematic review and meta-analysis on the effectiveness of CBT-informed anger management. *Aggression and Violent Behaviors, 25*(B), 280–292. doi:10.1016/j.avb.2015.09.011

Hofmann, S. G., Asnaani, A, Vonk, I., & Fang, A. (2012). The efficacy of cognitive-behavioral therapy: A review of meta-analyses. *Cognitive Therapy and Research, 36*(5), 427–440. doi:10.1007/s10608-012-9476-1

Juhnke, G. A., & Hagedorn, W. B. (2019). *Counseling addicted families: A sequential assessment and treatment model* (2nd ed.). New York, NY: Routledge.

Little, G. L. (2005). Meta-analysis of Moral Reconation Therapy®: Recidivism results from probation and parole implementations. *Cognitive-Behavioral Treatment Review, 14*(1/2), 14–16. Retrieved from https://www.moral-reconation-therapy.com/Resources/metaMRTprob.pdf

Skinner, B. F. (1974). *About behaviorism.* New York, NY: Random House.

Sudak, D. M., Codd, R. T., Ludgate, J., Sokol, L., Fox, M. G., Reiser, R., . . . Milne, D. L. (2016). *Teaching and supervising cognitive-behavioral therapy.* Hoboken, NJ: John Wiley & Sons, Inc.

Sukhodolsky, D., Solomon, R. M., & Perine, J. (2000). Cognitive-behavioral, anger-control intervention for elementary school children: A treatment-outcome study. *Journal of Child and Adolescent Group Therapy, 10*(3), 159–170. doi:10.1023/A:1009488701736

Wampold, B. E., & Bhati, K. S. (2004). Attending to the omissions: A historical examination of evidence-based practice movements. *Professional Psychology: Research and Practice, 35*, 563–570. doi:10.1037/0735-7028.35.6.563

Weisz, J. R., Jensen-Doss, A., & Hawley, K. M. (2006). Evidence-based youth psychotherapies versus usual clinical care: A meta-analysis of direct comparisons. *American Psychologist, 61*, 671–689. doi:10.1037/0003-066X.61.7.671

5

Systems of Care

No single counseling intervention can be applied to all students universally, eliminating every potential bullying and violent behavior. We do not believe all students should be allowed to return to school. Dangerous students and high-risk students require a significantly structured and managed milieu that is substantially more controlled than typical school environments, with greater immediate oversight, reduced student numbers, and a greater number of teachers who have been trained to address the needs of this population.

However, we believe the motivational interviewing and cognitive-behavioral therapy interventions described in the previous chapters, as well as the systems of care (SOC) modality described in this chapter and the next one, offer significant potential for change. This chapter introduces SOC, also known as wraparound services, with the next chapter covering its clinical use. All interventions can be adapted, as necessary, to the individual student's needs and uniqueness.

Systems of Care

SOC is broad enough to be used with students who present with bullying behaviors or mild to moderate violent risk factors but do not require restrictive environments.[1] It is part of an overall effort

[1] Such restrictive determinations should be made by multiple mental health professionals holding diverse state licenses and national certifications (i.e., school counselors; licensed professional counselors, clinical mental health counselors, and

to provide "seamless" care to students and their families (Adams & Juhnke, 1998; Adams & Juhnke, 2001; Brasheras, Davis, & Katz-Leavy, 2012; Erickson, 2012; Haber, Cook, & Kilmer, 2012; Juhnke & Liles, 2000; Miller, Blau, Christopher, & Jordan, 2012; Powell, Ellasante, Korchmaros, Haverly, & Stevens, 2016; Riebschleger, Day, & Damashek, 2015; Smithgall, Cusick, & Griffin, 2013; Snyder et al., 2012; VanDenBerg & Grealish, 1996; Whitson, Connell, Bernard, & Kaufman, 2012; Whitson & Connell, 2016). Students and their families benefit from a unified provider front versus compartmentalized treatment providers working from individual service silos with little if any service or goal commonalities.

SOC is a proven, evidence-based treatment that has demonstrated treatment efficacy (Crusto et al., 2008; Friedman & Drews, 2005; Green, Xuan, Kwong, Anderson, & Leaf, 2016; Painter, 2012). SOC has been identified as an innovative treatment and service treatment model that can be effectively used in both the juvenile justice and educational systems. In this approach, the student and family identify professional (e.g., school counselors, school psychologists, probation officers) and nonprofessional (e.g., grandmothers, deacons, dance coaches) persons they believe will be able to help them remain bullying and violence free. The approach encourages the development of an individualized treatment plan based on both traditional (i.e., individual, group, and family counseling) and nontraditional (e.g., photography, basketball, gardening) interventions. The intent is to help students and significant others identify behaviors and interactions they believe will

nationally certified school counselors; licensed social workers and certified school social worker specialists; licensed psychologists, nationally certified school psychologists, and licensed specialists in school psychology; and licensed marriage and family therapists) who have (a) administered appropriate psychological testing, (b) conducted face-to-face clinical interviews with the student, the student's family, peers, past victims, teachers, and important others, and (c) determined the student does not pose imminent danger. Concomitantly, the school's safety and risk committee must determine that no imminent danger or risk is foreseeable or anticipated, the student is committed to being bullying and violence free and able to consistently do so, and the school can adequately structure the student's day to ensure no harm to others and no adverse impact on the learning community will occur.

be totally devoid of bullying or violent ideation, thoughts, triggers, and behaviors.

Students who have bullied or been violent or who have been previously identified as a significant risk to others within the school milieu often receive mandated treatment that includes case management services from multiple mental health agencies and judicial system components (e.g., probation, detention services, case management). SOC establishes a unified treatment venture with active and ongoing communication among all providers and agencies. Services address the student's needs 24 hours a day, seven days a week, 365 days a year, at home and at school. Such efforts require significant commitment and collaboration by students, their families, and specialists.

Strengths Assessment

First, the student is assessed by the team and the safety and risk committee determines that he or she does not pose a danger to self or others and can be safely reintegrated back into a controlled school environment. Then, the student and family participate in a strengths assessment. Here, a meeting is held with specialists, professionals representing other agencies providing services to the student (e.g., speech therapists, juvenile probation officers), family members, and persons identified by the student, family members, and the safety and risk committee (McCammon, 2012).

The three primary goals of the strengths assessment are as follows:

1. Determining how the student and family members are currently meeting the student's needs (e.g., providing a nurturing and safe familial milieu for the students) and the family's needs (e.g., sufficient food and dental care)

2. Identifying ways in which mental health professionals and nonprofessionals can be helpful to the student and family members, especially related to keeping the student bullying and violence free

3. Providing the student and family members with kudos, positive feedback, and support for the effective behaviors they are implementing to enable the student's nonbullying and nonviolent behaviors and promoting family functioning (VanDenBerg & Grealish, 1996).

The underlying purpose of the strengths assessment is to provide the student and family members with information regarding what they are doing well. The intent is to help the family system build on their strengths while reinforcing the student's nonbullying, nonviolent, and pro-SOC behaviors. Persons attending the meeting participate in their designated professional roles to fulfill this purpose. A spirit of collaboration and equality is fostered as the nonprofessionals' suggestions and ideas are considered just as important as those made by the professionals.

To help you better understand the strengths assessment process, the following vignette is provided. In this vignette, 12-year-old Maria presents as an intelligent sixth-grade student. She is an only child and lives with her 33-year-old mother and 58-year-old maternal grandmother. Maria is a second-generation Mexican American who lives in a medium-sized southeastern city. Her family moved there when Maria was three, and she has had the same school peers since kindergarten. Approximately 25% of the students attending Maria's middle school identify themselves either as Hispanic or Mexican American, and 12% of the general school population has been identified as obese by the school system. Maria is markedly obese and has a history of fighting with those who tease her about her weight and her diabetes.

Last academic year Maria was suspended twice from school due to initiating fights. She was later expelled for a third fight. During that third fight Maria initiated a physical altercation with a female student who teased Maria about her weight. Maria sat on the teasing student and repeatedly struck her face, neck, shoulders, and arms. The altercation resulted in severe facial lacerations to the other student that required medical attention. Immediately following the altercation Maria was adjudicated and placed in a juvenile detention center. After two weeks in the detention center and one month at home with intensive case management, Maria and her mother petitioned the school requesting Maria be allowed to return to school.

Engaging the Student and Parent(s)

Typically the initial meeting is with the student and a parent or parents. This is especially true for students who have been mandated to attend counseling by the court or school system after a bullying or violent episode. In these situations the student's violence assessment has already been conducted, and the mental health professionals assessing the student (typically a team minimally composed of a board-certified child or forensic psychiatrist; a clinical, forensic, or school psychologist; a school counselor; and an SOC worker or marriage and family therapist) have determined that the student poses no immediate danger to self or others in the school milieu and is sufficiently invested to return to school without bullying or violent behavior. The initial portion of the session depicted below will focus on (1) engaging Maria and her mother, (2) describing what will occur within the SOC intervention, and (3) helping them to identify professionals and nonprofessionals to be included in the SOC intervention.

SCHOOL COUNSELOR: Ms. Diaz, thank you so much for bringing Maria to today's meeting. Mothers are vitally important to the successful reintegration of students back into the school environment. Your being here today demonstrates you are committed to Maria and invested in her school success.

MOTHER: No problem. Maria and I want her to return to school and continue her education.

Before we continue, it is important to discuss the reason for addressing the mother first rather than the student. Often, entry-level specialists engage students first. Although there may be some potential clinical advantage for doing so, we believe the intervention has greater clinical utility when the parents are engaged first. From a structural family therapy position, addressing the mother first confirms and supports her parental role and authority within the family system. It puts her in the "power seat." It confirms her position at the top of the family power hierarchy and emphasizes that she is the person in charge within the family system. Had both biological parents been in the treatment session, the specialist would have said "Mr. and Mrs. Diaz" or "Mom and Dad," thus placing both mother and father in the family authority positions.

Also, it is likely that Maria would neither attend nor engage in counseling had her mother not required it. In other words, the mother, or whoever represents the family's parenting team, is critical to Maria's engagement with counseling. Therefore, the more we laud the mother, the greater the probability that she will continue to require Maria's attendance at counseling and will ensure Maria arrives at the counseling office. Should the mother disengage or sabotage treatment, the harm will be irreparable. Hence, the specialist needs to ensure the mother perceives herself as a vital ally within the counseling and parenting process and experiences a welcoming and supportive atmosphere.

Furthermore, engaging the mother first has potential implications for this Mexican American family as well as many other families of diversity (A. Valadez, personal communication, May 18, 2009). Often within the Mexican American or Hispanic cultures the authority figure is the husband or oldest male figurehead (e.g., grandfather). In this case, the father is absent, so the mother is the figurehead. Failing to engage the mother first would likely be perceived as disrespectful to the mother and possibly even Maria (A. Valadez, personal communication, May 18, 2009). Thus, engaging the mother first is the most clinically and culturally appropriate technique with this family.

Next the specialist engages Maria by saying,

SOCIAL WORKER: Maria, how does it feel to be back at school?

MARIA: It is good to be back. I missed my friends.

SOCIAL WORKER: I bet. It is always good to reconnect with friends. What do you wish to accomplish though these system of care counseling sessions, Maria?

MARIA: Beats me. My mom and our attorney just told me to meet with you so I could get back in school.

SOCIAL WORKER: So, are you here because your mother forced you to come to these sessions, or because you really want to return to school, be with your friends, and most importantly learn?

MARIA: I'm here because I want to be.

SOCIAL WORKER: So, like an adult, you decided to attend these counseling sessions because you want to learn ways that will help you stop fighting and focus on your learning?

MARIA: Yes. My mom did not force me to come.

SOCIAL WORKER: Good. Your decision demonstrates a lot of maturity on your part, Maria. Lots of times little kids come because their mothers force them to attend counseling session. Unlike mature students like you, they don't understand learning in school is important. Without doing well in middle and high school it is difficult to get a good job or have the opportunity to get into college.

MARIA: I know how important school is. I'm not a little kid. I want to go to college to become a doctor. I can't be a doctor if I can't get back into middle school.

Engaging Maria may seem simplistic to some, but it is critically important. Some entry-level specialists fail to provide communication "balance." Despite having both the parent and the student present, they fail to equally engage one or the other. Maria needs to believe she is truly heard and understood. Given the specialist has already spoken to the mother, it is important to provide Maria communication time as well. In other words, it is imperative that both mother and daughter have the opportunity to provide input and actively participate in the counseling session.

In this case, the specialist validates Maria's response, but instead of lingering on that response, the specialist immediately asks Maria what she would like to accomplish by attending the sessions. Maria's flippant response is met with a strategically placed "forced choice" paradoxical question—either Maria was forced to attend or she wants to re-engage in school and learn. Most "tweens" (i.e., students between the ages of 10 and 12) and adolescents refuse to admit they are "forced" to do anything. Also, most want to prove they are adults. In other words, *they* make their own life decisions; *they* are not ruled by parents. Thus, the specialist's question provides an eloquent therapeutic paradox. Does Maria say her mother forced her to attending the counseling session? If she does, it suggests her mother has power and control over Maria. Furthermore, should Maria indicate that her mother forced her to participate in counseling, it suggests Maria is neither an adult nor capable of controlling her life. In other words, she cannot make mature, adult-like decisions. Hence, we can anticipate many students will respond in a manner denying they were forced to attend.

Here is the paradoxical hook. If Maria truly chose to attend the session without her mother's coercion, Maria will have to prove she is more adult-like than child-like. Thus, she will be forced to respond in a more adult-like manner within session as well as within the school and home milieu. This is exactly what the specialist wants. Thus, Maria's response to this strategically placed forced-choice paradoxical question catapults Maria toward healthier behaviors.

In this vignette, Maria indicates a desire to return to middle and high school so she can attend college and become a doctor. This clearly is a topic of importance for further discussion and may even include having a healthcare professional (e.g., physician, nurse, physician assistant) participate as a member on Maria's wraparound team.

Describing the Treatment Process

After engaging both the mother and Maria in balanced communication, the specialist will ask what they know about SOC counseling. The intent is not to test them or to determine what they don't know. Instead, the specialist wishes to provide an opportunity to successfully engage them by lauding them and providing positive strokes for whatever information they do know. At the same time, the specialist will help them gain a fuller perception of the process and answer questions.

PSYCHOLOGIST: Tell me a little bit about what you know about systems of care.

MOTHER: The way I understand it, Maria and I will identify people we think will keep Maria from getting in fights. We will ask those people to help us brainstorm ways to keep Maria out of trouble.

MARIA: Yes, so it's kind of like getting a group of friends and family and saying, "Help me so I won't get in fights."

PSYCHOLOGIST: It sounds as though you have done your homework, Mom. You are correct. Today we will create a list of professionals and nonprofessionals who Maria will invite to help her. Some people might not be willing or able to attend sessions. That will be OK. However, for those who agree to attend, we will be asking them to create new, nonviolent ways for Maria to interact. Remember, people we ask are only helpers. The real work will be done by Maria. So, it will really be up to Maria to do the things she agrees to do so she will remain violence free.

The specialist simply asks what the family knows about SOC. The mother responds first; then Maria adds her understanding. The specialist immediately compliments both of them. Then, the specialist describes key aspects of the SOC process. Both of these points are critical to building rapport and ensuring successful counseling.

Reader, would you mind if I asked you a question or two? Do you like to feel capable and competent? Do you like people to give you appropriate compliments? My suspicion is that you answered "yes" to these questions. Guess what? The same is true for parents and students. Every time you provide positive reinforcement to their attempts to appropriately engage, the experience builds rapport. No parent or student desires to be corrected or embarrassed in front of family or friends. Parents often are extremely anxious that others will perceive them as inept or, worse yet, *failures*. Often students are corrected so frequently they "turn off" to anything said by adults and specialists just because they are tired of being corrected. Thus, whenever specialists have the opportunity to provide a compliment or praise to a student (or parent), they should do so. Our belief is that only when the compliment-to-correction ratio is lopsidedly disproportionate on the compliment-giving side do parents and students later respond favorably to corrections.

Be careful not to overlook the specialist's final potent statement: The specialist reminds Maria and her mother that no matter who is present or what is said or done, the true change agent is Maria. To emphasize Maria's responsibility, the specialist states this construct twice in succession.

Identifying Participants

Next, the specialist helps Maria and her mother identify potential counseling team members. Appropriate member selection is critical to the success of SOC counseling and Maria's goal attainment. No more than 50% of the participants should be professionals (e.g., schoolteachers, speech therapists, specialists, juvenile probation officer). The other members should be nonprofessionals (e.g., grandparents, uncles, aunts, pastor or minister, family friends).

Number of Participants

Although the goal is to "wrap around" every aspect of the family and student's life (e.g., school, home, community) to reduce the student's violent behaviors by increasing familial and community functioning and interactions, counseling sessions can become very challenging if too many people participate. Based on our experience, meetings with more than six members tend to become too chaotic. Thus, we would recommend up to six highly committed participants.

Prerequisites for Participants

Persons selected by the student and family must be perceived as invested in the student and family's successful counseling outcome and must be respected by the student. Nonprofessional examples might include a revered teacher, a respected dance coach, or a favorite music instructor. It does little good to invite unknown persons who are unwilling to invest in the student's life. Students and family members will sabotage treatment if they perceive the nonprofessionals don't respect and value them.

Contraindications for Participants

Persons who might be contraindicated as team members would include the following: (a) people the student or family dislikes or mistrusts, (b) people with an evident substance abuse or addictions disorder, (c) people who fulfill criteria for personality disorders (e.g., antisocial personality disorder, borderline personality disorder) as set out in the fifth edition of the American Psychiatric Association's *Diagnostic and Statistical Manual of Mental Disorders* (DSM-5), (d) those who are actively engaging in criminal activities or have been recently convicted of criminal activities, (e) people who have been convicted, arraigned, or arrested for sex crimes, substance use, or violence or suspected of same, and (f) those displaying psychotic features such as hallucinations or delusions. In addition, persons who have demonstrated recent violent behaviors or who qualify for a DSM-5 disorder such as intermittent explosive disorder, oppositional defiant disorder, or conduct disorder should be ruled out as members.

Process of Identifying Participants

The following clinical vignette will help you understand how the strengths assessment and participant selection process works.

FAMILY THERAPIST: Mom, as both Maria and you already know, part of the systems of care strengths assessment process is identifying potential persons to invite to Maria's counseling sessions. Given I will facilitate those sessions and the court and school system have mandated both Maria's juvenile probation officer, Ms. Sanchez, and Maria's case manager, Mr. Osborne, be present, I believe it would be important for us to identify about three persons who Maria and you believe would be helpful in helping Maria be violence free.

MOTHER: Maria and I have discussed who we would invite. The first person we would like to invite is my mother, Rosa. She lives with us and helps me raise Maria. She loves Maria very much.

FAMILY THERAPIST: Grandmother sounds like an excellent suggestion, Ms. Diaz. Thank you for this suggestion. Help me understand how you believe she will help keep Maria violence free.

MOTHER: She is very strict, but, like I said, she is very loving. She loves Maria a lot and is home with her when I am working. Therefore, I believe Grandmother can lay down the law when I am at work.

FAMILY THERAPIST: What are your thoughts, Maria?

MARIA: Grandma is already very helpful. She and I do things together like shop and make dinner and stuff. I would like her to join us.

FAMILY THERAPIST: Who else have you thought about, Maria?

MARIA: Ms. Elms. She is my favorite teacher. She is the very best teacher I have ever had and she has diabetes like me, too. She always looks out for me and is really nice.

FAMILY THERAPIST: It sounds like you really want Ms. Elms to participate. Maria, tell me how Ms. Elms will help you eliminate your violent behaviors.

MARIA: It used to be when kids teased me about being fat, I would beat them up. If Ms. Elms were helping me, I could talk with her about how mad I am at those mean kids rather than fight.

FAMILY THERAPIST: Maria, that is an excellent idea. How did you come up with that?

MARIA: My case manager, Mr. Osborne, and I thought that up.

FAMILY THERAPIST: Well, you did a great job. Who else would be helpful to you?

Let's take a moment and review what just occurred. The specialist described those required to attend (e.g., Maria's juvenile probation officer). This is simply stated in the manner of Joe Friday from the old *Dragnet* television show: "Just the facts, ma'am." There is no apology about required participants; the specialist simply states who must attend.

Once these participants are stated, the specialist asks for names of three to five persons who will help Maria "be violence free." This is important for two reasons.

First, by indicating the limited number of persons, the statement encourages the mother and Maria to focus on only the people perceived as most helpful to Maria. Therefore, it precludes them from identifying dozens of people who may be only minimally invested or helpful.

Second, asking the mother and Maria to identify those who will help Maria establish her violence recovery empowers both the mother and Maria. It makes them the experts and implies that they are the ones who can make the best decision about who will attend the SOC sessions. Such empowerment is neither a gimmick nor a game. Who best knows the persons who can aid Maria in crystallizing her nonbullying and nonviolent behavioral patterns? Correct! It is Maria!

Reader, have you ever gone on a diet? How do you typically respond when someone *tells* you what dieting foods you *must* consume? I don't know about you, but whenever someone tells me what I *must* do, I typically resist. In fact, I'm going to prove them wrong. Instead, if someone provides me the information necessary to make a wise decision (e.g., "You are at significant risk of diabetes, stroke, and heart attack unless you lose 15 pounds"), then *I* am the one to decide what is in my best interests, and I do it. When I make that decision, I then am far more committed to successfully dieting. In other words, when I make the decision to diet, I am successful. However, should someone attempt to force me to diet, there is a significant probability I will waste valuable time and energy fighting the mandate, and I likely will not stay on the diet for very long.

Incidentally, who best knows your most tempting high-calorie foods? Do you crave salty potato chips, or are you more tempted by creamy, sweet, milk chocolate candy bars? Also, who knows the times of day you are most tempted to eat those high-calorie foods? For example, are you the type of person who can abstain from eating all day and then inhale everything in sight after 11 p.m.? The intent of asking these questions is not to make you hungry. Rather, we want to demonstrate that *you* know more about yourself and your eating patterns than anyone else. Thus, the empowerment we provide Maria and her mother specific to their identification of trusted persons whom *they* believe will be helpful in Maria's violence recovery is a fundamental part of SOC's foundation—that students and their families know what they need most, and they know who can best help them meet those needs.

Next, note that when the mother suggests the grandmother as a participant, the specialist lauds Ms. Diaz on her suggestion. As a specialist who had coursework in counseling theories, what do you remember about behavioral therapy? Exactly! Positive, rewarding behaviors typically result in replication of the desired behaviors. In other words, the specialist positively rewarded the mother for her suggestion. This potentially reinforces the mother's behaviors and increases the probability that she will continue to participate. Thus, we anticipate the mother will remain engaged in the treatment process and will suggest other potential participants as well.

Failure to provide such positive rewards creates participant disengagement. I suspect some of you likely experienced such disengagement at some point in your college experiences. Imagine a professor asking students to comment on a reading assignment or class-related topic. She is seeking a specific answer and brusquely dismisses all student responses until she finds the student who provides the exact, desired response. After three student responses are curtly dismissed, however, a funny thing happens: Students stop responding, and the professor has to "answer" her own question. When such dismissive behaviors occur over successive class sessions, students "give up" and stop answering the professor's questions.

The same is true for students and their parents who are identifying participants for SOC sessions. We need to ensure students and parents perceive they are adequately heard and understood whenever they present the name of a potential participant.

The specialist asks Maria's thoughts about her grandmother's involvement. It is important for Maria to perceive she has input into the participant selection process. Should Maria perceive the participants to be her *mother's* participants, she is more likely to sabotage counseling. However, should Maria be able to include persons she truly feels would be helpful to her, she will likely become more engaged in the counseling process. After all, how can you be dissatisfied with the participants if you were the one who chose them?

Furthermore, the specialist establishes a pattern of asking *how* the suggested person will help keep Maria violence free. By asking this question immediately following the proposed person's inclusion, both the mother and Maria will begin to think about this question before suggesting other names. Thus, once this pattern is established, the mother and Maria will initiate self-talk such as, "How will cousin Julie help keep me from fighting?" or "Bryce would be a good member because he always talks me down." This will help increase the probability that the mother and Maria will suggest persons they actually believe can help Maria maintain her violence recovery.

Throughout the clinical vignette we witness the specialist providing the mother and Maria with continued kudos. Here, Maria thoughtfully describes how Ms. Elms can help eliminate her violent behaviors. The specialist commends Maria's response and asks how Maria *developed* this intervention. Although Maria gives partial credit to her case manager for helping Maria come up with the idea, the specialist moves the focus off the case manager and instead heaps more kudos on Maria. The intent here is not to remove the case manager's recognition but to provide Maria with the maximum recognition for her plan. Again, this helps Maria perceive success and increases the probability of her continuing nonviolent behaviors.

Ruling Out Suggested Participants

After doing SOC with families in crisis and supervising doctoral and master's students in these interventions, we have come to understand that one of the most challenging situations occurs when students or parents suggest a potential participant who is clearly inappropriate for inclusion. Surprisingly, we have found such inappropriate suggestions are greatly reduced by asking *how* the suggested person will help eliminate the student's violent behaviors. This questioning is demonstrated in the above clinical vignette. If the student or parents suggest the inclusion of someone who is clinically inappropriate, we typically ask the student how that person will be helpful. Often this is sufficient for the suggested participant to be removed from consideration. However, when it is not, we attempt to determine how the presence of this person is perceived as potentially helpful, and then we suggest other means to address this need. This is demonstrated in the clinical vignette below:

MOTHER: The first person we want is our attorney, Mr. Vos.

COUNSELOR: Help me understand how Mr. Vos will be helpful in keeping Maria violence free.

MOTHER: No, that isn't why I want to invite him. I want to make certain that Maria doesn't get pushed around by her juvenile probation officer.

COUNSELOR: I can certainly understand you don't want Maria to get pushed around by her juvenile probation officer, Ms. Diaz. However, the persons we invite to participate should know Maria very well and be committed to helping Maria eliminate her violent behaviors. Would Mr. Vos's participation directly influence Maria to be safe and not fight?

MOTHER: No, I guess it wouldn't.

COUNSELOR: I'm assuming Mr. Vos agreed to Maria's participating in the systems of care so Maria could be allowed to return to school. Is that correct?"

MOTHER: Yes. He said the only way the school would allow Maria to return is if she participated in the systems of care counseling sessions.

COUNSELOR: Then your attorney thought it was in Maria's best interests to attend these sessions?

MOTHER: Yes. He said that.

COUNSELOR: So, he wouldn't have suggested that Maria attend if he had not felt it was in Maria's best interests to attend.

MOTHER: I guess you're right.

COUNSELOR: How about this, Ms. Diaz. Since I will be the person facilitating the sessions, should at any time within those sessions you feel Maria is getting pushed around or harmed in any way, will you promise me you will say something to me within the session?

MOTHER: I could do that.

COUNSELOR: Frankly, it is imperative that you let me know within session should you feel Maria is being harmed in any way. Although we have just recently met, Ms. Diaz, I believe you are very dedicated to Maria. So, should you believe at any time that Maria is being harmed, I need you to immediately tell me. That way we can address your concern right then and there. Will you make that promise to me?

MOTHER: Yes, I will do that.

COUNSELOR: Good, then I believe we can initiate these sessions without Mr. Vos as long as you promise to let me know if something is not going well.

In this vignette, we observe the specialist doing four very important things.

First, when the mother suggests Maria's attorney be present, the specialist does not panic. Instead, she remains in the cognitive realm and keeps the conversation on a cognitive level. She does not foolishly respond in an emotional manner. To keep the inter- action at a cognitive versus emotional level, she simply asks the very same thing she does whenever any potential participant is suggested: How will the suggested person help the student remain violence free? The mother responds by saying that Maria's attorney is desired for a different reason: She wants to ensure Maria isn't "pushed around" by her probation officer. I believe the mother's concern is legitimate. It has been my experience that many who are mandated into treatment feel disempowered. Here, the mother simply wants Maria's attorney to be present to empower her and Maria against a system that requires their successful completion of a process they don't control.

I don't know about you, but when I feel disempowered, I don't like it. Think about the last time you felt disempowered. Where were you? What happened? The last time I felt disempowered, a young store clerk was unwilling to refund my money for a pair of sunglasses I had purchased. The purchase had occurred the day be- fore with the same store clerk. At the time of purchase the clerk had clearly told me I had 90 days to return the purchase for a full money refund should I not like the glasses. As a matter of fact, the store's full cash refund policy was clearly described on the cash register re- ceipt. The situation got uglier by the moment as it became increas- ingly evident that no resolution amenable to both the clerk and me was going to come about.

Please note, this situation revolved around a pair of sunglasses! How would I have felt and behaved had the situation involved a loved family member! Clearly, students and parents who feel disempowered can present in an "ugly" manner. This is not the case with Ms. Diaz above. However, many parents believe they pay taxes and according to their thought processes their children are not a threat to others. As a matter of fact, these parents perceive their children as being *exploited* by an unfair counseling mandate. Mandated students and parents are often angry. They typically behave and respond on an emotional level rather than a cognitive one. When students and parents behave in this manner it is easy for specialists also to respond emotionally rather than cognitively.

Dr. William Purkey illustrates how specialists need to remain cognitive and professional in his anecdote about a Japanese samurai. The fictional samurai was employed by an emperor to behead persons who failed to pay their tax debts. As a professional, the samurai merely was fulfilling the charge assigned to him by the emperor. Thus, he had no malice or emotions toward those he was paid to behead. One day the samurai encountered a debtor he was assigned to behead. As the samurai drew his sword and prepared to behead the debtor, the debtor spit in the samurai's face and insulted the samurai's mother, wife, and children. Enraged, the samurai sheathed his sword and walked away. Later, when the emperor asked him why he had failed to behead the obnoxious and insulting debtor, the samurai simply explained it would be unprofessional to behead someone because of his own emotions.

This story contains a parallel meaning for specialists, who sometimes encounter angry students and parents. Often these students and their parents do not seek counseling to reduce their children's potential violent behaviors. Many times, these students and their parents have learned that when they intimidate or act in a threatening manner, others simply leave them alone or require little of them. Thus, when the school system or courts require these students and their parents to participate in counseling, they may attempt to intimidate or threaten the specialist. As professionals, specialists must remain at a cognitive level. They should never emotionally respond in anger toward previously violent or potentially violent students. Although this is sometimes difficult, it is critically important. Responding in an emotional manner will resolve little and often increases the student's or parents' emotions. Specialists need to remain professional and operate in a cognitive versus emotional or responsive realm. Thus, should the specialist perceive the student or the parents are threatening or dangerous, ask how these behaviors are helpful and describe what will happen should they choose to continue the threatening behaviors.

SOCIAL WORKER: Ms. Diaz, I guess I'm a little confused. I believe our goal is to be helpful to Maria. Is that correct?

MOTHER: Yes, that is correct.

SOCIAL WORKER: I'm very committed to helping Maria stay violence free and potentially return to school as she demonstrates her commitment to staying violence free. I believe you are committed to these things too. Is that correct?

MOTHER: Yes.

SOCIAL WORKER: Then help me understand how it is helpful for Maria to hear you say things to me such as, "I'm going to sue your butt off if you don't let Maria back in school" or "I should take you outside and whip your sorry rear end"?

MOTHER: I'm sorry. I didn't mean it to sound that way.

SOCIAL WORKER: Thank you for your apology. However, as you know, it is not up to me but rather up to Maria and you whether she is allowed back to school. If Maria continues to choose to act violently as she has in the past, then you will end up needing to find and pay for a private school that will accept her. That will be very expensive for you. Instead, I hope that I have both Maria's and your commitment to behave in nonviolent, nonintimidating ways that will demonstrate that Maria can return to Meadowbrook Independent School System.

We can see that instead of ignoring Ms. Diaz's intimidating statements, the specialist moves to a very professional and cognitively based interaction. Here, the specialist cognitively restates the goal, asks if the mother is committed to this treatment goal, and describes what will happen should Maria and her mother not demonstrate commitment to Maria's nonviolent behaviors (e.g., the mother will need to pay for private schooling elsewhere). After confronting the potentially intimidating statements made by the mother, the specialist then re-extends the opportunity for Ms. Diaz to actively join the specialist in seeking ways to solidify Maria's nonviolent behaviors.

The second important thing the specialist does in the clinical vignette earlier in the chapter is to agree with the mother and join in her noted concern. This is done by simply repeating the mother's voiced concern. Hence, the specialist agrees with the mother and also does not want Maria "pushed around" by Maria's juvenile probation officer.

Third, the specialist redirects the session back to the central theme: Will the presence of Maria's attorney reduce Maria's fighting? The mother confirms that the attorney's presence would not keep Maria violence free. However, understanding that the mother feels empowered by the attorney, the specialist asks whether the attorney had suggested Maria and her mother attend counseling sessions. In other words, the specialist perceives that the mother's confidence in the attorney can be used as a means to promote Maria's and her mother's engagement in counseling. Once the mother reports that the attorney had indeed made this counseling recommendation, the specialist capitalizes on her faith in the attorney and the attorney's recommendations.

Fourth, the specialist attempts to build rapport with the mother by saying that the specialist will facilitate the counseling sessions in a fair and impartial manner. Most importantly, she asks the mother to join her in creating a safe session for Maria. This is indirectly done by asking her mother to inform the specialist within session should she feel Maria is being "pushed around" or harmed. The mother agrees. However, the specialist doesn't simply discontinue the discussion. In fact, the specialist again provides kudos to the mother and observes that she appears "very dedicated" to Maria. Then, the specialist asks the mother to "promise" to bring up any concerns within the treatment sessions. This clearly denotes the specialist's commitment to Maria. It further demonstrates that the specialist heard the mother's concerns.

Contacting Participants

In most cases we believe it is important for the student to contact potential participants. There are three primary reasons for this:

1. We believe it is empowering for students to learn how to ask for help from others and to appropriately engage others without using dysfunctional techniques they had previously employed, such as bullying, threatening, violent, or conning behaviors. As students gain this new "help asking" skill, they acquire more appropriate, nonbullying, nonthreatening, and nonviolent ways to interact.
2. Given that students know and reportedly respect the persons they identified, it is far more likely that invited participants will respond to the student's request for participation than to a request made by an unknown specialist.
3. We have found that specialists and parents are far more invested in change than students. When specialists do the majority of the student's therapeutic work, there is little positive impact on the student.

Should the student be unwilling to make the contacts and seem minimally invested in the SOC process, he or she is simply referred back to the school district, judge, legal counsel, or agency that made the initial treatment request. Reports would then be sent to the initial referring sources (e.g., judges, probation officers). These reports document the student's unwillingness to comply with the mandated counseling or describe the student's lack of investment in the counseling process. Such reports likely mean the student will be sent to a long-term juvenile detention facility and will not be able to return to his or her former school milieu.

Of course, few things in counseling are inflexible. In some atypical situations, the specialist may perceive that the student is committed to changing her violent behaviors but presenting as exceedingly dependent, ashamed, or depressed. In such cases, the specialist may determine that it is clinically appropriate for him or her to contact potential participants. However, we would suggest the specialist and student make the telephone contacts together via conference calls so the student is continually engaged in the process.

Telephone Call Instructions and Role-Plays

Before phoning potential participants, the specialist, the student, and the parents again discuss each one. The discussion revolves around how the student knows the participant, previous helpful experiences the student had with the participant, and how the student believes the participant will be helpful in keeping him or her free from violence. Then, the specialist and student jointly complete a formal participant request sheet (Table 5.1). This sheet should be available to facilitate upcoming role-plays and the actual telephone invitations.

The specialist instructs the students not to tell potential participants that he or she is "making me call you." Instead, the specialist encourages the student to contact potential participants and start off by telling them they are valued and appreciated and the student believes they can provide important help. The student can describe how the potential participant has helped in the past and how his or her participation will help the student remain free from violence. The student can then ask the potential participant if he or she would be willing to attend an initial informational meeting with the student and others who have been identified as "required attenders" (e.g., juvenile probation officer, specialist, case manager).

Role-plays are then begun. During the first two role-play experiences, the specialist assumes the student's role and the student takes the potential participant's role. To make the role-play more realistic, the specialist uses the information on the participant request sheet. During later role-plays, the student plays himself or herself and the specialist assumes the potential participant's

Table 5.1 Participant Request Sheet

Participant's Name: Prefix (Dr., Mrs., Ms., Mr.)_____

_____

How do you know participant?_____

_____

_____

_____

Previous helpful experiences with the participant

When	Where	What Happened
_____	_____	_____ _____ _____
_____	_____	_____ _____ _____
_____	_____	_____ _____ _____
_____	_____	_____ _____ _____

Describe how the potential participant can be helpful to you in maintaining your freedom from violence.

_____

_____

_____

_____

Telephone Call:

Hello _____,

The last time we talked, you helped me _____

_____

Continued

Table 5.1 Continued

I've had some challenges related to _____
_____ and am wondering if you would be willing to help me by meeting
with my (parents, mother, father, grandmother, other) _____ and
me at my specialist's office on date_____ at (time)_____. The office is
located at 501 West Durango Street. I really would appreciate your help; may
I count on you?

---

role. After the role-plays, the specialist offers suggestions about the
student's verbal communications.

Making the Calls

After the student has created a fairly sincere and cogently stated request, the student makes the first telephone call from the specialist's
office, with the parents and the specialist observing and supporting
the student. From the sidelines, the parents and the specialist can
coach the student as necessary. After the call, the specialist asks the
parents to identify what the student did well during the call. Once
the parents have identified as many positive things as they can, the
specialist typically adds more positive things and commends the
student on an outstanding job. Again, suggestions are made.

If the student's telephone invitation was adequately stated, the
student then makes the remaining calls under the supervision of
the parents. However, if the student struggled or had difficulties
verbalizing the request, further role-plays are conducted as well as
another call supervised by the parents and the specialist.

Why Include Parents?

At this point some readers may be questioning why we encourage parental involvement in the role-plays and the actual

telephone calls. From a structural family therapy viewpoint, placing the parents in an administrative role over their children reestablishes the parents at the top of the family power hierarchy. In other words, this demonstrates to the students (and parents too) that the parents, not the children, rule the family system and the parents establish the appropriate family rules and boundaries.

It has been our experience with conduct-disordered, substance-abusing, and violent students that the students often have dethroned the parents in terms of having authority in the family system. This typically results in a chaotic home environment where the violent child rules the home via intimidation, threats, and violent behaviors. When parental control is eclipsed, violent and potentially violent students have nearly free rein. This leads to the student's misperception that he or she is free from all adult authority (e.g., school, judicial, police, corrections). Nothing could be further from the truth. Reestablishing parental authority within the home is crucial to addressing the student's violent behaviors. This is especially true with younger students who are ineligible to become emancipated minors and are a long time away from the age of majority.

Also, parents see the student far more often than the specialist. Even under the best circumstances where weekly counseling and case management is court mandated for formerly violent students, the number of interactions that specialists and case managers can have with students pales in comparison with the number of times parents can interact with these students. Clearly, some parents desire no interaction or are unable to invest time with their children. However, for the vast majority of students we counsel, parents want involvement. Such active parental involvement ensures students are supervised and under the watchful eyes of parents. In conjunction with counseling and case management, this can lead to more effective and lasting interventions.

Rejected Invitations

If a potential participant rejects the invitation to attend the meeting, it is important to monitor the student's responses toward that person. Should the student become upset and frustrated, the specialist can use this opportunity to help the student connect how internalized, cognitive self-talk influences violent behaviors. For example:

MARIA: That damn Mr. Pruitt! I am so mad at him! I can't believe he won't come to my counseling session!

PSYCHOLOGIST: Sounds like you're feeling pretty angry at Mr. Pruitt.

MARIA: Damn right I am angry at him. He is a good-for-nothing, self-absorbed jerk.

PSYCHOLOGIST: Maria, help me understand what you are saying to yourself, in your own mind, about why you are angry at Mr. Pruitt for not coming to the systems of care counseling session.

MARIA: What do you mean?

PSYCHOLOGIST: Well, you say you are angry at him for not agreeing to come to counseling to help you. Is that correct?

MARIA: Yeah. So what?

PSYCHOLOGIST: So, what are you saying to yourself about his not coming to counseling to help you?

MARIA: I'm saying he won't come because he doesn't like me.

PSYCHOLOGIST: And if he doesn't like you, what does that mean?

MARIA: That means he thinks I'm a loser.

PSYCHOLOGIST: And if he thinks you're a loser, what does that mean?

MARIA: It means I'm never going to amount to much.

PSYCHOLOGIST: And if you never amount to much . . .

MARIA: I'm failing my mom.

PSYCHOLOGIST: And if you fail your mom?

MARIA: (silence)

PSYCHOLOGIST: And if you fail your mom?

MARIA: She is going to leave me.

PSYCHOLOGIST: Maria, if Mom leaves you, then what?

MARIA: Then I will lose her love and I'm unlovable to anyone.

In an effort to help Maria better understand the connection between her internalized, cognitive self-talk and her violent behaviors, the specialist does three things:

1. Immediately after the specialist hears and senses Maria's anger at Mr. Pruitt, the specialist makes a comment related to her perception—Maria is in fact angry with Mr. Pruitt. This allows Maria an opportunity to admit, deny, or modify the specialist's comment. In this vignette, Maria verbally admits her anger.

2. The specialist asks Maria to notice her internalized, cognitive self-talk. Maria at first does not comprehend the specialist's comment. However, instead of dropping the comment and pursuing other interventions, the specialist simply rephrases the statement to make Maria's internalized self-talk more evident and comprehensible. Maria then verbalizes why she believes Mr. Pruitt rejected her invitation to attend the counseling session. According to Maria's internalized self-talk, Mr. Pruitt does not attend because he "doesn't like" her.

3. The specialist uses a "linking" technique to help Maria gain insight into the underlying issues that cause the behaviors resulting from negative self-talk (e.g., violent behaviors). When employing this technique, the specialist simply uses the student's previous responses and asks something like, "What does that [previous response] mean?" This is repeated until the student moves to the smallest identifiable feeling or thought. In Maria's case, if she fails her mother, her mother will leave. Mother's leaving would then prove that Maria is unlovable, and thus the anger and violence toward others.

Thus, should the student feel rejected, we use the experience to increase his or her insight and self-understanding. The hope is that we can then help the student gain the self-confidence to contact others who will accept the invitation to attend the counseling session. Most often, those who are truly invested in the student's success will at least agree to attend the first meeting. Usually these persons are less concerned with the details of the appointment and are focused on helping the student. They often have demanding schedules but usually make time. Typically, they are revered by students.

Quite a while ago, a young man contacted a family member to ask her to participate in an SOC experience. He believed her involvement was vital to resolving his addictions and intermittent explosive disorder. When he called her from the office, she was at work. She pleaded with him not to leave the office until she could arrive and pledge her support in person. In other words, this woman was so committed to him that she wanted an immediate, face-to-face interaction with him. Within 20 minutes she had arrived at the office and told him she had been aware of his alcohol abuse for years but had never taken the opportunity to speak with him about *her* recovery and *her* previously violent behaviors resulting from her drinking and drugging. The experience was quite moving for the young man, who said he had never known of her struggles with addiction and violence. Frankly, because of this family member's involvement, he readily progressed through his recovery from addictions and violent behavior.

Reticent Participants

Most who are contacted agree to participate in the first meeting. However, other are reticent to participate. In general, reticent invitees have one or more of the following characteristics:

1. They are less familiar with the student and the student's family than the student believed.
2. They have witnessed or heard about the student's violent behaviors and feel potential jeopardy or danger related to participation.
3. They are angry with the student for something the student said or did (e.g., the student had stolen items from the invitee).
4. They perceive little benefit or reward for attending.
5. They are friends or aligned with others who do not have favorable impressions of the student.
6. They do not perceive their involvement will be meaningful to the student or the student's family.
7. They are experiencing immediate personal or work-related needs that require their full attention.

Because often only two or three nonprofessional participants are needed, and one or two are often parents or family members, we encourage students to contact the next person on their list if someone is reticent to engage. In other words, if someone is reluctant to engage in the process, it would be better to select another person who is more invested. Also, should invitees attempt to establish unrealistic parameters regarding their involvement (e.g., "I will not attend if you don't cut your hair" or "I can only attend on the third Monday of the month"), we believe a different participant should be sought.

Confidentiality and Obtaining Releases

The specialist should inform the student and the parents that although the specialist will encourage participants to keep everything said within the interview confidential, embarrassing or hurtful facts may still be disclosed to those outside the meeting. Participants are not bound by professional ethics or confidentiality.

Therefore, before the first meeting with invited others, the specialist should inform the student and the parents about potential issues and implications. Also, before anyone is contacted regarding possible interview participation, students and their parents must sign release of confidential information forms. Furthermore, individual releases should be signed by all participants, thereby giving them permission to communicate with one another during treatment.

Specialists may also require participants to sign a pretreatment contract. Although not necessarily legally binding, by signing such a contract, participants relinquish their rights to seek case records or attempt to compel the specialist or other participants to divulge communications or occurrences that occurred during assessment or treatment.

Because students are typically minors, parents or legal guardians must approve their participation in the SOC experience and also approve those who are invited to participate. Typically, the rank-ordered list of invitees results from a brainstorming session with the parents and the student, so there are few surprises. However, *the parents, not the student*, are the ones who decide who is ultimately invited and allowed to participate. Approval is typically not a problem, because in most cases the parents or legal guardians desire the student to return to school and view participants as helpful in attaining that outcome. However, specialists should never initiate counseling without obtaining full approval from the parents or legal guardians and signed paperwork outlining their full support of inviting rank-ordered others to participate. As previously noted, participation by some is contraindicated, and only persons believed to be therapeutically appropriate should be included in the SOC experience.

If a minor is asked to participate in another youth's SOC experience, his or her parents will need to approve the minor's participation. Some parents may not allow their child to participate in another youth's SOC experience. The specialist should explain to the invited child's parents that the student values the invited peer and believes his or her presence will be helpful in attaining freedom from bullying and violence. Sometimes statements like these are enough to make the invited parents feel comfortable allowing their child to attend. At other times, the invited peers or their parents have experienced or witnessed the bullying and violent behaviors of the student requesting the peer's attendance. Thus, rightly, neither the peer nor the peer's parents will wish the youth to attend.

Management of Noncompliant, Treatment-Mandated Students

Because the impetus for bullying and violent students to enter treatment is so varied, it would be foolish to attempt to describe the management of each situation where a student may decline SOC involvement. This is especially true for voluntary students (e.g., students not ordered into treatment by the judicial system or required to participate by the school district). Many times, students who volunteer to participate feel coerced to do so by their parents and discontinue early in the process because of these feelings of coercion or the anger generated by feeling that they "must" participate.

However, the situation is somewhat different for students mandated to participate by the court or the school district. Mandated students must provide a release of confidential information and request the specialist to submit assessment findings to a specific court or school district. Depending on the specific circumstances of the student's refusal to be assessed and participate in the SOC process, the specialist can generally tell him or her that nonparticipation will likely result in the elimination of previous agreements with the judicial system or school district. The specialist should encourage the student to speak with legal counsel should he or she have legal concerns or refuse to participate. The intent of this statement is not to threaten or intimidate; it merely reflects reality. School administrators and legal counsel frequently offer first-time bullying or violent students or those with such ideation the opportunity to return to school if they participate in counseling. Those offered such opportunities pose minimal risk and are not viewed by school administrators as a threat to the safety of others. Students who refuse to participate in the school bullying or violence assessment or counseling process likely will not be allowed to return to school. Once this is verified by students and their parents, students often wish to "voluntarily" participate in the assessment and counseling process.

Summary

The literature demonstrates the utility of SOC interventions with students and their families. SOC interventions appear to offer students an opportunity to lessen the probability of bullying and violent behaviors by having regular meetings with significant others. The SOC approach seems well suited for multiservice interventions where professionals from various agencies jointly devise interventions with students, students' families, and significant nonprofessional others as ways to forestall bullying and violent behaviors and increase desirable behaviors. The participation of trusted and respected nonprofessionals who are identified by the student as important ensures a treatment approach that will meet the unique needs and goals of each student, thereby enhancing student motivation and treatment compliance. Coordination of the SOC approach with students at risk for bullying and violent behaviors increases treatment providers' collaboration and the promotion of integrated interventions to prevent bullying and violence and foster pro-social interactions. Chapter 6 will provide more in-depth information about how to use SOC interventions.

References

Adams, J., & Juhnke, G. A. (1998, November). *Wraparound services with school children and their parents.* Presented at the North Carolina Counseling Association Conference, Winston-Salem, NC.

Adams, J. R., & Juhnke, G. A. (2001). Using the systems of care philosophy to promote human potential. *Journal of Humanistic Counseling, Education & Development, 40,* 225–232. doi:10.1002/j.2164-490x.2001.tb00120

American Psychiatric Association. (2013). *Diagnostic and statistical manual of mental disorders* (5th ed.). Arlington, VA: Author.

Brashears, F., Davis, C., & Katz-Leavy, J. (2012). Systems of care: The story behind the numbers. *American Journal of Community Psychology, 49*(3), 494–502. doi:10.1007/s10464-011-9452-z

Crusto, C. A., Lowell, D. I., Paulicin, B., Reynolds, J., Feinn, R., Friedman, S. R., & Kaufman, J. S. (2008). Evaluation of a wraparound process for children exposed to family violence. *Best Practices in Mental Health, 4*(1), 1–18.

Erickson, C. D. (2012). Using systems of care to reduce incarceration of youth with serious mental illness. *American Journal of Community Psychology, 49*(3), 404–416. doi:10.1007/s10464-011-9484-4

Friedman, R. M., & Drews, D. A. (2005, February). *Evidence-based practices, systems of care, and individual care.* Presented at the Research and Training Center for Children's Mental Health, Tampa, FL.

Green, J. G., Xuan, Z., Kwong, L., Anderson, J. A., & Leaf, P. J. (2016). School referral of children with serious emotional disturbance to systems of care: Six-month clinical and educational outcomes. *Journal of Child and Family Studies, 25*(12), 3728–3738. doi:10.1007/s10826-016-0511-9

Haber, M. G., Cook, J. R., & Kilmer, R. P. (2012). Perceptions of family environment and wraparound processes: Associations with age and implications for serving transitioning youth in systems of care. *American Journal of Community Psychology, 49*(3), 454–466. doi:10.1007/s10464-012-9490-1

Juhnke, G. A., & Liles, R. G. (2000). Treating adolescents presenting with comorbid violent and addictive behaviors: A behavioral family therapy model. In D. S. Sandu & C. B. Aspy (Eds.), *Violence in American schools: A practical guide for counselors* (pp. 319–333). Alexandria, VA: American Counseling Association.

McCammon, S. L. (2012). Systems of care as asset-building communities: Implementing strengths-based planning and positive youth development. *American Journal of Community Psychology, 49*(3), 556–565. doi:10.1007/s10464-012-9514-x

Miller, B. D., Blau, G. M., Christopher, O. T., & Jordan, P. E. (2012). Sustaining and expanding systems of care to provide mental health services for children, youth and families across America. *American Journal of Community Psychology, 49*(3), 566–579. doi:10.1007/s10464-012-9517-7

Painter, K. (2012). Outcomes for youth with severe emotional disturbance: A repeated measures longitudinal study of a wraparound approach of service delivery in systems of care. *Child & Youth Care Forum, 41*(4), 407–425. doi:10.1007/s10566-011-9167-1

Powell, C., Ellasante, I., Korchmaros, J. D., Haverly, K., & Stevens, S. (2016). iTEAM: Outcomes of an affirming system of care serving LGBTQ youth experiencing homelessness. *Families in Society, 97*(3), 181.

Riebschleger, J., Day, A., & Damashek, A. (2015). Foster care youth share stories of trauma before, during, and after placement: Youth voices for building trauma-informed systems of care. *Journal of Aggression, Maltreatment & Trauma, 24*(4), 339–360. doi:10.1080/10926771.2015.1009603

Smithgall, C., Cusick, G., & Griffin, G. (2013). Responding to students affected by trauma: Collaboration across public systems. *Family Court Review, 51*(3), 401–408. doi:10.1111/fcre.12036

Snyder, F. J., Roberts, Y. H., Crusto, C. A., Connell, C. M., Griffin, A., Finley, M. K., & Kaufman, J. S. (2012). Exposure to traumatic events and the behavioral health of children enrolled in an early childhood system of care. *Journal of Traumatic Stress, 25*(6), 700–704. doi:10.1002/jts.21756

VanDenBerg, J. E., & Grealish, E. M. (1996). Individualized services and supports through the wraparound process: Philosophy and procedures. *Journal of Child and Family Studies, 5*(1), 7–21. doi: 10.1007/BF02234675

Whitson, M. L., & Connell, C. M. (2016). The relation of exposure to traumatic events and longitudinal mental health outcomes for children enrolled in systems of care: Results from a national system of care evaluation. *American Journal of Community Psychology, 57*(3–4), 380–390. doi:10.1002/ajcp.12058

Whitson, M. L., Connell, C. M., Bernard, S., & Kaufman, J. S. (2012). An examination of exposure to traumatic events and symptoms and strengths for children served in a behavioral health system of care. *Journal of Emotional and Behavioral Disorders, 20*(3), 193–207. doi:10.1177/1063426610380596

6

How to Implement Systems of Care

Chapter 5 introduced the systems of care (SOC) approach, and this chapter builds on your new knowledge by describing how to implement SOC interventions.

For reading ease we will continue using the same clinical vignette. As you will recall, Maria is an obese 12-year-old who is in the sixth grade. She is a first-generation Mexican American who lives with her single, 33-year-old mother and 58-year-old maternal grandmother. Maria has a history of fighting with those she perceives are teasing her about her weight. Maria was expelled from school after her last physical altercation, in which the victim required medical attention. Maria's mother now wishes for Maria to return to school. Maria and her mother have agreed to participate in the SOC process as required by the school district as a "first step" in considering Maria's potential re-enrollment.

In the initial SOC meeting:

1. The specialist welcomes participants, addresses releases of confidential information and confidentiality issues, and establishes procedural aspects for this and upcoming meetings.
2. The student introduces each participant.
3. The student's strengths are identified.
4. Nonbullying and nonviolent favorite activities are identified.

Specialist's Welcome

The intent of the specialist's welcome is to (a) reduce the first session's "uncomfortableness" and lessen the participants' anxiety,

(b) promote verbal commitment to Maria, and (c) establish procedural aspects of the first and upcoming sessions. Typically, whatever uncomfortableness or anxiety exists quickly dissipates as the
specialist introduces herself or himself, welcomes those present,
and describes what is going to happen in this and upcoming sessions. We suggest the specialist begin with a brief self-introduction
and welcome. Given most are present to help the identified student,
the participants are relatively indifferent to a detailed description
of the specialist's educational background and school counseling
credentials.

We have found it helpful to compliment participants for
attending and to characterize them as "expert consultants."
Therefore, we commonly say that the purpose of the meeting is for
invited participants to "help me understand the student and learn
how I can be helpful." We also encourage participants to make a
verbal commitment to the student and to each other. Therefore, a
typical introduction will likely begin similar to this:

> "Hello, my name is Jerry Juhnke. I am the supervising family ther-
> apist at Meadowbrook. On behalf of Maria and Maria's mother,
> Ms. Diaz, I'd like to welcome and thank you for coming. Your
> being here today demonstrates your commitment to helping
> Maria and your willingness to support Maria as she works toward
> her goals of remaining bullying and violence free. The intent of
> today's first system of care meeting is to describe the systems of
> care process and its rules, and for us to better understand how
> we can be helpful to Maria in her goal of successfully completing
> school in a nonbullying, nonviolent manner. Specifically, systems
> of care, or 'wraparound services' as it is sometimes called, is an
> evidence-based counseling intervention that has been found to
> be helpful with adolescents. Basically, students, with the help of
> parents and invited persons, *wrap around* the student and help
> the student stop bullying and violent behaviors. The belief is that
> when persons like you who are important to the student become
> invested in the student's success, they can help the student make

the correct choices and select the best behaviors to be successful. Your being here suggests that you are invested and want to help Maria."

As you can see, the introduction has an economy of words and doesn't get into details of Maria's past violent experiences. Instead, it is focused on the future. It describes how those present will *wrap around* Maria and help her make improved and nonviolent choices.

Typically, at this point, we attempt to promote verbal commitment by asking if anyone isn't interested in helping Maria. Given that the persons who are present have already taken the time to travel to the counseling office and are physically present, it is rare for participants to say they are not interested in helping. However, if persons indicate an unwillingness to help, we simply thank them for their time and if possible reframe their unwillingness to participate.

COUNSELOR: Is anyone not interested in helping Maria?

JORGE: I hate to admit this, but I don't think I can help.

COUNSELOR: Jorge, I know that Maria identified you as someone who could be helpful to her and really wanted you here. I'm sure your presence would mean a lot to Maria.

JORGE: I just can't help.

COUNSELOR: Is it that you don't want to help Maria or is there something else?

JORGE: I just can't take the time off work to be here. My boss just won't let me do it.

COUNSELOR: No problem. What I'm hearing you say is that you want to help Maria; however, work obligations won't allow you to come to sessions. Is that correct?

JORGE: Yes. I want to help Maria, but I just can't.

COUNSELOR: That makes sense to me. I thank you for coming today, Jorge. Let's let you return to work at this time.

Once those who are unwilling or unable to participate are thanked for their honesty, we quickly allow them to leave. Then, we focus on those who are present. The goal becomes helping those present to verbally disclose their commitment to Maria, her mother, and significant others, and their commitment to helping Maria achieve her new violence-free behaviors. This is begun by stating something like this:

> "Maria has identified each of you as someone very important to her who is able to meaningfully contribute to her attainment of a violence-free life. So, today, Maria, Maria's mother, Ms. Diaz, and I are asking you for your help. Your being here and not leaving means that you truly are committed to helping Maria."

These statements symbiotically frame the participants' continued presence as demonstrating their true commitment to helping Maria. We believe such a statement is important both for the student and those attending. In other words, it suggests to Maria "these people *want* to help you" and "they are invested in your success." For the participants, it implies that their involvement in Maria's life will be helpful to her.

Are you asking, "Why is such a symbiotic frame important?" The answer is simple. Have you ever been involved in a project where you anticipated few if any would benefit from your investment of time or energy? Exactly! When people are involved in a project they perceive as useless, they often have little enthusiasm and frequently fail to achieve related project goals. Conversely, have you ever been involved in a project where there was an air of excitement and expectation of success? Undoubtedly you have. Typically, the excitement increases as group members see positive indicators suggesting the goal is being achieved and realize the project's ultimate success is coming closer. Within those anticipated successful projects, few members drop out; instead, a robust loyalty develops.

You understand others are counting on you, so you make attendance and completion of your assigned duties a priority.

About this time, someone typically makes a comment suggesting a desire to help the student. However, should no one make such a statement, we will simply ask individual participants whether they are willing to make such a commitment. If we noticed any indications that participants are committed to helping, we often start with them. For instance:

SOCIAL WORKER: Ms. Sanchez, you are Maria's juvenile probation officer. When I asked, "Is anyone opposed to helping Maria?" I saw you shake your head "no." That said to me that you are not opposed to helping Maria and really want to help. Is that true?

MS. SANCHEZ: That is true. I want Maria to get back into school and be successful.

SOCIAL WORKER: Do you think she can be successful at school and not act violently toward others?

MS. SANCHEZ: I certainly do.

SOCIAL WORKER: Are you saying that just because you are her juvenile probation officer and are being paid to be here?

MS. SANCHEZ: Listen, I get paid to be here, but I don't think every kid can be successful. In this case, I believe Maria can be successful at school and can stop fighting and threatening others.

SOCIAL WORKER: Why do you say she can be successful at school and why do you believe she can stop threatening and fighting others?

MS. SANCHEZ: That's easy. Maria is smart. She is one of the smartest young ladies I have ever worked with. She also wants to please her mother and grandmother. Basically, she is someone who can be a leader at the school if she wishes, and I believe she will do just that.

SOCIAL WORKER: Maria, what did you just hear Ms. Sanchez say?

MARIA: She said I can be a leader at the school rather than a bully.

SOCIAL WORKER: Do you think Ms. Sanchez knows what she is talking about?

MARIA: I don't know. Maybe.

SOCIAL WORKER: Ms. Sanchez. How many kids have you worked with as a juvenile probation officer?

MS. SANCHEZ: Hundreds. This year alone I have served as a probation officer to 90 youth.

SOCIAL WORKER: That sounds like a lot. How many of those kids had the intelligence and leadership skills as Maria?

MS. SANCHEZ: Very few . . . Maria is quite able if she wishes to be successful.

SOCIAL WORKER: Maria, what did you hear Ms. Sanchez say?

MARIA: I heard her say that I can be a leader.

SOCIAL WORKER: Do you believe her?

MARIA: I don't know. I guess.

SOCIAL WORKER: Ms. Sanchez, were you lying to Maria and us when you said you think she has the potential to be a leader at her school? Because I get the feeling you are pretty honest with people and say what you mean.

MS. SANCHEZ: I don't lie. If I didn't think she had the potential to be a leader at her school, I wouldn't say so.

SOCIAL WORKER: Who else thinks Maria has the potential to stop her violent and intimidating behaviors at school and start being a leader?

MS. DIAZ: I know my daughter. She is a leader, and she can stop bullying others. I know we can help her become successful at school.

SOCIAL WORKER: So, I'm hearing you say that you are committed to being here at the systems of care meetings and helping your daughter become a leader at school.

MS. DIAZ: Very much so.

Let's summarize what happened here. First, after seeing the juvenile probation officer's favorable nonverbal behaviors toward the specialist's question, the specialist immediately turned to the probation officer. The specialist then informed the group that the probation officer had favorably shaken her head indicating that Maria can be successful. This is important. It suggests to Maria and those present that someone perceives Maria as having the potential to stop her violent behaviors and be successful in school. Also, by commenting on the probation officer's positive nonverbal behaviors, the specialist shows Maria that the probation officer perceives her strengths and is not "out to get her."

Next, the specialist confronts the probation officer and asks the obvious question, "Aren't you here because you are being paid to be here?" The probation officer eloquently responds, stating that she *believes* in Maria. This is a powerful statement. Maria is street smart. She knows how to con others, and she knows when she is being conned. When she hears her probation officer state that she can be successful at school, it encourages her to internalize the probation officer's positive belief in her. The specialist builds on this by asking the probation officer to describe Maria's strengths. The probation officer then describes Maria's intelligence and her desire to please her mother and grandmother. My guess is that Maria is internally agreeing with the probation officer and saying to herself, "That's right! I *am* smart. I *do* want to please my mother and grandmother!"

Next, the specialist asks Maria to state what she heard the probation officer say. This is done for four reasons:

1. It encourages Maria to pay attention to comments made within session.
2. It rewards Maria for successfully paying attention. Within solution-focused therapy, this is often known as "catching the client doing something right."
3. Having Maria restate her attributes promotes an internalized awareness of the qualities. In other words, Maria has heard the probation officer say that she is smart and able, but Maria may not be fully aware of these attributes. Verbally

repeating these attributes doesn't necessarily cause them to be internalized, but it does require Maria to acknowledge awareness that others believe she has these qualities. Over time these qualities may well become acknowledged and internalized by Maria as "who I am."

4. The restatement is not simply made for Maria; it is made to ensure that all members of the SOC group understand that Maria has strengths that can be used to be successful in achieving her nonviolent goals. Again, this instigates synergy within the group and promotes the perception that each member's investment of time and energy will help her achieve the desired outcome.

For even greater therapeutic punch, the specialist asks Maria's probation officer how many youths she has served. The specialist could care less what the actual number is; instead, the intent of the question is to help Maria understand she is perceived as unique in comparison to many of the others. Specifically, the specialist asks the probation officer how many of the youths had Maria's intelligence and leadership abilities. Maria's probation officer replies, "Very few" and adds that Maria can be successful.

The specialist quickly turns to Maria and asks Maria to repeat what her probation officer said. This is done so that Maria understands her unique opportunity for success and to emphasize that Maria has the potential to go down a different path than others. Then, the specialist asks if Maria believes her probation officer's opinion that Maria can be a leader. Maria's half-hearted response is immediately addressed by the specialist, who asks the probation officer if she is lying. The probation officer declares, "I don't lie." In other words, she is saying, "I wouldn't say Marie can be successful at school and be a leader if I didn't mean it."

The specialist then asks the other participants if they believe Maria has the potential to stop her violent and intimidating behaviors. This opens the doors for others to voice their beliefs. As more participants voice their agreement with the probation officer's perceptions, it challenges Maria's internal beliefs about herself and promotes the internalization, "If they believe I can be a leader without acting violently, then maybe I really *can* eliminate those violent behaviors. Maybe I *can* have a new identity as a school leader and get rewarded for those leadership behaviors."

Releases of Confidential Information and Confidentiality Issues

As we noted in Chapter 5, after the student and the student's parents identify those who will be invited to the SOC group, the student and the student's parents must sign appropriate releases of confidential information. Without obtaining such releases, the specialist cannot invite others to participate. Those who agree to attend the SOC group are sent releases and are asked to complete them before the first group meeting. At the first meeting, the specialist explains the importance of the releases ensures all the necessary releases are signed, dated, and signed by two or more witnesses (e.g., the specialist and the student's parents).

Next, the specialist explains confidentiality and its limits within the group experience, covering these topics:

The specialist is probably the only person present who must follow professional confidentiality ethics and laws.

Juvenile probation officers and other officers of the court or school are not bound by confidentiality. In fact, they are required by their jobs to divulge any disclosed information about illegal behaviors or potentially harmful behaviors directed at the students, community, or school.

These officers must also respond to divulged information related to the failure to uphold previous agreements between the student and the court or school.

Often at this point we ask such professionals to describe their roles and the topics they are required to divulge, such as drug use, truancy, or failure to comply with random drug screens.

Once the professionals finish their overview of their charges and what might constitute reasons for revealing discussions that occur within the SOC group, we typically say something like,

PSYCHOLOGIST: Correct me if I am wrong, but what I heard you say is that you aren't going to be telling others what happens in group unless you perceive that Maria is a danger to herself, is breaking the law, or is failing to comply with her release agreement. Is this correct?

PROBATION OFFICER: That is correct.

PSYCHOLOGIST: So, you wouldn't disclose information that was discussed within the group with your friends, or if you saw Maria at Wal-Mart you wouldn't reveal to others that she was previously expelled from school. Is that correct?

PROBATION OFFICER: I would never do that. If I did those kinds of things I would likely get fired.

The intent of this conversation is to help those present understand that professionals mandated to attend treatment are not going to frivolously gossip. Instead, they are required to report violations and potential behaviors that may be harmful to Maria or the community.

At this point we typically describe how people are reticent to speak freely if they believe others are going to gossip about them outside the group or if they feel information shared within the group is going to be bandied about. Often, I will turn to the student and ask if it would be important for him or her to learn that group participants wouldn't be sharing what they hear in the group with others outside the group. Most often the student *desperately* wants promises that information will not be shared outside the group. When we hear this, we simply ask if those present other than the court- and school-mandated officers would be willing to make this promise to the student. For example, the specialist might say,

FAMILY THERAPIST: Before we go any further, I need to bring up the topic of confidentiality. It is important for you to know that I cannot guarantee that everything said in this meeting will be confidential. I am unaware of any law which states that you cannot share information or report to others what is said or what happens in this meeting to persons who are not present. In other words, you should be especially cautious not to share sensitive information or information which could be potentially embarrassing or harmful. The law clearly states that I am the only one here who is bound by confidentiality. Therefore, I cannot discuss what happens here outside of this room unless I either have your permission to do so or I believe that you or someone else is in danger. However, knowing the importance of confidentiality and the need to have faith in each other, I am wondering if the group members invited by Maria would make a confidentiality pledge to one another. Although this pledge may not provide legal recourse for breaking confidentiality and understanding that it may not be legally binding, the pledge would state that whatever is said in today's meeting stays in the room and will not be shared outside this room to anyone unless someone is being a danger to herself or in danger of being injured. Would this be acceptable to you?

MARIA: I'd like that.

GRANDMOTHER: Yes, this makes sense.

MOTHER: Certainly.

FAMILY THERAPIST: OK. Maria, Mother, and Grandmother, I am hearing that each of you is pledging not to report anything that is said or done in this room to someone other than yourselves or me, is that correct?

Establishing Meeting Rules

Next, the specialist establishes the procedural meeting rules. Although these rules can vary from specialist to specialist and are at the complete discretion of the specialist, we have found that seven basic rules are important for the meeting:

1. *Each person should be treated with respect.* Participants should respect each other by treating others as they wish to be treated. No one should swear at another, call others derogatory names, or be caustically sarcastic. Threats of violence or implied threats will not be tolerated.
2. *Each person agrees to speak truthfully.* Participants promise to speak the truth at all times. No one should be accused of lying.
3. *Each person agrees to speak for himself or herself.* Participants may describe behaviors that they observed in others (e.g., "I saw Maria kick Joann"), but participants will not speak for others (e.g., "Maria is too scared to tell Oscar that she doesn't like him") or attempt to interpret observed behaviors (e.g., "I think Maria was crying because she thought John was breaking up with her").
4. *Each person agrees to participate.* Participants will contribute via their active participation. Nonparticipation suggests an unwillingness to support the student or an inability to provide necessary support. Thus, it is vital that participants invest themselves in the interview process.
5. *Each person agrees to ask questions.* Participants will ask questions and have the right to expect honest and thorough responses.
6. *Each person agrees to remain for the entire informational meeting.* Participants can leave the group for a personal break, but they must agree to return.

7. *Each person agrees to support the student and participating significant others.* Participants verbally agree to demonstrate their support of the student and others present by encouraging one another and helping in whatever ways are deemed appropriate and helpful.

After the rules are discussed, clarified, and agreed to, the specialist asks participants if there are any concerns or questions.

Student Introductions

At this point the specialist invites the student to introduce each participant, describe how the student knows each one, and how the student perceives this participant will be helpful in achieving the student's violence-free behaviors. For example:

SCHOOL COUNSELOR: Maria, I'm wondering if you would introduce everyone here, indicate how you know the person, and how they can help you achieve your new violent-free behaviors.

MARIA: OK. Well, this is my mom. I think everybody knows her. I know her because she is my mom! And I think she can help me learn how not to get mad and fight.

SCHOOL COUNSELOR: Thank you, Maria. Can you help us understand what kinds of things you believe your mother can do to help you "not get mad" and "not fight"?

MARIA: I don't know. I guess, like, having her tell me when she thinks I am getting mad and telling me things I could do instead of fighting?

SCHOOL COUNSELOR: So what would that look like?

MARIA: Well, when I'm starting to get really angry and my mom sees that I am getting angry, maybe she could say something like, "You look like you are getting angry. Go to your room and calm yourself down."

SCHOOL COUNSELOR: Would that really be helpful?

MARIA: Yeah, I think so. Sometimes I don't even know I am starting to get angry until I just explode. If she told me that I was starting to look angry, then I could think about what I needed to do to calm myself down.

SCHOOL COUNSELOR: Mom, is that something you would be willing to do?

MOTHER: Yes, I could do that.

SCHOOL COUNSELOR: What kinds of things might you tell Maria she could do in her room that might help her calm down?

MOTHER: Well, Maria likes to draw or make things. Maybe I could have some beads and bracelet wire in her room so when she gets mad, she can sit down and make some bracelets or something.

SCHOOL COUNSELOR: Maria, would that be helpful?

MARIA: Yeah, it would. I'd like that. Maybe Mom or Grandma could even go in my room and talk to me while we work on a new bracelet or something.

SCHOOL COUNSELOR: Why don't you ask your mom if she would be willing to do that?

MARIA: Now?

SCHOOL COUNSELOR: Yup.

MARIA: Mom, when you see that I am starting to get angry, can you tell me and then you or Grandma go with me to my room and maybe talk or help me make some new bracelets or something?

MOTHER: Certainly, baby.

SCHOOL COUNSELOR: Just one question, Maria. Are you attempting to make your mom responsible to either identify when you are angry or to solve your anger?

MARIA: I don't get what you are saying.

SCHOOL COUNSELOR: Are you saying to your mom, "I don't know when I am angry. So, it is *your* responsibility to tell me when I am angry and it is *your* responsibility to stop me from fighting"?

MARIA: No, I am not saying that at all. Sometimes I don't know how angry I am. Having my mom tell me that I seem really angry will help me figure out when I need to do something that will calm me down.

In this vignette, we notice some important interactions. First, given Maria's age and the fact she introduced her mother, we did not need to press Maria about *how* she knows her mother. Her response was age appropriate and fully acceptable. However, had Maria introduced an invited teacher, for example, we would ask Maria to provide more information. Here, we might query Maria regarding the course or grade the teacher had taught. We would further inquire how the teacher's past behaviors positively impacted Maria. Once Maria can identify and verbalize the teacher's past helpful and supportive behaviors, we can encourage replication of these behaviors in the future. Thus, the teacher can be a key group player by replicating previously prized behaviors toward Maria as Maria continues her violence abstinence.

This behavior replication potentially creates three important outcomes:

1. It produces security for Maria in the immediate SOC group. Hence, Maria's defenses will be reduced and she will be able to interact more freely within the group experience. This also means she will be more likely to accept constructive comments by this valued participant.
2. Replication of these teacher behaviors within Maria's immediate school milieu potentially reduces Maria's stressors in that environment, decreasing the likelihood of Maria's violent behavior.
3. Given that Maria believes this trusted teacher values her and is committed to her success, Maria will be more likely to seek her out should Maria consider acting violently.

The vignette demonstrates another critical element: the therapeutic sense of "baby steps," sometimes known as the "progression, not perfection" construct. We are not seeking immediate perfection. Instead, we use baby steps to progress toward the student's desired outcome of sustained, nonviolent behaviors. As we notice above, Maria is not asking her mother to implement overly demanding or superhuman behaviors. Instead, Maria merely asks her mother for three relatively easy behaviors: (a) informing Maria when she is perceived as presenting with an angry affect, (b) asking Maria to go to her room to calm down, and (c) talking with Maria while the two of them work on beading in Maria's room.

Some might argue this change construct is far too simplistic, but our experiences suggest otherwise. When combined, multiple small changes typically result in far greater change. When the smaller changes become ingrained within a person's recurring repertoire of behaviors, the larger changes become ingrained.

This same progression-versus-perfection construct is often used by successful dieters. Foolish dieters abstain from eating for a day or possibly two. Then they give way to their massive hunger and gorge on every edible food in near proximity. Successful dieters, however, understand that small changes in eating habits bring about weight loss. Instead of eliminating all foods, successful dieters exchange high-calorie foods for lower-calorie foods. Often, they begin walking to burn even more calories. Soon, the many small changes lead to big rewards on the scale.

In the same fashion, we are merely attempting to create multiple positive changes for Maria that will together provide opportunities for sustainable violence-free behaviors. Having her mother contribute to Maria's success by implementing the requested behavior is logical and a surefire way to begin the change process.

Two concluding comments regarding the introduction vignette are warranted. First, we have found it advantageous for participants to practice asking for help within the SOC group. Many tweens and adolescents do not understand how to effectively seek help or make requests. Instead, they have learned to bully or intimidate others to gain desired outcomes. In this vignette Maria reports that she would like to have her mother or grandmother participate in beading and conversation when Maria goes to her room to calm down. The specialist then asks Maria to formalize this request of the mother within session. Maria asks, "Now?" The specialist says "yes," and Maria asks for her mother's help. Having students making requests like this within the group is useful. Should the student report that she doesn't know how to ask for help or should she miserably fail at the request, the specialist can then demonstrate how such a request could be made. This then opens further opportunities to practice such requests within the group. We have found that understanding how to make requests effectively empowers students and often lessens their bullying and explosive behaviors.

Some within the mental health professions are hypersensitive to "codependency" issues. They view even the most appropriate requests for help as creating codependency or fostering continued codependent behaviors. Although we believe that codependency can be a significant clinical issue, we certainly don't believe this is the case in the above vignette. However, the specialist does address this concern by asking Maria if she is trying to make her mother responsible for Maria's behaviors. Maria denies such an attempt and the specialist believes her. Had the specialist believed Maria was attempting to make her mother responsible for Maria's behaviors, the specialist would have responded differently. The specialist might have said, "It seems that you are denying any responsibility for your violent behaviors and implying that your mother should simply tell you when you are angry and resolve your anger by paying attention to you. Is this what you are suggesting?" In most cases such a statement is sufficient to change the dynamics and allow a more therapeutic interchange to occur.

Identifying Student Strengths

The primary reasons for identifying the student strengths is to have significant others (a) describe healthy ways in which the student is meeting her current needs, (b) identify ways in which the specialist as well as other nonprofessionals can help the student secure the student's goal of being violence free, and (c) encourage continued positive behaviors by significant others toward the student (VanDenBerg & Grealish, 1996). This is done by providing students and their significant others feedback regarding what they are already doing well, reinforcing these healthy behaviors, and advancing students' and significant others' understanding of even healthier new behaviors that could be adopted (VanDenBerg & Grealish, 1996). The result is a collaborative assessment and data-providing venture in which significant others, the specialist, and the student jointly learn what is working and helpful and what is perceived to be helpful in the future. Such a collaborative and positively framed experience is foreign to most students who have perpetrated violent behaviors.

Despite the support occurring within this session, the intent of the strengths assessment is not to gloss over or minimize the student's concerns or difficulties. This would clearly be a harmful injustice to the student and the entire SOC process. Instead, the intent is to learn what is going well and to identify how the student, the specialist, and the significant others contribute to this process. Thus, the identification of student strengths encircles the student in a powerful, systems-oriented treatment milieu that continues to provide support opportunities for the student and her significant others.

Finally, identifying the student's strengths provides an opportunity to establish rapport and trust among participants. Building such rapport and trust is important because later the student will likely be challenged to change formerly familiar violent behaviors and will be held accountable by those in the SOC group to abstain from violence. Thus, the strengths assessment establishes the foundation on which students can be challenged. Therefore, the specialist must help the student and the significant others affirm and support one another during the strengths assessment. This can be accomplished by asking the student to respond to supportive statements made by significant others. For example:

SOCIAL WORKER: Maria, what was it like to have your mother tell you that she loves you?

MARIA: [Weeping] I can't fully describe what it was like, because it was so unbelievable. After all the mean things that I did to her and Grandma, to learn that she loves me means so much.

MOTHER: Maria, you know I love you.

MARIA: I know that now, Momma, but I didn't know that you still loved me until you told me. I had thought you hated me because I was so wicked and beat up other people.

SOCIAL WORKER: Sometimes when people love us, they don't know how to respond when we threaten, intimidate, or act violent. Mother, if you could say just one thing to your daughter about her committing herself to living without violence, what would you say?

MOTHER: You don't have to live this way. You are strong, just like your grandma. I know you don't have to fight. More importantly, though, Maria, I'll do everything I can to support you in your counseling. But I won't lie to you: If you start fighting again, I'll get right in your face and call your probation officer. I'd rather have you in juvenile detention for fighting than in prison for murder.

SOCIAL WORKER: What do you hear your mom saying, Maria?

MARIA: I hear her saying that she believes I don't have to fight.

SOCIAL WORKER: I hear her saying that, but I also hear her saying something else too.

MARIA: What?

SOCIAL WORKER :I hear your mother saying that she loves you, that you can eliminate your previous fighting behaviors, and she will support you. But I also hear her saying that she is going be truthful. If you start fighting again, she will call your probation officer. She will advocate that you be put in juvenile detention as a way of protecting you from potentially killing someone and going to prison for the rest of your life.

MARIA: I hear her saying that, too.

SOCIAL WORKER: Does that mean she doesn't love you or that she is not trying to be helpful when she tells the truth?

MARIA: No. It just means that she is trying to be helpful and knows telling the truth will help me.

SOCIAL WORKER: Then you want your mom to be truthful even if you don't like what she says?

MARIA: I might not like what she says. But if she is telling me something, I need to listen.

This vignette demonstrates two central elements:

1. The interaction offers an opportunity for the daughter and the mother to further build rapport and establish trust. The specialist does this by emphasizing the mother's statement that she loves Maria and by encouraging Maria to report what hearing of her mother's love means to her.

2. We hope that it will inoculate Maria from responding inappropriately to truthful statements during future SOC interactions. Thus, not only is the mother indicating that she will make truthful statements, but the daughter actually encourages her to make such statements and realizes that the purpose of these statements is to help Maria remain violence free and stay out of prison.

Identifying Nonviolent Favorite Things to Do

We have found one of the most important pieces of the SOC process is helping students identify nonviolent favorite things to do. This vignette demonstrates how to help clients identify such fun behaviors:

PSYCHOLOGIST: Maria, tell me about things you enjoy doing.

MARIA: I don't know. I really don't do much.

PSYCHOLOGIST: How about things you like to do with your mother or grandmother?

MARIA: Well, my mother and grandma sometimes take me to Fashion Beads and Jewelry.

PSYCHOLOGIST: What do you do there?

MARIA: We sit and talk and make bracelets and necklaces and stuff like that.

PSYCHOLOGIST: Is it fun?

MARIA: Yes, it is a lot of fun.

PSYCHOLOGIST: How do you make it fun?

MARIA: What do you mean?

PSYCHOLOGIST: Well, I have this belief that people make things fun by saying things to themselves that make the experience fun. You know, like those kids who like to do math problems.

MARIA: I hate math.

PSYCHOLOGIST: Me too. But I used to know kids who really liked math. They even thought math was a blast.

MARIA: Not me!

PSYCHOLOGIST: Me, either, but what do you think they were saying to themselves about the math problems that made doing math fun?

MARIA: I don't get it. What are you asking?

PSYCHOLOGIST: Well, I'm thinking to myself, "I don't like math problems. Maria doesn't like math problems. What must these kids who like math be saying to themselves when they do their math problems?"

MARIA: I have no idea.

PSYCHOLOGIST: I'm wondering if they are not saying things to themselves like, "This math problem is fun, because I know I can do it." And "Math problems are puzzles and I can't wait to see how to solve this puzzle."

MARIA: Yeah, I can see that. It makes sense.

PSYCHOLOGIST: So what is it that you are saying to yourself when you are making jewelry with your mom and grandma that makes the experience fun?

MARIA: Oh, I get it now. I'm saying, "I'm here talking with my favorite people. I'm having fun, because I'm making something pretty that I can wear and show everybody."

PSYCHOLOGIST: Cool! So you are not saying, "Mom and Grandma will not tease me about my weight or about not making a perfect bracelet"?

MARIA: No, I would never think that. I'm saying to myself, "Mom loves me; Grandma cares about me. They will never tease me about my weight."

PSYCHOLOGIST: Good. So, I'm hearing two things. First, when you are with your mother and grandma working on jewelry, you are making the experience fun by saying things like "Mom loves me" and "Grandma cares about me." Second, I'm hearing that you like being with your mother and grandma, and when you are with them you are not thinking about fighting.

MARIA: Exactly.

GRANDMOTHER: Well, then, I think your mother and I need to do more things with you.

PSYCHOLOGIST: Perfect! Because the more you are with her—

MOTHER: [interrupting specialist] the less she feels she is being teased and she doesn't feel she has to fight back.

PSYCHOLOGIST: You're good, Mom! Way to go. You and Grandma know exactly what needs to happen.

Let's analyze what happened in this vignette. The first thing this specialist so eloquently does is directly ask about fun things Maria likes to do. The assumption is that if the specialist can identify times when Maria is comfortable, her self-talk will be positive, and she is more likely having fun. The next assumption is that if we can identify just one "fun time," then Maria, her mother, and her grandmother can create others. The final assumption is that if Maria can begin to increase the amount of positive self-talk and have more "fun times" throughout the day, the probability of her violent behaviors occurring will be reduced.

Once the question is directly asked, Maria responds like most students by saying, "I don't know." Instead of stopping, the specialist immediately asks about things Maria likes to do with her mother and grandmother. In other words, the specialist doesn't accept "I don't know" as Maria's "final answer." The specialist understood that if she kept asking about things Maria liked doing with those with whom she spent time, sooner or later Maria would likely identify something "fun." The key is always asking about fun things being done with those the student likes or with whom she spends time. I have never met a student who hangs around with other students simply to enjoy the misery of the others' company. Even as adults few of us spend time with those we dislike if we don't believe the benefits outweigh the costs. Typically for students this means if they are not having at least some minimal threshold of "fun" with peers or significant others, they would disengage and begin spending time with others who *are* "fun."

As Maria identifies making bracelets and necklaces with her mother and grandmother as enjoyable, the specialist switches the conversation, asking how Maria "makes" the experience fun. In cognitive-behavioral terms, the specialist begins to train Maria that the self-talk that she initiates can make experiences either positive or negative. In particular, the specialist talks about something that we have found almost universally inconceivable to the students we counsel—some students like math! This resonates with Maria, and her response is that she "hates" math. Instead of arguing that Maria should like math, the specialist immediately joins with the student and replies, "Me too." In other words, the specialist is indirectly saying, "Hey, you and I are alike. You hate math. I hate math." More importantly, the implication for Maria is that she and the specialist have something in common. This cognition promotes the perception, "Hey, this specialist is rather similar to me."

Such therapeutic joining is imperative. It helps Maria, her mother, and her grandmother see the specialist as invested and similar to each of them. My guess is that the grandmother does not have an internal discussion such as, "What? This specialist doesn't like math? How dare she say she doesn't like math!" Instead, I would anticipate that the grandmother is probably saying, "That specialist is more like me than I originally thought."

Next, the specialist challenges Maria to understand "how" students who like math internally reframe math problems. Here, the specialist suggests that students who like math experience math problems as "enjoyable puzzles." In other words, the specialist encourages Maria to understand a "parallel process." Here, math problems are "paralleled" to making jewelry. In other words, one's self-talk (e.g., "I'm having fun finding the answers to this math puzzle") influences how one interprets the experience or task. The specialist also helps Maria understand her internal dialog regarding her mother's and her grandmother's thoughts about Maria. Further, she points out that Maria is not fighting when Maria is in the presence of her mother and grandmother and doing something enjoyable. The grandmother immediately understands this nonviolence construct and identifies Maria's need to increase activities with her mother and grandmother. The mother even completes the specialist's statement, making it apparent that she also understands that when Maria is with her mother and grandmother making jewelry, Maria is not fighting. The specialist then lauds both the mother and grandmother for identifying Maria's needs and their willingness to agree to spend more time with Maria.

After we identify favorite things the student likes to do, we slightly shift our focus. In particular, we move toward other nonviolent times. Specifically, we want to identify persons the student is with, what she is doing, where she is, and what she is saying to herself during these nonviolent times. The discussion might sound something like this:

FAMILY THERAPIST: Maria, tell me about the times when you are not fighting.

MARIA: What do you want to know?

FAMILY THERAPIST: My belief is that you don't fight every moment of the day, right?

MARIA: Yeah.

FAMILY THERAPIST: So tell me about the times you weren't fighting yesterday.

MARIA: Well, let's see. I was at soccer practice with my friends and I didn't fight.

FAMILY THERAPIST: OK. Who was there?

MARIA: Annie, Karl, Juan, and Olivia.

FAMILY THERAPIST: Have you ever gotten in a fight with Annie or fought when you were with Annie?

MARIA: [Giggling] Of course not. She is my friend! We never fight. We are having way too much fun together to fight.

FAMILY THERAPIST: How about Karl, Juan, and Olivia? Do you ever fight with them, or have you ever fought when they were around?

MARIA: Never.

FAMILY THERAPIST: I'm confused. How is it that you don't fight with Annie, Karl, Juan, or Olivia?

MARIA: That's easy. We are always having fun together. We don't argue or fight.

FAMILY THERAPIST: Maria, when you are with Annie, Karl, Juan, and Olivia during soccerpractice, what kinds of things do you say to yourself?

MARIA: I guess I am thinking to myself, "This is fun, these are my friends, they like me, and I don't have to worry that they are going to make fun of me."

Let's stop here. Maria has just reported four persons she enjoys and does not fight with. She also has told us what the five of them are doing when Maria doesn't fight: They are practicing soccer. Maria also reports her self-talk. At this point, the specialist may wish to engage Maria and the SOC group members to identify noted commonalities occurring when Maria is not violent. The specialist might say,

> "Maria, I don't know about others here, but I'm hearing some common themes related to times when you are not acting violently. Specifically, I am hearing that when you are with people you consider to be your friends, like Annie, and when you are places that are fairly structured such as Girl Scouts, church, and soccer practice, you frequently are telling yourself that you are 'having fun' and 'enjoying' yourself. What are the rest of you hearing?"

After the group has thoroughly discussed perceived commonalities among nonviolent times with Maria, the specialist might ask something like,

> "Maria, given that you invited each person here and you know they all want the very best things for you, what do you believe they are suggesting about who you should spend more time with, activities you should be more involved in, and places you should be more often?"

The intent is to have Maria self-identify the people, activities, and places she should become more involved in.

Next, the specialist will investigate the people, activities, places, and self-talk related to times when Maria is violent. The specialist might say, "Tell me about the last time you fought. Who was there, where did the fight occur, and what were you saying to yourself?"

Again, the specialist is going to be listening for commonalities in times when Maria acts violently. Once these commonalities become clear, the specialist will say something like,

> "Maria, just like the commonalties you described during times when you choose not to fight or act violently, I'm hearing some other common themes related to times when you do act violently. Specifically, I am hearing that when you are around Chrissie and when you don't have much adult supervision, you tend to do things that get you in trouble. Are others hearing the same thing?"

At the conclusion of this investigation of violent times, the SOC group will make suggestions about people Maria should stay away from, places she should not go, and things she should not be doing. The specialist should then ask Maria her commitment to following through with the recommendations of the group:

> "This is what I heard people you value say today. I heard them say you should spend more time with Annie, Karl, Juan, and Olivia and that playing soccer with your friends was important. I also heard the people you value say you should stay away from Chrissie and places where there is little or no adult supervision. On a scale of 1 to 10, how likely will it be that you do these things?"

Should Maria indicate a high number (6 or above), she should be lauded and congratulated for choosing to do the best things. Should she provide a low score of (5 or lower), the specialist may ask something like, "You have said you would give yourself a 1 on the scale, meaning that you likely aren't going to do the things this group suggested. How is it helpful for you not to do the things that this, your group of friends, have suggested?"

Summary

The SOC process provides opportunities for the student and the student's significant others to learn how to change. The intervention is relatively easy to implement, and the outcomes can produce significant results. Like a team of coaches, the SOC participants support the student by offering sincere and nurturing directions. These directions provide new behavioral and cognitive patterns that ensure student success.

This chapter described how to use SOC and builds on the fundamentals provided in Chapter 5. We illustrated how the specialist should facilitate an SOC meeting, address issues of confidentiality, create group rules, help participants identify and focus on the student's strengths, and help students identify favorite nonviolent behaviors and interactions they can use.

Reference

VanDenBerg, J. E., & Grealish, E. M. (1996). Individualized services and supports through the wraparound process: Philosophy and procedures. *Journal of Child and Family Studies, 5*(1), 7–21. doi: 10.1007/BF02234675

7

Psychological First Aid

The First Four Core Actions

This chapter cover psychological first aid (PFA) and describes the first four core actions: (a) contact and engagement, (b) safety and comfort, (c) stabilization, and (d) information gathering. The next four will be covered in Chapter 8.

General Overview

According to the *Psychological First Aid: Field Operations Guide*, PFA is "an evidence-informed modular approach to help children, adolescents, adults, and families in the aftermath of disaster and terrorism" (National Child Traumatic Stress Network and National Center for PTSD [NCTSN/NCPTSD], 2006, p. 1). In a nutshell, PFA was developed to reduce the emotional trauma experienced by disaster survivors and to promote "short- and long-term adaptive functioning and coping" (NCTSN/NCPTSD, 2006, p. 1).

Professionally speaking, PFA matches the basic tenets and general broad underpinnings of most mental health professions (i.e., professional counseling, social work, psychology, and marriage and family therapy). Specifically, PFA is health based and does not focus on psychopathology. In other words, those who developed PFA believed most survivors are resilient. They believed many survivors will adequately cope with whatever event they experienced without developing debilitating, long-term, trauma-related symptoms. They also believed that if trauma-related symptoms did develop, they will fall somewhere on a broad continuum from mild to severe. In short, not all trauma-related symptoms will be severe. This model stands in stark contrast to those who view school bullying and violence survivors as "broken" and in need of "fixing." Instead, PFA suggests that survivors' response depends on multiple factors, such as their perception of the experience, their previous levels of emotional and interpersonal health, and their sense of hope and perceptions of the future.

We will use the same clinical vignette in this chapter and the next one:

Angel is a 13-year-old seventh-grader who attends Cactus Bluff Middle School in a large southwestern city. She and her best friend Katrina play on the school's seventh-grade girls' basketball team. Both wore school basketball team spirit wear and cheered the seventh-grade boys' basketball team during a home Thursday evening game. At the game, Angel and Katrina "talked smack," hurled trash talk, and made negative comments toward opposing players. The sister of one of the opposing team's players, and her two female friends, threatened to "beat up" Angel and Katrina if they didn't stop their obnoxious trash talk.

Angel and Katrina continued their verbal bashing and began taunting the sister and her friends. At halftime the opposing team member's sister shoved Angel and Angel fell from the third row of the bleachers. The school resource officer ejected the sister and her two friends from the game. After the game Angel and Katrina exited the school building and began walking home. However, as they crossed the dimly lit school parking lot, the sister and her two friends appeared. The sister said she had a knife and stated she was going to "carve [Angel] up." The sister grabbed Angel, threw her to the ground, and put Angel into a martial arts type of chokehold.

Katrina escaped from the assailant's friends, ran back into the gym, and sought help. Immediately, the school resource officer, the vice principal, and the specialist ran to the parking lot. When the sister and her friends saw the officer coming, they ran away. Angel was crying and trying to catch her breath when the specialist knelt down next to her. Angel had the wind knocked out of her and had abrasions to her knees, elbows, and face from being thrown to the ground. Katrina, who remained in the gym with two teachers, was badly shaken and tearful.

Core Action 1: Contact and Engagement

The goal of the first core action, contact and engagement, is to initiate contact with bullying and violence survivors or to respond to the survivor's contact. Key components are (a) demonstrating respect and compassion for those who have experienced bullying and violence and (b) presenting in a calm, professional manner. Often this first core action is initiated by the specialist via a brief introduction.

In the scenario, the specialist was at the basketball game and was the first to respond to Angel after the parking lot attack. Here, the specialist might say to Angel,

SCHOOL COUNSELOR: Hello, Angel. I am Ms. VanderPaul, your counselor. I remember talking with you last week when you needed a hall pass. Do you remember me?

ANGEL: Yes, I know you. I remember you helping me get a hall pass.

SCHOOL COUNSELOR: Good. Are you OK?

ANGEL: I don't know. Katrina and I were walking across the parking lot and we were attacked.

SCHOOL COUNSELOR: I thought I would just check in with you to see if you're OK.

ANGEL: [long pause] I don't know.

SCHOOL COUNSELOR: What may I do to help you right now?

Given that specialists are often on campus grounds when school violence occurs, and because students are already familiar with them, these professionals are uniquely positioned to be "first responders" to school bully and violence survivors. Typically, students immediately recognize the specialist, and this familiarity often engenders feelings of security and comfort for survivors. In the vignette, the specialist recognizes Angel and reminds her of their recent benign school interaction. This is done simply to connect with the student in a nonthreatening, nonintrusive manner. Angel immediately acknowledges she knows the specialist. The specialist then simply affirms Angel's statement and asks if she is OK.

This statement is vitally important. The specialist doesn't gush, "Oh, you poor thing. I bet you are scared to death!" Instead she provides the student the *opportunity to engage* in a counseling interaction. She neither demands interaction from the student nor conveys that the student must have experienced severe psychological distress as a result of the violent event. Had the student said, "I'm fine," the specialist would simply have asked if she needed anything (e.g., a ride home) or wanted to talk. She then would have allowed the school resource officer and vice principal to talk with Angel and to follow up on school policies and possibly to make a police report. The opportunity to engage in counseling is entirely up to the student; the specialist should never force counseling engagement to occur.

The specialist also asks what the student needs from her right now. This is important as well. The student may indicate a need to talk, a need for someone to talk with her parents about the bullying or violent event, or any of a million other things. The critical component is the specialist acts interested in the student and asks about the student's immediate need. Whatever needs requested by the student should be followed by at least an attempt to secure them. For example, when survivors are provided PFA they often will simply request an opportunity to sit, talk, or drink some water. Giving student survivors full attention and providing an opportunity to sit, talk, or have a bottle of water gives them a chance to feel comfortable, to talk with the specialist in a way that is not focused on psychopathology, and to meet their basic needs. These safe experiences create feelings of immediate normality and provide further opportunities to engage in discussions about what happened, what the student wishes to do, what the student needs, or feelings about the bullying or violent experience.

In the vignette, the specialist initiates contact with the student, but there are also times when the specialist will respond to a survivor's contact. For example, on Friday morning, Angel may present at Ms. VanderPaul's office. In this case, Angel is seeking help from the specialist.

ANGEL: Ms. VanderPaul, do you have a minute to talk?
SOCIAL WORKER: Certainly, Angel. Would you like to sit down here in my office? How about a bottle of water?
ANGEL: No, thanks.
SOCIAL WORKER: Angel, how are you doing after the basketball game incident?

Again, notice what happens. Ms. VanderPaul immediately invites the student to sit down in her office and offers bottled water. Then the specialist asks how Angel is doing after the basketball game experience. This interaction conveys her interest in Angel and shows the specialist wants to be helpful. Such interactions convey safety and provide opportunities for students to discuss what happened, air their concerns and needs, or simply "just talk."

Core Action 2: Safety and Comfort

The primary goals of this core action are "to enhance immediate and ongoing safety and provide physical and emotional comfort" (NCTSN/NCPTSD, 2006, p. 12). In particular this core action is designed to let students know that they have survived the immediate event and they are in a "safe zone" protected from immediate threat. It also allows the specialist to assess the student impacted by the bullying or violence for shock and threats of harm to self (e.g., suicidal ideation) or others (e.g., retaliation). If such issues are noted, immediate intervention with documentation must occur. For example, if the student presents with irregular breathing, dizziness, lack of bladder or bowel control, or clammy skin, the specialist would immediately contact emergency medical services personnel and ensure appropriate medical intervention is provided. Should the student express an intent to harm those who perpetrated the bullying or violence, the specialist would intervene or, if imminent danger is perceived, contact police authorities to ensure safety.

Had Angel and Kristina been stabbed, the specialist as part of this core action would establish an immediate safe zone away from danger where the survivors can simply "be" without feeling mobbed by those who wish to help or stared at by onlookers and passersby. For example, the specialist might immediately secure and cordon off a safe zone where the two girls are in the parking lot, or if it would be important to get them back inside the school, a safe zone could be established in the library, the teachers' lounge, or the specialist's office. Cordoning off such an area will keep everyone except the survivors, the specialist, and medical responders away from the survivors. To accomplish this, the specialist will need to get others involved. This might include charging the school resource or peace officers, vice principals, nurses, teachers, coaches, or custodial staff the task of creating a safe zone area. Typically, a place out of site is best until police and loved ones (e.g., parents) arrive. Loved ones can then be escorted to the safe zone to reunite with the survivors.

Depending on the circumstances, including the age and popularity of the students and type of event and location, the specialist may wish to allow one or two close friends of the survivors to enter the safe zone. Once in the safe zone, friends can support the survivors until parents arrive. For instance:

PSYCHOLOGIST: Angel, let's go to my office. School Resource Officer Richards is going to stand guard outside my office door to ensure we are safe inside. From there, I will contact your parents and ask them to meet us in the safety of my office. Is that alright with you?

ANGEL: Yes . . . I just want to be safe. I don't know what to do.

PSYCHOLOGIST: Angel, I'm going to stay with you until your parents arrive. You will be safe with Resource Officer Richards and me until your parents arrive.

In this vignette, the specialist takes administrative control. She includes the school resource officer and ensures Angel understands she will be safe until her parents arrive. When Angel reports she doesn't know what to do, the specialist again takes administrative control and states that she will stay with Angel until her parents arrive. The specialist's overriding messages are "You are safe," "I am here with you," and "Your parents and help are on the way."

The specialist may determine it will be therapeutically supportive to have one or two of Angel's friends who attended the basketball game stay with Angel in the safe zone. Instead of making this decision herself, the specialist would ask if this is what Angel desires:

PSYCHOLOGIST: Now you are safe within my office with the school resource officer standing guard outside the door to ensure you are safe. Principal Valadez is calling your mother and will make certain she gets here as quickly as she can. In the meantime, I am wondering. I saw you sitting with Gina Gonzalez and Erin Jones in the bleachers at tonight's game. Would you like me to ask one or both of them to join us here in the safe zone while we await your mother's arrival?

This is an important interaction for three reasons:

1. The specialist continues to communicate Angel's safety. She states "you are safe" and augments that message by reminding Angel the school resource officer is standing outside the safe zone door to ensure no one can harm Angel.
2. The specialist's statements inform Angel what is happening outside the safe zone. The specialist tells her the principal is contacting her mother and the mother will be arriving quickly.
3. The specialist tells Angel she'd noticed that she was sitting in the bleachers with two other students. However, instead of merely allowing those students into the safe zone without Angel's permission, the specialist gives Angel a sense of control by allowing Angel to determine if both, one, or none of the students should be allowed to support Angel in the safe zone until Angel's mother can arrive.

Returning to the situation in which Angel presents at the specialist's office the morning after the violence, the core action continues to revolve around safety and comfort. However, because the violence occurred the previous evening and the violent students do not attend the school, the specialist's response will be different. Here, instead of whisking Angel to a safe zone, the specialist will promote safety and comfort in a slightly different manner. Again, the specialist will consult with others such as the school resource officer to ensure Angel's safety within the current school milieu. However, this may require informing the school resource officer, the principal and staff, and Angel's teachers about the incident after the basketball game. Descriptions or pictures of the alleged assailants may be provided. Of course, given how significantly laws differ among states, the specialist must first contact the school district's legal counsel and seek their direction.

In Angel's situation, after the specialist obtains relevant directions from legal counsel and the principal, she informs Angel of the exact measures being taken to protect her, describes what she should do should she feel threatened while at school or if she should see the perpetrators elsewhere (e.g., at a store, movie theater, band concert), and discusses available services to help Angel cope. In particular, the specialist will most likely meet with Angel and her parents to ensure that they all have information regarding the previous night's violence and identify how to respond should the assailants reappear. Meeting with Angel and her parents will also provide an opportunity to describe the manner in which students Angel's age typically present immediately following experienced violence. The interchange might go like this:

FAMILY THERAPIST: Mr. and Mrs. Jones, thank you so much for coming to discuss Angel's situation. Your being here conveys to Angel that she is very important to you and you are committed to helping ensure her safety and needs are met.

MRS. JONES: Thank you for having us. We are very concerned.

FAMILY THERAPIST: Angel, have you told your mom and dad what happened last night?

ANGEL: Yes, they came to the safe zone and the police told them what happened.

FAMILY THERAPIST: What did the police tell you, Mrs. Jones?

MRS. JONES: The officer was very nice. He indicated that a verbal altercation had occurred. Angel and her best friend Katrina had argued with some girls from Smith Middle School. The Smith girls were ejected from the game and when Angel and Katrina walked to the parking lot, they were attacked.

FAMILY THERAPIST: Did the police say anything else?

MR. JONES: They took Angel down to the police station and she identified two of the girls from the Smith High School yearbook. The assistant district attorney contacted us this morning and said charges would be filed against the girls. Their names were Penny Anderson and Veronica Wareht. They still didn't know the name of the third girl but thought they would have that information this afternoon.

FAMILY THERAPIST: Would you mind if I conveyed this information to our school resource officer and principal?

MR. JONES: Please do.

FAMILY THERAPIST: This is what we are doing at Cactus Bluff to help ensure Angel's safety. First, the resource officer, principal, vice principals, and Angel's teachers have been informed of the situation. Specifically, a description of the alleged assailants has been provided to the resource officer, principals, and Angel's teachers. Should these girls come to Cactus Bluff, the school resource officer will arrest them for trespassing on school property. Second, Angel and I have devised an action plan. Angel knows what to do should she see any of these girls or any others she perceives as threatening. Angel will immediately tell a faculty member, staff member, resource officer, or administrator should she feel in danger. Additionally, we have asked that Angel use the "buddy system" over the remainder of the semester and have at least one friend with her at all times. This includes coming to and leaving school.

Let's review this clinical vignette. The first thing the specialist does is to thank Angel's parents for attending the session. She also frames their attendance aloud in very positive terms so that Angel, her mother, and her father hear very positive things about one another. This is done to promote Angel's positive perception of her parents' attendance. In other words, rather than Angel perceiving her parents as being there to "control" or "sanction" her, the message is that the parents' presence means Angel is important to them, and her parents are committed to ensuring her safety. At the same time, the specialist compliments the parents, which can reduce any potential defenses about "having" to attend this school-requested meeting.

Next the specialist empowers Angel by sharing administrative control. By asking Angel if she has shared the situation with her parents, it promotes Angel's active participation in the discussion and allows her to feel a significant part of the conversation. Had Angel not shared information about the events, this would provide an opportunity for her to describe what happened within a safe environment controlled by the specialist. For example, if Angel had not described the situation to her parents and her parents became angry at her for not doing so, the specialist might positively reframe this behavior like this:

ANGEL: No, I didn't tell them.

MR. JONES: What! You were attacked at school and you didn't tell us?!

MRS. JONES: Why didn't you tell us? We are your parents! I can't believe—

COUNSELOR: [gently interrupting Mrs. Jones] Pardon me, Mrs. Jones, I don't mean to interrupt, but if you wouldn't mind, please allow me to provide my professional opinion here. It sounds to me as though Angel had been through a very traumatic event— someone verbally attacked, threw her to the ground, and then choked her. Undoubtedly, Angel was in emotional turmoil from the event and responded like many 12- or 13-year-old students would: She bottled everything up. In psychological terms, she "compartmentalized" the situation because it was incredibly scary for her and because she likely wanted to protect both Mr. Jones and you from worrying. Now, given that Angel probably did this subconsciously rather than consciously, she probably doesn't fully remember why she did this. All she knows is the situation was emotionally overwhelming at the time and short-circuited her ability to respond. Again, this would be common for most 12- or 13-year-olds and is not atypical. I believe the important thing here is that Angel wanted both of you to be present here in my office so she could tell you about the events in a safe place where she knew both Mr. Jones and you would be able to feel safe and know that she is OK.

Here the specialist respectfully interrupts Mrs. Jones. She apologizes for the interruption and inserts her "professional opinion." This interruption is therapeutically relevant. In layman's terms, the specialist gets between the dog and the fire hydrant. She diverts the mother's negative verbal salvo by reminding Angel's parents of the trauma Angel likely experienced. Without inappropriate harsh confrontation the specialist reminds Angel's parents that their daughter is a 12-year-old child and that her behaviors are consistent with most 12-year-olds who experience life-threatening trauma. The specialist also reframes Angel's behaviors in psychological terms and then suggests that subconsciously Angel was attempting to "protect" her parents. Our experiences suggest when such positive reframing occurs, the parental arguing or "attack" ends. Even a semi-plausible explanation proposed by the specialist stops the negative discourse long enough for parents and students to thoughtfully consider the explanation. Such an interruption is enough to refocus the session and move back to the needs at hand.

Getting back to the original vignette where Angel had informed her parents about the previous evening's traumatic events, the specialist again promotes the core action of safety and comfort by providing Angel and her parents a summary of what will be done at the school to protect Angel. This both reminds Angel of how she should respond if she sees the alleged perpetrators and encourages her to remember the action plan that she had developed to help ensure her safety.

this core action, the specialist continually reminds students (and parents on their arrival to the school) that the students are being cared for and are safe. If the bullying and violence are over and there is no imminent danger, it is helpful to frequently repeat to survivors they are safe. Doing so implies that the immediate danger has passed. Here the specialist might say, "Angel, you are safe now. We are here for you. Everything is going to be OK." This affirming mantra is comforting to students. It reminds them and their parents that the immediate crisis has passed. Such reassurance is vitally important and can do much to quell the presenting anxiety and fear.

Depending on the students' ages and the emotional stability of their parents, it is helpful to describe typical trauma responses. Whenever working with parents of students who experienced bullying or violence, it is critical to inform them that youths often respond and behave differently. Many times, when multiple students experience the same bullying or violent event, their clinical presentations widely differ. Some will experience depressed affect, will feel hopeless and sad, and will demonstrate fatigue or report low energy levels (Perry, 2002). Other survivors may respond by becoming overly "clingy" with their mother and primary caregivers. They may have a heightened sensitivity to perceived rejection. Many times, they will have difficulties separating from their mother or primary caregivers, and they may be perceived as overly "whiny." Some will "regress," acting younger than their chronological age. They will present and act younger than they have in years. Some survivors may present with enuresis (wetting oneself) and/or encopresis (feces soiling in clothes) (Krill, Jr., 2009) and want extreme coddling and nurturing from their parents. Others may present at the other end of the continuum. Students who had previously presented without attention-deficit/hyperactivity disorder symptomatology may suddenly present as highly distractible, impulsive, or aggressive.

Specialists must inform parents about these potential symptoms. It is our belief that informing parents decreases the probability survivors will be punished for symptoms and increases the probability parents will both attend to the symptoms and seek immediate mental health counseling should the symptoms escalate. In Angel's case the specialist might say,

SOCIAL WORKER: Over the years we have found student survivors respond to incidents like Angel experienced in many different ways. A few experience no clear symptoms. Others will suddenly present as sad, depressed, or fearful. Others will become "clingy" or "whiny" and won't want to be separated from their mother or family members. Still others will become angry, defiant, impulsive, or distractible. All these are normal trauma response behaviors.

MOTHER: Makes sense.

SOCIAL WORKER: This is what we would ask you to do over the next few days and weeks. Are you up to it?

FATHER: Yes.

SOCIAL WORKER: Good. First, keep an eye on Angel. I realize that I don't have to tell you this, so, I am preaching to the choir here. It is evident you are highly invested parents who love your daughter and will help her. However, some parents punish their children should they begin to demonstrate some of the post-violent symptoms. Instead, I know that you won't do that with Angel.

FATHER: We would never punish her for experiencing symptoms. They attacked Angel; she didn't attack them.

SOCIAL WORKER: I agree. After getting to know you for just a few minutes it is strikingly evident you both love Angel.

MOTHER: Very true.

SOCIAL WORKER: Knowing what great parents you both are, I suspect that you will make special times for Angel and the two of you to do things together. Maybe you will decide to take walks or play board games together. Or maybe you will do something else like make family dinners together or write stories together. The key is spending extra time with Angel until she is back to her normal self. Can I count on you both doing this?

MOTHER: No question we will do that.

SOCIAL WORKER: Good. I've got just one more thing to say. Should you find that Angel begins to get worse in any way, call me. Here is my number [the social worker hands a business card to the mother and another one to the father]. So, if she begins to demonstrate increased depression, anger, or an inability to concentrate, give me a call so we can meet.

FATHER: We certainly will.

SOCIAL WORKER: Angel, this goes for you too. If you begin to feel overwhelmed, like hurting yourself or others, or feel really sad or depressed and you don't know why, come to my office or call me at this number [the specialist hands a business card to Angel].

Let's review what happened here. First, the specialist describes the types of symptoms Angel may present or develop. This is rather psychoeducational and provides Angel's parents a general description of potential post-trauma symptoms that Angel *may* present. Next Ms. VanderPaul invites Angel's parents to respond to a potential therapeutic directive. However, instead of simply telling them what to do, she asks them if they are willing to follow the directive. Although the implication is subtle, the inference is significant. Angel's parents now agree to follow the specialist's instruction. Stated differently, they are "buying into" treatment. Too often specialists simply tell parents what to do. Many times, parents simply agree without truly investing in their child's trauma recovery. In this instance, however, the parents had the option to refuse the directive. Instead, they pledged their commitment to comply with it.

Immediately, the specialist both lauds Angel's parents and establishes a paradox. The paradox suggests that inept parents punish children who experience post-trauma symptoms. Further, the paradox clearly differentiates Angel's parents from the implied inept parents. Can you imagine any caring parent responding, "No. I want to be an inept parent and inappropriately punish my child due to her genuine post-trauma symptoms?" Of course not! Angel's parents are invested in helping their daughter. They quickly report they would never punish Angel for legitimate symptoms. Such seemingly inconsequential communication nuances are in fact quite consequential. They promote appropriate responses by Angel's parents.

The specialist then provides a smorgasbord of potential ways in which Angel's parents can engage Angel in additional parent–child time. Thus, instead of merely providing one example describing how Angel's parents could engage Angel, the specialist suggests four. More importantly, the specialist imbeds the suggestion that Angel's parents can come up with "something else." The suggested engagement activities are then "capped" with a question: The specialist asks if the parents will provide special engagement time. Who could possible answer "no"? If they did, the specialist might simply ask something like, "I guess I am a little confused. How will it be helpful to Angel *not* to provide special opportunities to spend time with you?"

Two final powerful interactions are noted. First, the specialist provides her business cards with her telephone number to each person—the father, the mother, *and Angel*. This is important. No one is left out. If the specialist provided the mother and father with cards but failed to hand a card to Angel, it would suggest that Angel is not part of the solution. It would further suggest that Angel's parents control Angel's recovery and that she is utterly powerless. Second, the specialist asks each person—including Angel—to call if Angel decompensates. Again, making a special invitation for Angel to participate in her personal trauma recovery empowers her and suggests that she can positively impact the success of her treatment.

Core Action 3: Stabilization (If Warranted)

The primary goals of this core action stage are to calm and orient emotionally overwhelmed and disoriented violence survivors. This core action is often appropriate when students experience severe violence (e.g., an on-campus shooting or an assault that results in the death of or significant injury to a highly regarded classmate). However, this core action may be unnecessary if the violent event was less serious in terms of severity (e.g., a single veiled threat made by a non-menacing person) or outcome (e.g., no injuries were sustained). For example, if the event involved a veiled threat made by a smaller, younger student, the threatened student may not perceive potential danger. Thus, stabilization may be unwarranted.[1]

However, should survivors' post-violence presentations be extreme, specialists will need to stabilize them or refer them for stabilization by other mental health professionals. Examples of such extreme presentations might include students who (a) are unresponsiveness to verbal questioning, (b) demonstrate severe regressive behaviors such as assuming the fetal position, aimless rocking back and forth, or thumb sucking, (c) cry, tremble, or shake uncontrollably, or (d) rant or speak nonsensically aloud to themselves.

Do you remember Angel's friend Katrina in the earlier case vignette? She had escaped the attack in the school parking lot and, although emotionally shaken, had reported the incident so that Angel could be rescued. Let's slightly modify that case vignette so that it is relevant to this core action. This time, when Katrina escapes let's say she was so emotionally distraught that she hid between parked cars in the school parking lot. Later that evening, she was found sitting with her lower back against the wheel of a parked car. Her knees were drawn tightly to her body with her arms wrapped around her shins and her hands clasped around her ankles. She is aimlessly rocking back and forth, trembling, and just audibly crying. Her face is tear-soaked and her mascara is smeared from weeping. She is unresponsive to the school resource officer who found her. Here, it is quickly apparent that stabilization is relevant and necessary.

---

[1] It should be noted all threats are considered legitimate and potentially dangerous despite the physical stature or age of the persons making the threat.

In such a situation, and depending on the immediate presenting dangers in the parking lot (e.g., traffic, at-large assailants), the most therapeutic stabilization intervention will include going to the student rather than having her brought to the specialist's office. For example, the specialist may ask the school resource officer to summon additional staff or police to create a safety zone around the student. If possible, the student should have at least a six-foot radius around her where no one except immediately intervening persons can enter. In full view of the student, the specialist would quietly and slowly approach. She would then ask if the student would mind if the specialist sat next to her. The specialist identifies herself as a specialist who is going to help the student. The specialist's voice is soft and caring. The tempo of the communications is very slow. The specialist speaks slowly and allows silence between questions or statements. Specifically, the specialist might say something like this:

PSYCHOLOGIST: I'm Ms. VanderPaul. [Pause and wait for student response. If no response is given, continue.] I'm a psychologist at Cactus Bluff. [Pause and wait for student response.] Would you mind if I sat by you and talked with you?

STUDENT: [Unresponsive; staring ahead with no direct eye contact; continuing to weep]

PSYCHOLOGIST: [After a minute or so of silence] Everything is going to be alright. You are safe. I'm going to take care of you. Can you tell me your name?

STUDENT: [Unresponsive]

PSYCHOLOGIST: You are going to be alright. Can you tell me your name?

STUDENT: [Unresponsive]

PSYCHOLOGIST: You are OK now. I am here to help you. You are safe. I won't leave you until I know that you are OK. Can you tell me what happened?

STUDENT: Un-nah. [Katrina slowly and almost unnoticeably shakes her head side to side indicating "no."]

PSYCHOLOGIST: That's OK. We won't talk about what happened. It is over. You are now safe. I see you have a Cactus Bluff Middle School T-shirt. Do you attend Cactus Bluff?

STUDENT: Uuhhh-huh. [Katrina slowly nods her head indicating "yes."]

PSYCHOLOGIST: Who's your favorite teacher?

STUDENT: [almost inaudible] Ms. James.

PSYCHOLOGIST: Ms. James is one of my favorite teachers, too. She is a very kind lady. Let's see if we can find her, OK?

STUDENT: Uuhhh-huh. [Katrina nods her head.]

PSYCHOLOGIST: What classes do you have with Ms. James?

STUDENT: [Unresponsive]

PSYCHOLOGIST: We are looking for Ms. James right now and will try to get her here or get her on my cell phone. Everything is going to be alright. You are safe with me.

STUDENT: [Unresponsive]

PSYCHOLOGIST: Sometimes when I get really scared or bad things happen to me, I want to talk with my mom or dad. Can we call your mom or dad for you?

STUDENT: Yes. I want my mom.

PSYCHOLOGIST: OK, we are going to get your mom. What is your name so we can call her?

STUDENT: Katrina. Katrina Marlboro.

PSYCHOLOGIST: OK, Katrina, we are going to call your mom right now.

In this vignette, Ms. VanderPaul, the Cactus Bluff middle school psychologist, was informed by the resource officer that an un-identified student appeared nonresponsive and emotionally overwhelmed in the school parking lot. For safety reasons the specialist goes to the student *only* after understanding that the parking lot is safe and makes certain that other persons go with her. On seeing Katrina, Ms. VanderPaul approaches her slowly and in full view. This ensures two things:

1. The student is aware of Ms. VanderPaul's approach and is not startled.
2. If the student becomes agitated or hostile, Ms. VanderPaul can observe this change in physical or emotional presentation and if necessary escape.

Next Ms. VanderPaul identifies herself by name and position. This is important. It helps Katrina understand that she is not a stranger who is attempting to revictimize her. Ideally, the statement triggers positive memories of seeing or interacting with Ms. VanderPaul at school. Such memories may provide Katrina a sense of security and promote her engagement. If the student has not interacted with Ms. VanderPaul, the specialist's introduction may still foster a sense of safety. This is because most students favorably perceive school counselors, school social workers, school psychologists, and marriage and family therapists who work in the schools and are known by students (E. Zambrano, personal communications, December 23, 2009). Hence, by reporting her position and affiliation with Cactus Bluff Middle School, the specialist makes an attempt to connect with or engage the student.

Ms. VanderPaul asks permission to join and speak to Katrina. Asking permission is an excellent therapeutic intervention with violence survivors. It provides students a sense of control and indirectly indicates that the student controls whether the specialist will enter her space or not. Such perceived control by those in post-violence situations often engenders a sense of security. Typically, violence survivors had no control whatsoever during the violent episode. Verbalizing their current control of who is allowed to interact with them suggests they are no longer helpless and denotes they have regained their control.

The student responds by "not responding." Instead of immediately saying anything, Ms. VanderPaul provides a period of silence. Again, this is an excellent therapeutic intervention. It empowers the student by suggesting that *she* controls the interaction. In other words, Katrina, not the adult, controls whether Katrina responds. Therefore, Katrina controls with whom she will verbally engage. Katrina also controls the session's tempo, ensuring that topics will be discussed at Katrina's pace, not the specialist's. If questions or topics are too disconcerting or are perceived by Katrina as too threatening, she can discontinue responding or slow her responses. This ultimately ensures that Katrina directs the tempo of the questions. Thus, she has regained power and controls what happens next.

During this time, it is important not to continually stare at the student. Instead, it is best to demonstrate that the specialist is fully listening but for the specialist to briefly and slowly shift eye contact. Often, we teach our supervisees to sustain full eye contact when first asking questions. However, if the student is still unresponsive after a few moments, they should slowly lower their heads and slowly and nonchalantly look at their hands in their laps. Once supervisees look at their hands they are instructed to slowly rub their left index finger with their right thumb, and then slowly look back at the student's eyes. If the student still does not engage, the specialist repeats the "thumb look and rub" technique. This process is completed two or three times as needed before the specialist makes any further statements.

At no time should the specialist look far away. In other words, the specialist should not look at the distant school building or football field. Looking at distant or far objects may be misperceived by the student as a desire by the specialist to escape from the student's presence. Instead, by slowly and briefly looking at the specialist's own hands, the experience keeps the specialist in the student's "relationship bubble." It suggests, "I am still here with you. I am paying attention to you. And I am not leaving this immediate relationship."

Next the specialist tells Katrina that everything is alright; she is safe. The specialist also says she is going to take care of Katrina. Stated differently, the specialist is saying, "I am here for you. I am committed to you." This conveys to Katrina that she has someone who is committed to helping her and that nothing is going to harm

Katrina while the specialist is present. Again, these statements promote a sense of safety and allow the specialist to ask the next question, "Can you tell me your name?"

Here, Katrina is unresponsive. The specialist repeats that the student is safe and asks her name again. Instead of asking the same question over and over again, the specialist repeats the mantra, "You are safe now" and changes the question to "Can you tell me what happened?" The specialist never challenges the student to respond (e.g., "Come on, answer my question. Who are you?"). Instead she gently continues the mantra "You are safe now." Often badly shaken violence survivors do not want to recall what happened; the memories are overwhelming and frightening. Notice that when Katrina shakes her head no, the specialist provides a supportive response, "That's OK. We won't talk about what happened. It is over." This response is key and conveys that the traumatic event is over. In other words, the survivor doesn't have to relive what happened. The response further indicates the safety mantra and clearly conveys that the school survivor will not be forced to respond. Again, this says to the student, "You do not have to re-experience the overwhelming memories. *You control* what topics we discuss."

The specialist then asks a new question. This further indicates that the survivor continues to control the interaction. It suggests, "OK, you don't want to talk about the violence. However, I am not going away. Instead, I am committed to helping you. I'm going to ask more questions to learn who you are. You are important to me." Here the specialist reports a benign observation and asks a different question ("I see you have a Cactus Bluff School T-shirt. Do you attend Cactus Bluff?"). This question has nothing to do with the violence. She asks, "Who's your favorite teacher?" The question, too, is totally safe and has nothing to do with the trauma. More importantly, it potentially introduces positive memories of someone who has cared about the student in the past—someone with whom the student felt comfortable and safe. The question produces a verbal response from Katrina.

The specialist then talks favorably about Ms. James, the student's reported favorite teacher. These positive statements are an attempt to build rapport and continue the student's engagement. The statement that the specialist will seek Ms. James is designed to convey the message, "More safety is coming. Someone you like and who cares about you is coming." Contacting Ms. James also gives the specialist a clue as to the student's identification if no further student responses are forthcoming.

The specialist then reports that when she is scared, she often wants to talk with her parents. She then asks if Katrina would like to speak with either her mother or father. Angel immediately responds, provides her name, and helps the specialist learn her mother's telephone number.

Core Action 4: Information Gathering

This core action involves identifying the student's immediate needs and concerns: "What does this student need right now?" In particular, the specialist determines how the student perceives the severity of the violent experience. Remember, those who directly experienced the threat of death or severe harm have survived a potentially terrifying experience. Those who witnessed the death or trauma of close friends or peers may experience emotional trauma. Depending on their resiliency, coping mechanisms, and available support, individual survivors' needs greatly vary.

When gathering information from students about their experiences, specialists will follow each survivor's lead. Some may present as reluctant or reticent to engage. They may provide terse or cursory responses to questions. Others may "gush" information and present as overly loquacious. The key for specialists is to provide a balanced response. Should survivors be reticent to engage, the specialist should allow the students "space." Instead of asking further questions, the specialist should simply provide contact information (e.g., handouts with emergency counseling contact numbers and directions for students and their parents) and mingle with other nearby survivors. In this way, reticent students experience the presence of the specialist and have a means of access *if needed*. Simply "being in the presence" of a specialist might provide a sense of security and comfort to those who are reticent to engage.

In the case of a reticent high school student who witnessed the shooting of a friend at a school track meet, the specialist might respond in the following manner:

FAMILY THERAPIST: How are you doing?

STUDENT: I'm fine.

FAMILY THERAPIST: Did you know Johnny?

STUDENT: Yes. We were stretching out together and waiting to be called to the track relay race when he was shot.

FAMILY THERAPIST: Did you see him get shot?

STUDENT: You know, I really don't want to talk right now.

FAMILY THERAPIST: OK. Here is my office telephone number and a 24-hour school crisis line [handing the student a school counseling business card]. If you want to talk, I will be close by. Just let me know.

STUDENT: Right.

Here, the specialist simply asks the student how he is doing. The student's response is terse. The specialist then asks if the student knew the violence victim. The survivor reports they were stretching out together when his friend was shot. The specialist then asks the survivor if he witnessed the shooting. The survivor tersely extinguishes the communication. But instead of "pushing" the survivor for further details of what he saw or experienced, the specialist matter-of-factly validates the student by stating "OK" and complies with the student's request. However, before disengaging, the specialist provides contact numbers and informs the student that she will be mingling about and will be available if the student changes his mind.

Notice the specialist doesn't say something such as "I understand." This statement would inaccurately convey that the specialist "knows" exactly what the survivor has experienced. Such a therapeutic mistake can quickly result in a verbal assault on the specialist by a survivor. Survivors often feel angry that persons not present at the violent event could claim to understand their experience. The specialist also doesn't say, "I bet that was awful to see your friend shot." This would imply that the survivor *should* feel "awful."

Violence survivors who present as loquacious and seemingly wish to discuss every aspect of their experience need to be validated. However, the specialist should state that at this particular time only important basic information is being gathered about all the survivors' potential pressing needs. The survivor should gently be reminded that in a short time after the basic information is gathered, survivors will be given an opportunity to express their experience more fully. The interaction might go like this:

COUNSELOR: How are you doing?

STUDENT: I have no idea. Johnny and I were stretching out and the next thing I knew there were gunshots. Johnny fell to the ground. There was blood everywhere. I didn't know what to do, so I ran and hid by the bleachers. Once the shooting stopped I ran over to Johnny, but he was already dead. I can't believe this happened. I mean, like, this was something right out of a movie. It was unbelievable. One moment I'm stretching out with my teammate and the next thing he is dead! I was so afraid. I think everyone was very afraid.

COUNSELOR: Can I do something for you right now?

STUDENT: I wasn't the one who got shot. I'm perfectly fine, but it scared me. It scared me really bad. I was thinking, "This can't be happening. This is like in the movies or something." I'm so glad you are here, Ms. VanderPaul, because I've got so many things running through my head that I want to process.

COUNSELOR: What I am doing right now is merely trying to help understand what survivors need. Are you OK?

STUDENT: Yeah, I'm fine. I just really can't believe this just happened here at Jefferson High. But, I'm so glad I can process this with you, Ms. VanderPaul.

COUNSELOR: At this time I'm just gathering basic information. You've provided me with yours. Once things settle down and we learn what everyone's basic needs are, we will be coming back through. Let's talk more then. How does that sound?

STUDENT: I'd like that a lot.

As in the previous interaction with the terse student, the specialist again simply asks how the student is doing. This time, however, the talkative student rambles on, describing what he saw, thought, and felt. The specialist allows him to talk for a little while, but when he takes a breath and slows down, the specialist truncates his account by rephrasing the original question. Now, the specialist asks if she can do something for the student "right now." In other words, "Do you have an immediate need?" The student concretely responds and reports a desire to process the event with the specialist. Instead of allowing the student to do so and continue his rambling, the specialist explains that she is attempting to determine what survivors' immediate needs are. She then repeats, "Are you OK?" This final, direct, and closed-ended question is designed to stop the flow of words; the student has the choice to answer either "yes" or "no." Stated differently, the specialist gently closes off the opportunity for a continued discussion. The student responds he is "fine." The specialist tells him that the information he provided was exactly what she needed and informs him that he will have the chance to talk with her after she determines all the survivors' pressing needs. She concludes with the question, "How does that sound?" This final question is very empowering because it suggests that the student has some control over whether the specialist will leave.

Commonly asked questions in this information-gathering stage revolve around the survivor's experience or needs. Questions might include, "Were you injured?" or "How well did you know the person who was shot?" or "Is your friend missing?" For survivors who are confused and don't know what to do next, the specialist might say something like, "How about we call your parents?" For survivors who are overwrought with feelings of guilt or shame because they rather than their friend survived, the specialist might say, "It sounds as though you believe you should have been the one who was shot rather than your friend." Notice that each of these questions or statements simply attempts to gather information about the survivor's needs or concerns. The intent is not to use the questions or statements as an entrée into talk therapy. Rather, the intent is merely to allow survivors to voice their needs, concerns, or feelings and to identify their specific needs.

Summary

This chapter has provided an overview of PFA and the first four core actions and goals: (a) contact and engagement, (b) safety and comfort, (c) stabilization, and (d) information gathering. The chapter has described techniques and interventions for each stage. PFA is an intervention that is relatively simple to implement and appears to provide clinical utility depending on the specific student's needs and pressing concerns. The interventions presented can be readily modified as necessary.

References

Krill, Jr., W. E. (2009). Encopresis and enuresis in stress disordered children. Retrieved November 13, 2009, from http://hubpages.com/hub/Encopresis-and-Enuresis-in-Stress-Disordered-Children

National Child Traumatic Stress Network and National Center for PTSD. (2006). *Psychological first aid: Field operations guide* (2nd ed.). Retrieved June 6, 2009, from www.nctsn.org

Perry, B. D. (2002). Childhood experience and the expression of genetic potential: What childhood neglect tells us about nature and nurture. *Brain and Mind, 3*, 79–100. doi:10.1023/A:1016557824657

8

Psychological First Aid

Advanced Core Actions

Chapter 7 provided a general overview of psychological first aid (PFA) and its use with school bullying and violence survivors and described the first four PFA core actions. This chapter will cover the other four core actions: (a) practical assistance, (b) connection with social supports, (c) coping information distribution, and (d) collaborative services linkages. This chapter also introduces the reflecting "as if" intervention for school bullying and violence survivors. Table 8.1 lists all eight core actions.

Core Action 5: Practical Assistance

Here specialists offer practical help related to the information gathered in core action 4. Providing violence survivors with help for pressing or anticipated concerns is paramount. This core action has four steps:

1. From the list of needs identified in core action 4, help the client identify the most pressing need or concern.
2. Clarify the need.
3. Discuss an action plan.
4. Act to address the need.

Table 8.1 Psychological First Aid Eight Core Actions and
Corresponding Goals

Core Action 1: Contact and Engagement

Goals

• Initiate contact with survivor and parents.

• Respond to survivor or parental contact.

Core Action 2: Safety and Comfort

Goals

• Ensure the survivor's immediate safety.

• Provide physical and emotional comfort.

• Assess student's specific intent to harm self (i.e., self-injury, suicide) or
others (e.g., violent retaliation).

Core Action 3: Stabilization (if warranted)

Goals

• Calm survivors.

• Orient emotionally overwhelmed and disoriented survivors.

Core Action 4: Information Gathering

Goals

• Identify survivors' needs.

• Identify survivors' concerns.

• Assess students' perceptions of the severity of the violent experience.

Core Action 5: Practical Assistance

Goals

• Offer survivors help regarding immediate or future needs.

• Offer parents or primary caregivers help regarding survivors' needs.

Continued

Table 8.1 Continued

Core Action 6: Connection with Social Supports

Goals

• Help survivors and their families establish contacts with primary support persons (e.g., professional specialists, clergy, physicians).

• Establish survivors' and their families' contact with resources or groups as needed (e.g., survivor support groups, medical support groups, 12-step programs).

Core Action 7: Coping Information Distribution (Psychoeducational)

Goals

• Provide survivors and their families with information about potential adverse reactions to experienced violence.

• Describe effective coping strategies used by other school violence survivors and their families.

• Identify coping strategies that survivors and their families believe will work best for them.

Core Action 8: Collaborative Services Linkages

Goal

• Link survivors and their parents to specific persons at services (e.g., medical, counseling, school, police, district attorney) that are immediately needed or may be needed in the future.

Identify the Most Pressing Concern

Identifying the most pressing concern is therapeutically helpful because it helps survivors determine what is most important to them at this specific moment in time. It also helps survivors to articulate what they want and how that would look.

Before moving on, it is important to comment regarding age-appropriate needs and concerns. In general, very young, elementary-age children will simply want their nurturing parents or caregivers to arrive on scene. In this case, once the parents arrive, the specialist will provide PFA to both the student and the parents. The specialist will help them identify the student's most pressing need and the parents' most pressing need. Often parents want assurances that their child is safe and will suffer no lasting physical or psychological harm. The specialist might say something like this to a young student and his parents:

COUNSELOR: Johnny, you are safe now. Mom is here.

MOTHER: John-John, I was so very worried!

JOHNNY: Mommy, it was horrible!

MOTHER: I can't believe this happened. Are you hurt?

JOHNNY: No.

COUNSELOR: Ms. Samuels, it is so good to have you here. Johnny really needs to hear you tell him that he is safe, everything is going to be alright, and you are with him.

MOTHER: John-John, everything is going to be alright. Oh, I was so worried about you.

COUNSELOR: The thing we need to do right now is to help Johnny know that he is safe and that things are going to get back to normal as quickly as possible.

MOTHER: Will he be alright? I mean, is he psychologically damaged because he saw that jerk attack his best friend Tommy with a knife? This whole thing is insane. I hope they kill that kid for doing what he did!

COUNSELOR: Mom, John-John really needs you to focus right now. Tell John-John he is safe. The attack is over, and Tommy is in route to the hospital where the doctors will do all they can to make him better. John-John needs you to tell him this. Hold him in your lap. Look him in the eyes. Tell him he is safe. You are here to protect him. And Tommy's going to the hospital and the doctors there are going to do all they can for him.

MOTHER: John-John, Momma's here. It's over. That bad man is gone. The police are going to put him in jail. Tommy's mommy is going with him to the hospital and everything is going to be OK.

JOHNNY: [crying softly] OK.

COUNSELOR: Good work, Mom.

MOTHER: But can you promise me that John-John is going to be alright?

COUNSELOR: The EMTs looked John-John over pretty well and didn't find any injuries. Isn't that right, John-John?

JOHNNY: [Nods affirmatively]

MOTHER: But I mean psychologically. Can you promise me that he won't have psychological problems because of this?

COUNSELOR: One thing we know about young kids like John-John is that they are usually very resilient. Often when they have support from loving and devoted parents like you, they do very well. Of course, I can't promise anything, but I believe the big thing right now is to get things settled down, get you back home, and make things as normal as possible. How does that sound to you?

MOTHER: Pretty good. I just want to get John-John home.

COUNSELOR: How does that sound to you, John-John?

JOHNNY: [Nods affirmatively]

COUNSELOR: Good, then that's what we are going to do. Mom, I'm going to give you a couple of handouts related to emergency contact numbers should John-John begin to have some difficulties or if you have concerns or questions that pop up later. The handout also describes some typical behaviors kids can have after a situation like this. [The specialist goes on to explain potential psychological trauma responses of children as described earlier in Introduction Chapter, p. 11]

COUNSELOR: So, Mom, what is your most pressing concern?

MOTHER: I just want to get John-John home.

COUNSELOR: OK, let's do that. I'm going to walk you over to Command Officer Smith, who will have a couple of forms for you to sign, and he will make certain that you get to your car.

COUNSELOR: John-John, what is your biggest concern?

JOHNNY: I don't know.

COUNSELOR: OK. Do you need anything right now?

JOHNNY: No, I don't think so.

COUNSELOR: Good. So, if you think of anything, tell your mom and have her or you call me, OK?

JOHNNY: OK.

Let's discuss this exchange in greater detail. As in previous vignettes, the specialist continues the mantra that the student is safe. The specialist suggests things are back to normal and the student is safe because his mother has arrived. This implies to the mother that she is in control and knows what is best for her son. It gives her power and authority. Thus, instead of stating or implying that the specialist is in control, the specialist places the mother at the head of the immediate power hierarchy. From a structural family systems perspective, this places the mother in authority over Johnny and suggests that Johnny needs to follow his mother's authority. The statement conveys the message, "Things are back to normal. Mother is taking over."

Following the brief exchange between the mother and Johnny, the specialist therapeutically *joins* the mother by indicating it is good to have her at the scene. Then, the specialist tells her some important things she needs to say. This establishes a tone for the mother's communication with Johnny. It conveys the message, "Mom, you've got to be strong for Johnny. Don't get overwhelmed by emotions. Tell Johnny he is safe. He will be alright. And you are going to ensure his safety." This statement informs the mother that she is critical for Johnny's healthy recovery.

When the mother asks if Johnny will experience psychological repercussions or dysfunction due to the violent trauma and then starts to emotionalize the situation by describing what she wants done to the perpetrator, the specialist refocuses the mother to the charge at hand. The specialist tells her exactly what to say and describes how to place her child on her lap. Besides directing the mother on what she will say and do, the specialist's directives serve another important purpose: They tell Johnny what is going to happen. Knowing what is going to be said and done provides immediate structure with no surprises for Johnny. Having the specialist say the attack is over and Tommy is on his way to the hospital, and having the mother repeat these same things, signifies that indeed Johnny *is* safe and all the things that can be done for Tommy are being done.

As an aside, did you see the slight but important rapport-building technique used by the specialist? Good work! You saw it. The specialist initially called the student "Johnny." However, when the mother spoke, she addressed her son as "John-John." Once the specialist heard this, she immediately started calling him "John-John" and did so during the remainder of her interactions with him and his mother. This is another way specialists can engage students and parents and suggest they are committed to the family.

Also important to note is the manner in which the specialist responded to the mother's request for a *promise* that Johnny was not psychologically harmed. The specialist first described the resiliency of children. Then, the specialist implied how the mother's love and devotion could favorably impact Johnny. Finally, the specialist said, "I can't promise anything." This is important. Parents want reassurance that their child will be the same as before the violent trauma, but no matter how much we wish this were true, we cannot make such a promise. Instead, the best thing to do is simply state that we can't make such a promise while providing hope and expectations that the student's resiliency will prevail.

Given that this core action stage involves providing practical assistance to the previously reported pressing needs and concerns noted by mother and student, the specialist next addresses their desire to return home. Specifically, the specialist describes what will happen next. The specialist does not simply leave this core action stage at the mother's discretion; she invites Johnny's input as well. When Johnny does not identify a pressing need or concern, the specialist lauds him and gives him the opportunity to continue engagement with the specialist should a concern arise. Finally, the specialist again empowers both mother and student by stating that either can call the specialist should a need or concern arise.

Clarify the Need

The next step in this core action stage is to *clarify the need*. The specialist will talk with the student and likely the student's parents to clarify the identified pressing need. Then, the specialist will help the student and family realistically examine the need and understand its underlying core. Thus, instead of chasing a vague and global need (e.g., "I want to feel better"), the specialist works to help the student and family understand the crux of the need. Here, it is important to help students behaviorally describe the need (e.g., "I want my mother here" or "I want to drink some Gatorade"). Describing a behavior-based need increases the probability of a successful outcome.

Like the beauty pageant contestant announcing her desire for "world peace," on occasion students or parents may identify unrealistic pressing needs. When such clearly inappropriate or unrealistic "needs" are presented (e.g., "We need the school to send us to Disney World for a month so we can forget about the violent trauma"), it is helpful to respond in a manner that does not argue or engender contention. Here, one might say:

> "You know, Dad, your idea of going to Disney World to help your son and family recover from this experience makes sense. But unfortunately I have never heard of a school system sending violence survivors to Disney World, nor do I believe the school system has the money to fund such a trip. However, I am wondering: Might there be another place that your family and you might consider going that would be affordable and provide a respite for your son and family?"

The intent of this communication is to validate the underlying purpose for the request and redirect it in a way that provides a chance to consider and discuss other potential opportunities.

Discuss an Action Plan

The specialist next will *discuss an action plan* with the student and family. Responding specialists often are aware of available services to help survivors and their families. For example, students often want to know the condition of fellow victims who were rushed away by ambulance or who are being treated for physical injuries sustained in the violent episode. Depending on the specific situation, specialists will want to use their clinical judgment regarding divulging information.

For example, in Chapter 7's vignette about Angel and Katrina, the most pressing need identified by Katrina might be to learn Angel's whereabouts and condition. If the specialist knew Angel had survived the attack and was at a nearby hospital, it may be therapeutically logical to provide this information to Katrina. As a matter of fact, if Angel and Katrina considered each other to be their very best friends and this was common knowledge to the specialist, it might be therapeutically appropriate to reunite the two at the hospital if Angel was physically stable.

Conversely, if the specialist was aware Angel had been abducted and found murdered, the specialist will need to weigh the potential therapeutic benefits of informing Katrina now versus allowing her to learn of Angel's murder later. Many factors will need to be considered. For example, based on the specialist's brief interaction with Katrina's mother, does the specialist perceive her to have sufficient cognitive, psychological, and physical resources to respond adequately to Katrina's current post-violence trauma and her anticipated severe bereavement response to Angel's murder?

On the treatment side of the equation, if the specialist is aware she has the immediate support of other mental health providers on scene with Katrina, that the school resource officer can provide transportation to a nearby hospital if deemed necessary, and that the local hospital has indicated that psychiatric hospitalization is available, this may well be the best time to inform Katrina of Angel's death.

Act to Address the Need

The final step of the core action 5 is *act to address the need*. Here, the specialist will assist the student and the student's parents to respond to the most pressing identified need. Thus, if the student wants to know about the whereabouts of other violence survivors, a plan is generated with the student to help gain that information.

Typically, these four steps occur in succession, with rapid movement from one step into the next with little hindrance. If the student states a vague need like, "I want to feel better," the specialist might ask, "What would feeling better look like?" or "What would you be doing if you were feeling better?" The specialist might say something like:

SOCIAL WORKER: You say you want to feel better. I would like you to feel better, too. What would feeling better look like to you?

STUDENT: I don't know.

SOCIAL WORKER: Sometimes it is helpful to identify how you might be acting or what you might be doing if you were feeling better.

STUDENT: Well, if I were feeling better, I probably wouldn't be here.

SOCIAL WORKER: So where exactly would you be if you were feeling better?

STUDENT: I would be at the basketball court shooting hoops.

SOCIAL WORKER: That makes sense to me. So, what would you have to do to go to the basketball court and start shooting hoops?

STUDENT: I guess my parents would have to say it was OK for me to shoot some hoops so I could clear my mind of all the junk that happened today.

SOCIAL WORKER: Well, what would you have to do to ask your parents if you could go shoot some hoops to clear your mind?

STUDENT: I guess I would just have to ask them.

SOCIAL WORKER: Might that be something you want to do?

STUDENT: I think so. I think I just need to ask them.

Reviewing this vignette, we see the specialist merely repeats the student-stated vague need ("You say you want to feel better"). Stating that the specialist would like this student to fulfill his stated need suggests to the student that his need is supported by the specialist and the specialist is working with him to have the need satisfied. Next the specialist asks, "What would feeling better look like to you?" In other words, how would you be acting? Where would you be? What would you be doing? If the student can identify each of these, the specialist can begin creating a plan to satisfy the identified need. The student responds he wouldn't be "here"; instead, he would be at the basketball court shooting hoops. Again the specialist agrees with the student, and then she asks what he would have to do to allow him the freedom to do what he wishes. The student reports he would simply need his parents' permission. The specialist then asks if the student wishes to ask his parents to go to the basketball court. The student replies that he just needs to ask his parents for their permission and that playing hoops would eliminate a major source of discomfort and stress for him.

Core Action 6: Connection with Social Supports

The goal of this stage is to help survivors and their families establish contacts with primary support persons and other potentially helpful resources. The degree and length of contact may vary according to immediately presenting and developing needs. Both professional (e.g., specialists, clergy, physicians) and nonprofessional (e.g., family members, friends, neighbors) contacts are included. Specifically, survivors and their families will need connections that can provide psychological, physical, social, and spiritual support.

Of particular relevance to school violence survivors is parental and family support. With younger students, parents are key. Immediately following any threatened or realized violence, younger children want significant parental contact. Thus, specialists should seek parental involvement immediately after any violent or potentially violent trauma. However, once students reach high school, the degree of desired parental support can greatly fluctuate. Some high school students will want substantial contact with their significant peers (e.g., boyfriends, girlfriends, selected friends from band or sports teams) and limited contact with parents or family members. Although parental support should be sought, parents should also be informed that older students may tend to seek the majority of their support from peers and that such peer support is common for this age. Here the specialist might say something like:

"Mr. and Mrs. Valadez, in situations such as this where violence was threatened toward your son, it can be particularly challenging for students, parents, family, and friends. Something that you may wish to be aware of is that high school seniors about Joel's age often want more peer support than parent support. This is sometimes difficult for parents, but desiring peer support is often developmentally appropriate for persons of Joel's age."

The specialist positively reframed Joel's desire for more peer than parent support as age appropriate and normal.

Core Action 7: Coping
Information Distribution

The primary goals of this core action are to provide students and their families with information about potential adverse reactions to the violence. Specialists will both suggest effective coping strategies should such reactions occur and help survivors and families determine which coping strategies *they* believe will be most helpful. This stage is psychoeducational in nature and often is conducted with both the student and parents. It repeats information previously provided in Introduction Chapter; p. 11 in greater detail and describes how students may respond to the violent experience.

All discussions about potential symptoms should be presented in an age-relevant fashion. For elementary-age pupils, the specialist could create presentations suitable to their cognitive, social, and emotional development, using common, non-"psychobabble" words that students will understand. For example, the specialist wouldn't say something like "enuresis"; young students certainly wouldn't understand it, and parents might not either. Instead, a specialist talking to the mother of a kindergarten student might say something like this:

> "Sometimes when five-year-olds like Melanie witness or experience violence, they may begin a pattern of wetting their pants or beds. This is relatively common. If it happens, don't freak out. It is not unusual for five-year-olds to pee in their pants or bed after seeing something really scary. Of course, not all five-year-olds begin this pattern. But if they do, don't punish them. They simply can't help this unfortunate physical response and probably don't like sitting in their wet pants any more than adults would."

The specialist here normalizes post-violence enuresis by saying it is "relatively common." Next, the specialist states, "*If* it happens, don't freak out." This statement is powerful. Notice the specialist doesn't say "*When* it happens." Thus, Melanie is not banished to life-time of enuresis. However, should it occur, her mother and father are forewarned that it is a symptom of the violence she experienced. Therefore, should Melanie wet her pants or bed, she is not *being bad* but instead simply *suffering post-violence symptoms*. To further her point, the specialist reports that, like adults, the girl won't like sit-ting in her wet pants. Also notice that the specialist begins by saying "wetting" and then says "peeing." This ensures that parents and the student truly understand the symptom.

Undoubtedly some specialists will be bothered by the fact that these statements are made with both the parents *and Melanie* pre-sent. They may be concerned that remarks made about enuresis in front of Melanie will result in her intentionally wetting herself. We disagree: Forewarning the parents regarding potential enuresis prepares parents (and students) for what may happen. Thus, should enuresis occur, it is not experienced as a scary, uncontrollable, and unforeseen behavior that suggests students are intentionally being "bad."

When discussing potential post-violence symptoms within this psychoeducational format, the specialist should clearly de-scribe age-appropriate symptoms. In other words, it makes little sense to talk about common reactions of adolescent violence survivors when speaking to five-year-olds and their parents. Also, the specialist should speak candidly, without using innuendos or insinuations.

Another helpful technique is to ask younger students to ex-plain what they "think" happened. Very young elementary school students may not understand the construct of death as being per-manent or the injuries to friends as impacting future interactions. Thus, the specialist should listen to how students describe the vio-lence experience and answer questions as simply and honestly as possible.

If student survivors are very young, drawing may help them more effectively communicate what they seen or experienced.

Conversely, for high school students, the specialist can create a presentation that takes into consideration their developmental stages and needs. Because adolescents typically want to be viewed as adults, the specialist should use age-acceptable communications. In other words, specialists should use their clinical judgment when intervening. Varsity football players who wish to portray themselves as self-reliant, tough, and strong likely won't readily embrace drawing with crayons as a viable option.

No matter what form the violence took, potential post-violence reactions should be discussed with both survivors and their parents. At a minimum, the following should be included: (a) intrusive experiences, (b) avoidance and withdrawal, (c) physical arousal reactions, (d) repetitive play and social interactions, (e) grief and bereavement reactions, and (f) anger. Intrusive experiences, avoidance and withdrawal, and physical arousal are often associated with post-traumatic stress disorder. Intrusive experiences typically include distressing memories of the violent experience or associated images (e.g., a bloody knife, the face of the assailant, the scream of a fellow survivor). These memories or images continually return despite the survivor's active attempts to keep them from entering consciousness. Such memories or images are very frightening for younger students and can be disabling. Violence survivors often feel powerless to stop the recurring memories or images. Thus, they feel increasingly vulnerable to the feelings connected to these memories or images. Letting students know that such memories and images are common among violence survivors can help normalize these symptoms and can help survivors understand that they are not "going crazy." It is also important to discuss survivors' potential feelings of vulnerability brought about by their inability to control such intrusive memories or thoughts.

One technique our post-violence survivors have reported helpful is "the hot fudge sundae memory." Depending on the individual student's emotional, cognitive, and social presentation, age, and pressing needs, we might say something like this:

FAMILY THERAPIST: I'm hearing you say that as an honors high school senior who is also a strong and tough district champion wrestler, you *should* be able to stop the memories of the attack from coming into your mind. Is that correct?

JOE: Right! I should be able to do that.

FAMILY THERAPIST: Would you be willing to help me for a moment?

JOE: Sure. What do you want me to do?

FAMILY THERAPIST: Do you like hot fudge sundaes?

JOE: Yes. But what does that have to do with anything?

FAMILY THERAPIST: Help me out for a moment. Will you promise me that you won't think about a hot fudge sundae for the next few moments?

JOE: Sure, that's easy.

FAMILY THERAPIST: Good. Are you ready to start?

JOE: Yup! I won't think about hot fudge sundaes.

FAMILY THERAPIST: Good. So, I don't want you to think about a hot fudge sundae. I don't want you to think about the vanilla ice cream in an ice cream bowl. I don't want you to think about the steamy hot fudge cascading down the vanilla ice cream. I don't want you to think about the whipped cream on top or the nuts or the cherry. So, what are you thinking about?

JOE: You got me! I was thinking about the hot fudge sundae.

FAMILY THERAPIST: So tell me, Joe. How is this visualization similar to the memories that keep coming to you about the attack?

JOE: They are not similar at all.

FAMILY THERAPIST: Really. Were you trying *not* to think about the hot fudge?

JOE: Exactly! I was trying not to think about the hot fudge sundae.

FAMILY THERAPIST: The more you tried to not think about the hot fudge sundae, what happened?

JOE: "OK. I get it. The more I tried not to think about the hot fudge sundae, the more the hot fudge sundae was on my mind.

FAMILY THERAPIST: Right. So, what did you learn?

JOE: The more I try not to think about the attack, the more I keep the memories coming.

In the same way violence survivors attempt to exclude the memories and images that continually bombard their consciousness, some survivors will also attempt to avoid the vicinity of the violent episode, persons connected to the violence, and anything they associate with the experience (e.g., guns, clothes worn the day of the event, songs played during the event). In other words, survivors often attempt to "shield" themselves from memories of the violence by avoiding anything that reminds them of the experience. Thus, survivors may withdraw from friends who may wish to talk about the survivor's experience or even previously enjoyable hobbies or activities that the survivor may believe are connected to the experience. For example, a student who was attending a choir event when the violence occurred might drop out of choir or even stop singing songs that might engender memories of the violence.

Using the psychoeducational process, the specialist should inform students and their families about potential physical arousal actions associated with violent experiences. An example is hypervigilance, which occurs when students constantly scan their environment for real or imagined threats. In other words, they may constantly be on the lookout for another violent episode. Other common post-violence physical arousal responses might include a heightened startle response, where a loud sound may cause the student to jump, or a sleep disturbance, where the primary presenting issue is an inability to relax. Some students may present with underlying anger and associated angry outbursts that appear inappropriately severe. Younger students may even enact repetitive play about the violent event and attempt to portray themselves as a hero disarming the perpetrator.

Many times, younger students cannot describe the emotions they are experiencing. Instead of asking students about their experienced emotions, it is more useful to have them describe their physical sensations and to ask closed-ended versus open-ended questions. For example, instead of asking, "What emotions are you experiencing?" the specialist may say:

SCHOOL COUNSELOR: Sometimes when students tell me how they feel after being shot at, they tell me things like their heart is beating really, really fast or they feel shaky. Other times they tell me that they keep hearing the sounds of the gunshots in their heads. Is your heart beating really, really fast or do you feel shaky?

STUDENT: No. But I feel really strange, like I'm in a bad dream and I can't breathe.

SCHOOL COUNSELOR: What is that like for you?

STUDENT: I don't like it. Sometimes it gets so bad I think I'm going to throw up.

SCHOOL COUNSELOR: What do you do when that happens?

STUDENT: I get scared and think I'm going to get sick all over the place.

SCHOOL COUNSELOR: And if you got sick, what would happen?

STUDENT: My teacher would send me to the school nurse.

SCHOOL COUNSELOR: And if you went to the school nurse, what would happen?

STUDENT: I'd guess she would clean me up and send me back to class.

SCHOOL COUNSELOR: And if she sent you back to class?

STUDENT: I would be right back where I started from. I'd be fine.

SCHOOL COUNSELOR: That makes sense to me. Sometimes students I know who start to feel like they are in a bad dream and scared like they can't breathe find it helpful to do something like count to 10, sing, or say something like "I am safe." Do you think any of those things or something else might be helpful?

STUDENT: Hmmm. When I was a little kid and I got hurt, my grandpa taught me to say *estoy bien*.

SCHOOL COUNSELOR: What does *estoy bien* mean?

STUDENT: It means, "I'm OK. I'm not hurt."

SCHOOL COUNSELOR: Did it help?

STUDENT: Yes.

SCHOOL COUNSELOR: Do you think it would help you should you feel strange like you are in a really bad dream and can't breathe?

STUDENT: My grandpa taught me that when you say *estoy bien* all your fear leaves. I will try it.

Let's first review three important things that happened here:

1. Instead of asking the student to discuss nebulous or difficult-to-describe feelings or emotions, the specialist asks the student to describe the physical sensations experienced. This is important. Even young students can accurately describe the physical sensations they are experiencing.
2. It is safe to describe your physical sensations because no one can say they are "incorrect." The student knows his sensations. Although the physical sensations cannot be physically held in the student's hand or handed to the specialist, the sensations are tangible to the student. They are real. Thus, the student's reported physical sensations cannot be incorrect. He can say what he *feels* and his feelings can never be suspect.
3. The language used is not psychological jargon. The sensations described are presented in age-appropriate language that is easy to comprehend.

These first three points provide safety for the student. Students who feel safe are more likely to engage in the counseling process.

Next, the specialist describes some sensations reportedly identified by other students who experienced the same type of violence (e.g., being "shot at"). The specialist doesn't describe sensations identified by students who, say, were struck by a car or fell off the roof of the school. In other words, the specialist states that students who experienced a similar situation identified these types of sensations. The specialist then focuses on three symptoms: heart palpitations, feeling shaky, and intrusive memories. This is a forced-choice response, also known as a closed-response statement. Less experienced specialists might not understand the importance of using such a forced-choice or closed-response question here. They might inaccurately believe that all presented questions should be open-ended. However, with younger students or persons exposed to violence, the use of only open-ended questions can actually be counter-therapeutic. Often younger students and persons overwhelmed by a violent experience require the structure and safety provided by closed-ended questions. Limiting potential responses to three provides a feeling of control for the student and addresses potential concentration issues common to many violence survivors.

The student denies having any of the three symptoms. Instead, he reports different sensations—feeling "strange," living in a bad dream, and an inability to breathe. Immediately, the specialist engages the student and provides an opportunity for him to further describe or comment on the sensations. The student reports he doesn't like the sensations and is worried he might vomit. The specialist then uses a "linking" intervention, trying to help the student realize the final outcome of the presenting concern. In this case the student is encouraged to respond to the next thing that would happen until the final outcome (i.e., vomiting) occurs. In this case, the student reports that if he actually vomited, nothing too overwhelming would occur. Eventually he would be safely returned to his room.

Once this acceptable outcome is verbalized, the specialist introduces the idea of initiating a new behavior should the student experience the noxious post-violence feelings like those previously experienced. The specialist suggests counting to 10 or singing and provides a third "you create it" option. The student goes for the third option. The specialist welcomes the student's response and learns that the student's revered grandfather formerly taught the boy a Spanish phrase. Based on the student's comments it seems the use of the phrase (positive self-talk) had been helpful in the past. When the specialist asks if the student thought it would be useful to employ the phrase related to his post-violence symptoms, the student embraces the coping option. Other coping options that might be suggested include behaviors such as (a) talking with trusted significant others (e.g., parents, friends, teachers), (b) journaling, or (c) engaging in counseling. The interchange might go like this:

SOCIAL WORKER: I wonder what other coping behaviors you might wish to try.

STUDENT: What do you mean by that?

SOCIAL WORKER: Well, sometimes students who experience violence report that it is helpful to start not just one coping behavior, like saying *estoy bien*, but to start a couple new coping behaviors like writing in a journal and describing what you are thinking or sensations that you are feeling.

STUDENT: I don't like to write. Journaling wouldn't be good for me.

SOCIAL WORKER: I wonder what else might be helpful to you.

STUDENT: I like to play catch with my grandpa. He and I always talk. I bet that would be helpful.

SOCIAL WORKER: That sounds good. Let's talk with your grandpa and see if we can't make a schedule when the two of you could get together.

As you see, the specialist attempts to engage the student in multiple coping behaviors. Journaling is proposed first, but the student reports journaling is not a match. Instead of continually listing other coping options, the specialist asks what options the student believes would be helpful. This is an efficient intervention, and the student quickly identifies a behavioral coping option he believes would be best. Some students seem to have truncated abilities to identify coping options after a violent experience. These students and their parents typically want lists and ideas from which to

choose. Others refuse all presented ideas and seem to find it important to create their own coping behaviors. Who suggests or creates
the coping behavior is inconsequential. The important factor
here is simply that students and their families use multiple coping
behaviors and do what they believe is most useful in helping themselves respond the best they can.

Core Action 8: Collaborative Services Linkages

The primary goal of the final core action is to link student survivors
and their parents to specific people at agencies, programs, and
institutions that provide needed survivor services. Many times,
these linked services offer (a) medical services for physical injuries
sustained during the violent episode or psychotropic medications
for post-violence anxiety or bereavement, (b) counseling services for individual or family members related to the post-violence
symptoms or the pre-violence substance abuse that led to the violence, and (c) legal services for restraining orders or petitions. Such
petitions often involve a request that property confiscated during
the violent event (e.g., bicycle, jewelry, clothes) be returned to the
victim. Specialists will want to link students and their families to
immediately needed services (e.g., medical services for a lacera-
tion sustained in the violent episode) as well as services that may
be needed in the future (e.g., legal services for a possible restraining
order).

As part of this final core action stage, specialists introduce the
idea of participating in a debriefing experience. No pressure is
placed on the student or parents to participate. Instead, specialists
simply provide the time and location of the debriefing along
with a little background specific to the intent of the debriefing.
Participation in a debriefing is often influenced by a person's
perceptions of how the debriefing will benefit him or her. It may

be helpful if specialists communicate that the debriefing experience is more about helping others to process and cope with the violence than helping themselves. The specialist may say something like, "Although the debriefing experience may be helpful to you, the debriefings are often more helpful to others who need to process what happened. Your presence and participation in a debriefing experience will likely be more helpful to others than yourself." Hence, the stigma of attending is eliminated. Survivors and parents can say they attended to help others rather than feeling that they need help with their psychological responses or symptoms.

Specialists may wish to remind themselves of the 20-60-20 rule related to debriefing participation. About 20% of those who participate in the debriefings find the experience to be of little help. About 60% find the experience either helpful or not based on perceived supportive interactions within the debriefing experience among themselves and other participants. The final 20% seem to find debriefings overwhelmingly positive no matter what happens.

Reflecting "As If"

We have found the reflecting "as if" intervention easy to use and helpful. Reflecting "as if" is founded on proven, widely accepted, evidence-based practices (Sommers-Flanagan & Sommers-Flanagan, 2012; Watts & La Guardia, 2013) and based on ideas and procedures from Adlerian therapy and constructivist and social constructionist perspectives (Watts, 2013; Watts & La Guardia, 2013; Watts & Phillips, 2004; Watts, Williamson, & Williamson, 2004). Specifically, the reflecting "as if" technique is relationship focused, optimistic, and present and future oriented; it anticipates positive change outcomes and places emphasis on the student's existing strengths, skills, and abilities (Watts, 2013; Watts & La Guardia, 2013). The intervention invites students to both identify and implement new or alternative behaviors. Survivors perceive these new and alternative behaviors as potentially helpful in changing their negative behaviors and relationships. Given that the new or alternative behaviors are created by students seeking counseling rather than being created or forced on students by a specialist, students are more likely to feel ownership of them (Watts, 2013; Watts & La Guardia, 2013). Thus, students are more likely to commit to implementing the behaviors and expect positive outcomes when the behaviors are used. Furthermore, given that students completely control if and when they use their newly devised behaviors, students will likely use the new behaviors when they believe they will bring about desired and intended outcomes.

Reflecting "as if" comprises three distinct phases, each with a specific task: (a) brainstorming, (b) refining and ranking, and (c) implementing the behaviors.

Phase 1: Brainstorming

Phase 1 consists of brainstorming with students. Here students identify new or altered behaviors they believe would be help change their reactions and behaviors resulting from bullying or violence experiences. Watts and La Guardia (2013) encouraged specialists to use thought-provoking questions—for instance, "You say you're sick and tired of being scared of being bullied again. When you begin acting like the survivor you are and acting like you would like to be, how will you be acting differently?" or "If a good friend would see you several months from now and you were more like the person you desire to be, what would this person see you doing differently?"

Phase 2: Refining and Ranking

This phase is what Watts described as a "plausibility check" (Watts, 2013; Watts & La Guardia, 2013). Here, students and specialists work together to help students refine their identified new or altered behaviors. Specialists help students ensure the new or altered behaviors are specific, behaviorally oriented, measurable, and relevant to the desired outcome. Once the plausible new or altered behaviors are behaviorally described and measurements for the behaviors are devised, clients then rank order the behaviors from easiest to most difficult to implement.

Phase 3: Implementing the Behaviors

Phase 3 has three steps:

1. The student selects two of the easiest behaviors from the list generated in Phase 2 and initiates these behaviors during the upcoming week.
2. The specialist and the student discuss the student's experiences with the new or altered behaviors. Specifically, the specialist focuses on successful behavioral attempts and discusses how the student may see and experience others, his or her interpersonal relationships, and himself or herself differently.
3. The specialist encourages the student in his or her continued pursuit of change, focusing on the student's strengths and abilities, differentiating between what people do and who people are, and communicating affirmation regarding student efforts (Watts & Pietrzak, 2000).

Reflecting "As If" Vignette

The following vignette illustrates the application of the reflecting "as if" technique with Andrew, a 15-year-old Caucasian male who is a junior at Central High School. In the high school cafeteria, a larger senior shoved Andrew and then poured milk on Andrew's head. Andrew cried and ran out of the cafeteria. Two weeks later, he comes to the counseling office to speak with the specialist about the incident. He presents with above-average intelligence and maturity for his age. He says crying in front of his peers was "embarrassing." He denies resulting anxiety or depression and denies suicidal ideation or thoughts of retaliation toward the other student: "I'm not that kind of guy. He's just a football player who doesn't know how to use his words to get what he wants."

Phase 1: Brainstorming

FAMILY THERAPIST: Andrew, I'm very impressed by you. Coming here to talk about how you can get over your feelings of embarrassment is quite mature and impressive.

ANDREW: Yes, I am tired of feeling embarrassed about crying in front of my friends at the cafeteria because of what Tom Clark did to me. After all, I didn't shove him; he shoved me. He weighs at least 200 pounds and is much larger than me. He scared me. Yet I'm the one who feels embarrassed!

FAMILY THERAPIST: If you were behaving as if you were the person you want to be who isn't embarrassed, how would you be behaving?

ANDREW: I guess I would be behaving friendly to everyone rather than trying to stay away from everyone.

FAMILY THERAPIST: So, how would behaving friendly look, Andrew?

ANDREW: I would stop hiding and start smiling and talking to my friends.

FAMILY THERAPIST: Makes sense. How would you not be hiding?

ANDREW: I don't know. Maybe I would just begin walking down the hall and not care if others saw me.

FAMILY THERAPIST: What else would you be doing?

ANDREW: I guess I would be smiling and say "hi" to people rather than being silent.

FAMILY THERAPIST: OK. So, you would just walk down the hall, smiling, and you would be saying "hi" to people. Is there anything else you would be doing if you were acting like the person you want to be who isn't feeling embarrassed?

ANDREW: Nope. Those would be the things I would concentrate on.

In phase 1 the specialist and Andrew are brainstorming how Andrew would act if he were acting like a person who isn't embarrassed. Although the above responses are limited for demonstration purposes, they describe how to ask a bullying survivor how to identify new, desired behaviors. It is critically important to ensure that the responses are behaviorally described. Andrew first reports he would begin behaving friendly. The specialist then asks, "So, how would behaving friendly look?" The intent of this question is to have Andrew behaviorally describe how he would be acting. He does this by saying he would stop hiding, start smiling, and start talking to friends. The specialist then asks what else Andrew might do. Andrew reports he would say "hi" to people rather than be silent. This brainstorming helps Andrew envision the behavioral manner in which he can choose to act, and it provides a template of options from which he may select.

Phase 2: Refining and Ranking

COUNSELOR: Andrew, how plausible is it that you will start walking down the hall, actually smile, and say "hi" to people when you walk around the school?

ANDREW: It wouldn't be that hard to do.

COUNSELOR: But on a scale from 0 to 10, with 0 indicating you likely won't walk around the school smiling and saying "hi" and 10 indicating that you will walk around the school, smiling as you walk, and saying "hi," how realistic is it that you actually will walk around the school smiling and saying "hi"?

ANDREW: I think about a 6. I will be smiling more than half the time I walk around the school.

COUNSELOR: So, I'm hearing that you would be willing and able to smile and say "hi" to others more than half the time you are walking around the school. How can you check yourself to see how often you are walking, smiling, and saying "hi"?

ANDREW: Well, I could write "smile" and "hi" on the back of my hand, and every time I look at my hand, I can remember to smile and say "hi."

COUNSELOR: You seem pretty dedicated. I bet you would do that.

ANDREW: Yup.

COUNSELOR: So, what could you do to remember to walk, smile, and say hi?

ANDREW: Every time I look at the back of my hand and see "walk," "smile," and "hi," I will start doing it.

COUNSELOR: That's a good idea. Which of these things will be the easiest for you do and which will be the most difficult?

ANDREW: I don't think any of these things will be hard to do. I think smiling will be easiest, followed by saying "hi," and then walking around.

COUNSELOR: So, we would order these behaviors from easiest to hardest by saying smiling is easiest and number one, saying "hi" would be second easiest or number two, and third easiest would be walking around the school.

ANDREW: You got it!

In phase 2, specialists create a plausibility check by asking if students will use their newly self-identified and desired behaviors. This specialist challenges Andrew by asking if he actually will do the new identified behaviors and how he will monitor his use of these behaviors. Andrew says the new behaviors will be useful in helping him get over his embarrassment. He then devises a method to measure or monitor his compliance by writing "smile," "walk," and "hi" on the back of his hand. He reports that he will implement the new behaviors each time he sees the words on the back of his hand. Finally, the specialist has Andrew rank order the behaviors from easiest to most challenging.

Phase 3: Implementing the Behaviors

Step 1

SOCIAL WORKER: Given that the anti-embarrassment behaviors you identified are pretty straightforward, which two behaviors will you want to begin this week?

ANDREW: I can do all three this week.

SOCIAL WORKER: I really believe you could. However, let's identify just two that you will use and practice this week. Once you are successful with those two new behaviors you can add your third anti-embarrassment behavior the following week. Which two will you want to use this week?

ANDREW: I know I can smile and say "hi."

SOCIAL WORKER: Good. Between now and the next time we meet next Monday, why don't you smile and say "hi" when you see people? Keep track of how that goes and tell me how things improve between now and next week.

The specialist asks Andrew which two anti-embarrassment behaviors he will use. As is often the case with relatively easy-to-implement behaviors, Andrew reports he can implement all three. Although it is highly plausible that he could, the specialist wants Andrew to have a high probability for success and focus on two limited behaviors that can quickly become an ingrained habit. Thus, the specialist says she believes Andrew could successfully implement all three but encourages him to focus on just two behaviors in the upcoming week and then report his success at their next session. The specialist sets an expectation for success by stating, "Tell me how things improve between now and next week." This statement has two significant therapeutic implications: (a) it implies the specialist believes in Andrew and his ability to implement these new anti-embarrassment behaviors and (b) it establishes her expectations for Andrew's success.

Step 2

PSYCHOLOGIST: Welcome back, Andrew. Tell me how often you smiled and said "hi" to others this past week.

ANDREW: It was easy. I smiled and said "hi" wherever I went.

PSYCHOLOGIST: Cool! So, on a scale of 0 to 10, with zero meaning you never smiled or said "hi" and 10 meaning you were smiling and saying "hi" all the time, what kind of score would you give yourself?

ANDREW: I'd say an 8. Most days I smiled and said "hi" to most everyone.

PSYCHOLOGIST: An 8 is a pretty high score and tells me you smiled and said "hi" a lot. What kinds of things did you do to remind yourself to keep on smiling and say "hi"?

ANDREW: I really didn't have to do much. I wrote "SMILE" and "hi" on the back of my hand the first day. But after I started smiling and saying "hi," it was easy to continue and I didn't write on my hand anymore.

PSYCHOLOGIST: So, will you continue smiling and saying "hi" this next week?

ANDREW: Yes. I plan to.

PSYCHOLOGIST: Tell me how smiling and saying "hi" reduced your feeling of embarrassment and helped you.

ANDREW: It changed how I felt about myself. I wasn't embarrassed because I controlled how I acted and what I did and people responded very favorably to me. It was like the whole incident was in the past and no one remembered what happened.

PSYCHOLOGIST: You also said you wanted to walk and not hide from
   people. Are you ready to do all three this week?
ANDREW: No problem. I can do that.

The specialist asks Andrew a scaling question to learn the frequency of his smiling and saying "hi." She also asks how Andrew
reminded himself to smile and say "hi." She asks if Andrew planned
to continue his new behaviors and whether the two behaviors
helped him reduce or eliminate his feelings of embarrassment.
Andrew reports that his smiling and saying "hi" behaviors resulted
in people smiling back at him and speaking to him. Given the favorable outcome, the specialist then asks if Andrew was ready to
implement the third anti-embarrassing behavior, walking around
and not hiding from people. Andrew reports he is ready to do
so. Hence, the specialist encourages him to start walking around
campus and monitor all three behaviors in the upcoming week.

Had Andrew reported he was not ready to begin walking around
campus, the specialist would ask something like, "What things will
you need to do before you start being ready to walk around campus?"
Once Andrew identified the things that he would have to do before
using the new behavior, the specialist would help him establish a plan
and timeline to accomplish what needs to be done. Had Andrew
reported that his newly implemented behaviors had been ineffective, the specialist would ask something like, "How can you modify
the smiling and saying 'hi' or identify new behaviors that can help
you reach your goal of non-embarrassment?" The intent is to help
Andrew understand that he ultimately controls his behaviors and can
identify and establish behaviors that will help him achieve his goals.

Step 3

FAMILY THERAPIST: Andrew, I am impressed with the progress
   you have made and your commitment to be free from embarrassment. You have really set your mind to stopping the
   embarrassment.

ANDREW: Thanks. I want to go to college, and being embarrassed all the time would keep me from being able to achieve what I want in life—a college education and a good job.

FAMILY THERAPIST: You have many strengths and abilities, Andrew. You are a good communicator, you are intelligent, and you have many excellent interpersonal skills. I know you will be very successful. It is fun to see you becoming the person you are and to watch your dedication to continuing the change you want to achieve your goal of college.

In this interchange the specialist does many things. She verbally praises Andrew, reports his progress, and begins to differentiate between Andrew and his former behaviors. The specialist also describes a few of Andrew's strengths and abilities. She concludes by communicating her perceptions of Andrew's future success and her belief in him.

Summary

This chapter has described core actions and goals 5 through 8 of the psychological first aid technique. As with all interventions, specialists should strongly consider the potential positive and negative ramifications for implementing the psychological first aid intervention and ensure the intervention matches the survivor's needs and poses no significant dangers or threats for participants. The chapter also described the reflecting "as if" intervention and provided a clinical vignette demonstrating its use.

References

Sommers-Flanagan, J., & Sommers-Flanagan, R. (2012). *Counseling and psychotherapy theories in context and practice: Skills, strategies, and techniques.* New York, NY: Wiley.

Watts, R. E. (2013, April). Reflecting as if. *Counseling Today*. Retrieved from http://ct.counseling.org/2013/04/reflecting-as-if/

Watts, R. E., & La Guardia. A. C. (2013, November). *Reflecting as if: An encouragement-focused brief counseling process*. Paper presented at the Texas Counseling Association 57th Annual Professional Growth Conference, San Antonio, TX.

Watts, R. E., & Phillips, K. A. (2004). Adlerian psychology and psychotherapy: A relational constructivist approach. In J. D. Raskin & S. Bridges (Eds.), *Studies in meaning: Exploring constructivist psychology* (Vol. 2, pp. 267–289). New York, NY: Pace University Press.

Watts, R. E., & Pietrzak, D. (2000). Adlerian "encouragement" and the therapeutic process of solution-focused brief therapy. *Journal of Counseling and Development, 78*, 442–447. doi:10.1002/j.1556-6676.2000.tb01927.x

Watts, R. E., Williamson, J., & Williamson, D. (2004). Adlerian psychology: A relational constructivist approach. In *Adlerian yearbook 2004* (pp. 7–31). London, UK: Adlerian Society (UK) and Institute for Individual Psychology.

Epilogue

The focus of this book has been on responding to perpetrators and survivors of bullying and violence. Given the frequency of bullying and violence, and the emotional and physical suffering that often results, we hope this book has been useful in helping you to respond to your students. We have described a detailed and coherent assessment and intervention strategy believed to offer relatively broad clinical utility. However, you already know the truth: Because students come from varying backgrounds and cultures and present with diverse personalities, concerns, levels of intelligence, social supports, and strengths, no easy or simple assessment or intervention will match every student or situation.

We have a close friend, Steve, who, like his father before him, is an expert carpenter. When he comes to our house to build or fix things, he drives a pickup truck filled with all sorts of saws, drills, and carpentry tools. Depending on the individual job, he grabs multiple toolboxes and one of his many immense tool belts from the bed of the pickup truck. Each toolbox and each tool belt is brimming to capacity with very specific tools that he needs for the exact job at hand. When tearing down walls, he uses heavy sledgehammers and large crowbars. However, when he is doing "trim work," the hammers he brings in are dainty and small. He knows exactly which tool to use, when to use it, and how to use it.

Like expert carpenters, specialists must be experts with many assessment and intervention tools. Each assessment and intervention must match the individual student and his or her specific needs. No single technique can be applied to every student and every situation. The intent of this book is to provide a starting point for you to consider how best to serve your students and address their clinical needs. However, it must be adapted and used in conjunction with your clinical skills and counseling knowledge. At the same time, this book and your assessments and interventions must be used in conjunction with an experienced clinical supervisor and your school safety and risk committee to ensure that your assessments and interventions are safe, appropriate, and effective. The overriding mandate is to ensure safety and to use assessments and interventions that help rather than harm.

We are most honored to have had the privilege of sharing our book with you. You serve one of the most noble causes within any profession—helping ensure the safety, protection, and development of America's next generation. We thank you for your dedication to students and for committing yourself to their psychological, emotional, social, intellectual, and physical health.

Index